for General McClellan. Perhaps he will say, in respect to the latter, "it has been difficult for him to procure exact returns of divisions, brigades, &c." No doubt. But why not have given me proximate returns—such as he so eagerly furnished the President and certain Secretaries?
Has, then, a senior no corrective power over a junior officer, in case of such persistent neglect and disobedience? The remedy by arrest and trial before a Court Martial would probably soon cure the evil. But it been feared that a conflict of authority, near the head of the army, would be highly encouraging to the enemies, and depressing to the friends, of the Union. Hence my long forbearance; and continuing (though nominally) on duty. I shall try to hold out till the arrival of Major General Halleck, when, as his presence give me increased confidence in the safety of the Union—and being, as I am, unable to ride in the saddle, to walk, by reason of dropsy in my feet and legs, and paralysis in the small of the back, I shall definitively re from the army.

I have the honor to remain, with high respect, your most obedient servant,
WINFIELD SCOTT.

On the 1st of November the sad, insulted patriot retired before a young courtier, who is not worthy to undo the shoe-lachet of the brave old hero, General SCOTT. From July, 31, to January, 1862 (a period of six months), McClellan had been in command of the ay. The autumn and winter had been unparalleled for the beauty of the weather and the ness of the roads. The army under his immediate command numbered 224,135 soldiers, fectly equipped, and as brave men as ever went to battle. The Potomac, the gate-way to Capital, was blockaded by the enemy. Rebel outposts were within sight of Washington. The Rebel army lay near. No forward movement of our vast forces had been made. Not in a plan of action was developed; *only a persistent plan of inaction.* I read McClellan's own words from his own revised report:

But about the middle of January, 1862, upon recovering from a severe illness, I found that *excessive* anxiety for an immediate movement of the army of the Potomac had taken possession of the minds of the Administration.
A change had just been made in the War Department, and I was soon *urged* by the new secretary, Mr. nton, to take immediate steps to secure the re-opening of the Potomac and Ohio Railroad, and to free the ks of the lower Potomac from the rebel batteries which annoyed passing vessels.
Very soon after his entrance upon office, I laid before him, verbally, my design as to the part of the plan campaign to be executed by the army of the Potomac, which was to attack Richmond by the lower Chesapeake.
He instructed me to develop it to the President, which I *did.* The result was, that the President disapproved it, and by an order of January 31, 1862, substituted one of his own.

* * * * * * *

WASHINGTON, EXECUTIVE MANSION, Jan. 31, 1862.
SIDENT'S SPECIAL WAR ORDERS, No. 1.
Ordered: That all the disposable force of the Army of the Potomac, after providing safely for the defense Washington, be formed into an expedition for the immediate object of seizing and occupying a point upon railroad southwestward of what is known as Manassas Junction, all details to be in the discretion of the nmander-in-Chief, and the expedition to move before or on the 22d day of February next.
ABRAHAM LINCOLN.

I asked his Excellency whether this order was to be regarded as final, or whether I could be permitted to mit, in writing, my objections to his plan, and my reasons for preferring my own. Permission was acceded.

McClellan, in objecting to the plan of the President, and in giving reasons for prefering own, says:

The second base of operations available for the Army of the Potomac, is that of the lower Chesapeake , which affords the shortest possible land route to Richmond, and strikes directly at the heart of the my's power in the east.
The roads in that region are passable at all seasons of the year.

* * * * * * *

Should it be determined to operate from the lower Chesapeake, the point of landing which promises the st brilliant results, is Urbana, on the lower Rappahannock. This point is easily reached by vessels of heavy ught, it is neither occupied nor observed by the enemy, it is but one march from West Point, the key of region, and thence, but two marches to Richmond. A rapid movement from Urbana, would probably cut Magruder in the Peninsula, and enable us to occupy Richmond before it could be strongly reinforced. uld we fail in that, we could, with the co-operation of the navy, cross the James and show ourselves in rear ichmond, thus forcing the enemy to come out and attack us, for his position would be untenable, with us on southern bank of the river.
Should circumstances render it not advisable to land at Urbana, we can use Mob Jack Bay—or, the *worst* ing *to the worst,* we can take Fort Monroe as a base, and operate with complete security, although with celerity and brilliancy of results, up the Peninsula.
The total force to be thrown upon the new line would be, according to circumstances, from 110 to 140,000.

The President yielded to the General, who had his own way (p. 107), and his plan was pted.

At page 154, General McClellan says:

On the 1st of April I embarked, with the head-quarters on the steamer Commodore, and reached Fort nroe on the afternoon of the 2d.

* * * * * * *

As to the *force* and *position* of the enemy, the information then in our possession *was vague and untrustrthy.* Much of it was obtained from the staff-officers of General Wool, and was simply to the effect that cktown was surrounded by a continuous line of earth-works, with strong water batteries on the York River, I garrisoned by not less than 15,000 troops, under the command of General J. B. Magruder. Maps which I been prepared by the Topographical Engineers under General Wool's command were furnished me, in ich, the Warwick River was represented as flowing parallel to, but not crossing the road from Newport News Williamsburg, making the so-called Mulberry Island a real island; and we *had no information as to the e course of the Warwick across the Peninsula,* nor of the *formidable line of works which it covered.*

So, then, according to McClellan's own report, he had been in command of this splendid my of the Potomac for six months when he found, as he says, "that excessive anxiety for an immediate movement had taken possession of the minds of the Administration; and the new Secretary *urged* him to take immediate steps to free the Potomac from rebel batteries, and instructed him to develop his plan to the President."

Was it not about time to do some of these things? His reason for insisting on going down the Peninsula two hundred miles to find an enemy, which had lain within twenty miles of him all winter, was that "the roads in that region are passable at all seasons of the year." And yet, if his dispatches are correct, he could not move a step there in early June, because "the roads were impassable." This new development of his plan was sent to the President on the 3d of February; and yet, in April following, he writes that, even then, his information as to the enemy was vague and untrustworthy, and that he did not know whether Mulberry Island was a real island or not, and that he did not even know which way the Warwick River ran! This will be found at page 154 of his report; and at page 106 of the same report, he states that the total force to be thrown upon the whole line was to be from 110,000 to 140,000 men! The army of the Potomac, according to the returns in the War Department certified by McClellan himself, numbered as follows:

ABSTRACT of returns received from the Army of the Potomac, from the time General McClellan took command to August 1st, 1862.—On file in the Adjutant General's office:

Date of Return.	Aggregate Present for Duty.	Aggregate Present and Absent.	
September 30, 1861	118,537	144,005	
October 10, "	123,724	157,723	
October 20, "	148,581	163,340	
*November 12, "	154,364	175,731	
*November 21, "	156,853	180,902	
November 30 (monthly)	162,731	198,238	
December 10, 1861.	168,996	195,403	
*December 20, "	174,384	209,445	Forces around the city of Washington and line of the Potomac, before the opening of the campaign, April 1st, 1862.
December 31, "	183,507	219,781	
*January 1, 1862.	194,159	224,085	
*January 10, "	190,695	225,935	
January 31, "	182,313	222,227	
February 28, "	185,418	222,018	
*March 2, "	192,424	221,578	
March 31, "	179,362	214,983	
June 10, 1862.	101,697	139,868	
June 20, "	115,102	156,833	
June 30, "	98,258	148,755	Forces of the Army of the Potomac on the Peninsula.
July 10, "	99,826	157,088	
July 20, "	101,691	158,314	
July 30, "	96,044	156,001	

I certify that the above is a correct statement, taken from the official returns made by Major General McClellan (those marked thus * are signed only by his Assistant Adjutant General, the others by Major General McClellan himself) on file in this office, for the respective dates.

(Signed) SAMUEL BRECK, *Assistant Adjutant General.*
ADJUTANT GENERAL'S OFFICE, WASHINGTON, D. C., October 25th, 1864.

THE PLAN.

"FAIRFAX COURT-HOUSE, March 13, 1862.
"The council of commanders of army corps have unanimously agreed upon a plan of operations. Gen. McDowell will at once proceed with it to Washington and lay it before you.
G. B. McCLELLAN, *Major General Commanding.*
Hon. E. M. STANTON, *Secretary of War.*

"HEADQUARTERS ARMY OF THE POTOMAC, Fairfax Court-House, March 13, 1862.
"A council of the generals commanding army corps at the headquarters of the army of the Potomac were of the opinion—

"First. That the enemy having retreated from Manassas to Gordonsville, behind the Rappahannock and Rapidan, it is the opinion of the generals commanding army corps that the operations to be carried on will be best undertaken from Old Point Comfort, between the York and James rivers, upon Richmond; provided, First, that the enemy's vessel, the Merrimac, can be neutralized. Second, the means of transportation sufficient for an immediate transfer of the force to its new base can be ready at Washington and Alexandria to move down the Potomac. Third, that a naval auxiliary force can be had to silence, or aid in silencing the enemy's batteries in York river. Fourth, "*that the force to be left to cover Washington shall be such as to give an entire feeling of security for its safety from menace.*" (Unanimous.)

This was the Peninsula plan submitted by McDowell, and McClellan telegraphs on the same day:

FLINT HILL, March 13, 1862—6.15 P. M.
Your dispatch was received at 6.10 P. M., at this place, about three miles from Fairfax Court-House, where I am moving a division. The members of the council, together with myself, were unanimous in forming the plan which was presented to you by General McDowell. Steps have already been taken, so that if the plan meets your approval, the movement can commence early to-morrow morning. I will communicate more fully as soon as I return to my camp.
Your speedy action will facilitate the movement.   G. B. McCLELLAN, *Major General.*
Hon. E. M. STANTON, *Secretary of War.*

WAR DEPARTMENT, March 13, 1862.
The President having considered the plan of operations agreed upon by yourself and the commanders of army corps, makes no objection to the same, but gives the following directions as to its execution:
1st. Leave such force at Manassas Junction as shall make it entirely certain that the enemy shall not repossess himself of that position and line of communication.
2d. Leave Washington secure.
3d. Move the remainder of the force down the Potomac, choosing a new base at Fortress Monroe, or anywhere between there and there; or, at all events, move such remainder of the army at once in pursuit of the enemy by some route.
Seven o'clock, forty minutes.   EDWIN M. STANTON, *Secretary of War.*
Major General GEORGE B. McCLELLAN.

SPEECH

OF

HON. EDWARDS PIERREPONT,

DELIVERED AT THE CONVENTION AND MASS MEETING OF THE DEMOCRACY OPPOSED TO THE CHICAGO PLATFORM,

HELD AT THE

Cooper Institute, New York, November 1, 1864.

FELLOW-CITIZENS: A little while ago those of the Democratic party who meet here to-[nig]ht, earnestly desired a change in the Administration; to that change we looked as the [on]ly safe way to bring peace to our country. We trusted that the Chicago Convention would [ex]hibit wisdom, honor and patriotism; we hoped that they would drop all minor dissensions [an]d strive to bring about an honorable adjustment of our difficulties.

Many of us believed that the Convention would propose that the insurgent States lay [do]wn their arms and return to the Union; and this being done, that a convention of all the [St]ates be called for the purpose of trying to harmonize the real or imagined grievances. [Up]on that simple platform we had hoped to place two eminent civilians, whose wisdom, [wh]ose moderation, and whose statesmanship the country could trust. With such a platform, [an]d with such candidates, we had intended to go before the people and urge them to make [th]is change as the surest means of restoring the Union. But when we find that the enemies [of] our Government, traitors to Democratic principles, ruled that assembly, and virtually sur[re]ndered the honor, the valor and the manhood of the North, we denounce the crime and [ref]use to stand silent by and witness the completion of our country's humiliation.

The Democratic party were defeated in the Presidential contest four years ago, because [th]e southern politicians wished it defeated; they deliberately planned and persistently [ex]ecuted that defeat. Mr. Lincoln was elected because the southern politicians wished him [el]ected, and did all in their power to make *our defeat* and *his election* sure. Their object was [to] destroy the Democratic party, and thus destroy the Union, as they themselves openly said, [th]rough their journals, they "hated free schools, free speech, free institutions, free labor, and [fre]e men." No man of our time had a more complete knowledge upon this subject than that [tru]e Democrat, brave patriot, and great man, Stephen A. Douglas. Death summoned him [fro]m this scene of strife, and in his last farewell he said:

"The election of Mr. Lincoln is a mere pretext. The present secession movement is the result of an enor[mo]us conspiracy formed more than a year since—formed by leaders in the Southern Confederacy more than [tw]elve months ago. They use the slavery question as a means to aid the accomplishment of their ends. They [des]ired the election of a northern candidate by a sectional vote, in order to show that the two sections cannot [liv]e together. When the history of the two years from the Lecompton question down to the Presidential elec[tio]n shall be written, it will be shown that the scheme was deliberately made to break up this Union.

"They desired a northern Republican to be elected by a purely northern vote, and then assign this fact as [the r]eason why the sections cannot live together. If the disunion candidate in the late Presidential contest had [ca]rried the united South, their scheme was, the northern candidate successful, to seize the Capital last spring, [an]d by a united South and divided North, hold it. Their scheme was defeated, in the defeat of the disunion [ca]ndidates in several of the southern States.

"But this is no time for a detail of causes. The conspiracy is now known; armies have been raised, war is [lev]ied to accomplish it. There are only two sides to the question. Every man must be for the United States or [aga]inst it. There can be no neutrals in this war; *only patriots or traitors!*"

This last speech of Douglas was delivered just before he died. It was delivered in [Ch]icago. Three years after a great convention assembled at that place; in it were many [wh]om Douglas had cherished as his best friends, as true to Democratic faith, as patriots [up]on whom his country could rely in her most trying hour. Many in that convention were [Do]uglas' friends—steadfast in Democratic faith, and real patriots at heart.

A committee on resolutions entered that assembly and said:

"This Convention does explicitly declare, as the sense of the American people, that, after four years of [fai]lure to restore the Union by the experiment of war, during which, under the pretense of a military necessity [of] war power higher than the Constitution, the Constitution itself has been disregarded in every part, and pub[lic] liberty and private right alike trodden down, and the material prosperity of the country essentially im[pai]red, justice, humanity, liberty, and the public welfare demand that immediate efforts be made for a cessa[tio]n of hostilities, with a view to an ultimate Convention of all the States, or other peaceable means, to the [en]d that at the earliest practicable moment peace may be restored on the basis of the Federal Union of the [Sta]tes."

We are told, when that resolution was read, that a strange sensation ran through the [as]sembly, that the members looked into each other's faces, and that in the stillness you could

Published by the War Democratic State Committee of the State of New York.

hear the heart beat. It is no wonder! they were standing by Douglas' grave! and they saw his handwriting on the wall, and they heard his warning voice say, "There can be no *neutrals* in this war—*only patriots or traitors.*"

I shall show that the sentiments embodied in this resolution were not the sentiments of any friend of Douglas, of any true Democrat, or of any lover of the Union. The resolution was forced upon the Convention against its real sentiments, and by noisy, bold, and fraudulent threats of a Northwestern secession. It is to be regretted that the friends of Douglas, the friends of his principles, the friends of the Union, did not firmly say, "*There can be no neutrals in this war—only patriots or traitors.*" But all real friends of the Union will soon shake off the galling fetters with which Vallandigham, Pendleton, and other southern sympathizers have bound them, and return to the true principles of the Democratic party, from which these friends of the Union's enemies have for the moment beguiled them.

The hour is near when all will see that "there are only two sides to this question; every man must be for the United States or against it."

Vallandigham and a few active, noisy, adroit and audacious enemies of the Union, and friends of Toombs, Jeff. Davis and Judah Benjamin, have assumed to give voice to the Democratic party; they have skillfully tried to make honest Democrats believe that no supporter of an administration placed in power by Republicans could be a Democrat. By this false and specious logic, many honest men have been deceived. When the Democrats of the South, by their own treachery to the Democrats of the North, placed Mr. Lincoln in power, what was a patriotic Democrat to do, but to sustain the only government which Southern traitors had left us? Were Northern Democrats to sacrifice their country, to surrender their manhood, to become the doughfaced cowards and poltroons which Southern braggarts always said we were? When, in April, 1861, Fort Sumpter fell, and the Rebel Secretary of War, amid the roar of cannon and the shouts of the enemies of our Government, announced to the world that the Confederate flag floated over the walls of Sumpter, and that the same flag would float over the Dome of the Capitol at Washington before the first of May, what were Northern Democrats to do? What did their good instincts prompt them to do, and what did they do? They rose in their might, and swore to defend and to preserve our country entire; they hastened to the field, nor stopped to ask who for the time was at the head of their beloved government. This great uprising struck the South aghast—so long had we been accustomed to yield to their arrogant pretensions; so long had they ruled us as they pleased; that they verily thought, when they chose to deprive us of power and to put Mr. Lincoln in place, in order, as they expressed it, "to fire the Southern mind and hurry the cotton States into revolution," that Northern Democrats would tamely submit to the destruction of their party, and the ruin of their country. They soon found out their mistake; they also found that Northern Democrats would fight, and that they were dangerous foes to meet in the field. They found that Northern Democrats retained their valor; that they still loved their country, their government and the Union; that the dear old flag which waved so proudly over every sea, and whose bright stars gladdened the heart of freedom on every shore; which no tyrant, king or emperor dared insult; they would not allow to be pulled from the high Dome of the Capitol, nor let the rebel rag there float in the morning air, to flap shame and menace in the face of LOYAL MEN. When Davis, Mason, Slidell, Toombs and Judah Benjamin saw this, they took counsel together, and they did "explicitly declare" that war, thus conducted, would be "a failure," and they concluded that upon Northern Democrats they had better "exhaust all the resources of statesmanship," and so they commenced. Emissaries were sent abroad to write in foreign journals; secret agents were sent to every part of the North; efforts were made in every possible way to delude, deceive, and to corrupt the mind of the Democracy; skillfully to excite their prejudices, their passions and their fears.

Arbitrary arrests, the fanaticism of abolitionists, the currency, the draft—labor too low, and labor too high—the short-comings of the administration, the love of peace, and the evils of war, were each seized upon in turn, in order to divide the party, and to prejudice the public mind against the Government—and for what end? Was it to restore the Union? No! every one now knows that it was to stop the war, and to destroy the Union.

The Englishman who fought for the Sultan in the Crimean war was not thereby made a Turk or a Mahomet. We do not turn Republicans to sustain this war. We fight for our Government—for patriotism—not for party. We go into this war Democrats, we shall come out of it Democrats. We shall preserve our Democratic Government, our Democratic principles, and our Union entire. Can any dullard be made to believe that our brave officers and soldiers who have periled their lives in the war are changed from Democrats to Republicans? It is the strength of their Democratic faith and the devotion of their Democratic patriotism which makes them fight so nobly.

The South had well nigh exhausted "all their resources of statesmanship" upon the Democratic party when they forced the second resolution upon the Chicago Convention and placed "their own familiar friend," Pendleton, on the ticket.

But the South had other resources, as they confidently believed; they supposed that cotton ruled the world; that England could not live a year without this staple of the South—

that without cotton England would soon be in revolution—be forced to recognize the Confederacy and raise the blockade. England *did* want the cotton; England did desire to recognize the South; England did eagerly wish to rend us asunder; to cripple our commerce, to have free trade with the South, and to destroy our manufactures; and she encouraged the Southern revolt in every possible way. She allowed the Alabama to be built in her waters, and to be manned with English seamen, and under false pretences to leave her shores to prey upon our commerce. She saw with joy the havoc which that swift steamer was making upon our merchantmen; — that our shipping was rapidly driven from the seas, and that England was taking the trade of the world! Emboldened by the success of the Alabama, she allowed the formidable steam rams to be built for the destruction of our Navy, and to break up the blockade. Our Government protested against the hostile act; England shuffled, prevaricated, excused herself—said she had no *law* to stop them; and they were nearly ready to come out upon us, when Mr. Seward said if English law could not stop the rams— English law could not stop war with the United States. The trading English are a considerate people; they keep the ledger carefully, and they know how to cypher; slow, to be sure, but pretty accurate in calculating profit and loss. Lord Russell sent out to Lord Lyons to know whether these Yankees would fight? His lordship replied that they were a strange, obstinate, fanatical sort of people, and that he thought they *would* fight; that he had been through the North with Mr. Seward, and the people seemed to have a great deal of property and a great deal of pluck; and besides that there were a good many of them, and they did not seem to be *afraid of anything*—in short that they were a dangerous nation to quarrel with. England began to reason, that if the Alabama, without a single port in the wide world within which to take a prize—without a single harbor for a resting place—could destroy the commerce of the United States, what would a hundred American cruisers do when let loose upon English ships? England soon contrived to stop the rams. England is harmless *now*; she has given bonds secured by all her shipping upon the ocean; she will keep the peace; she is old, heavy and rich; she keeps shop; does a profitable business; makes things to sell; and peddles them in her vessels all over the world. Fighting is not her profession; she says war is unchristian, is wicked. The South have "exhausted all their resources of statesmanship" upon England, and have given it up.

But the South relied also upon France. France is a warlike nation, with vast armies in perfect discipline, and ready for the field. France don't cant about the "wickedness of war;" France is not so thoroughly of the shop as England. France cares less about money, and has more love of glory. France is prepared and ready for a fight—she needs only the occasion and the motive. We have been in real danger from France. The motive has been widely different in the two countries. England wants to see us broken up, our commerce and manufactures destroyed; France has no such wish. The present Emperor, like his great uncle, sees that our greatness is useful as a restraint upon England. But he had certain designs upon Mexico and the Isthmus, bearing upon the trade with the Pacific and China, which made our temporary disunion seem desirable; and the evidence is clear that the South believed that, for the surrender of Louisiana and Texas, the Emperor would lend the Confederacy his aid. It is now too late to purchase his intervention even at that price. The restoration of the Union will not interfere with any known designs of that far-seeing statesman. On the contrary, he wishes it restored, and he will soon throw his influence in that direction. France gives the laws of taste, luxury, and fashion to the civilized world. Nations who are at war—poor or demi-barbarian—are of little value to France; but every nation which cultivates the arts of peace, grows rich, luxurious, and refined, pours its treasures into France. If stable governments can be established in Mexico and upon the Isthmus, those countries will rapidly grow rich, refined, luxurious, and make a new market for the wines, the silks, and the countless fabrics of France. Our own country had become the best of her customers; the war has now nearly destroyed all trade with France. I learned from our Consul in Paris that the trade had literally ceased. The Emperor understands all this—he watches every phase of our politics and every movement of our armies with intensest care. He wishes peace in America for the good of France; and you may be sure that he will try to hasten peace by every means in his power. During the month of July it was confidently whispered by the Secessionists in Paris, that the next steamer would bring news of Lee's entry into Washington, and that the Confederacy would forthwith be recognized by France. No Union man could then understand upon what this confident hope was based; we now know—the Northwestern conspirators were to aid Lee, and the Rebels in Paris were advised of it. The plot failed. Many of the conspirators have fled, others are secreted, some have been arrested, and are now on trial in Indiana. The Rebels have "exhausted all their resources of statesmanship" in this direction, and have "explicitly failed." The Emperor, as you know, has lived in this country—he understands our Government—he waits the result of this autumn election to determine his action. I had it direct from those who have the best means of information, and before the result of the Chicago Convention was known, that, if Mr. Lincoln should be re-elected, it would assure the Emperor that the North were determined to put down the Rebellion "at all hazards;" and that they had the ability to do it. But if the opposition candidate were elected, then it would assure him that the North were too much divided to succeed against the Confederacy—that he was determined, if possible, to bring about an early peace, and that the re-election of Mr. Lincoln would be conclusive evidence that there could be no peace but in *Union*, and that the election of the opposing candidate would make it equally conclusive that there could be no peace but in *disunion*. It may be safely said that soon after the election of Mr. Lincoln, the hand of Napoleon will be seen in favor of the speediest Peace and Union of all the States; urging the North to offer, and the South to accept, re-union with every right guaranteed under the old Constitution.

But it may be safely said that the South will not accept even this. Not a Secessionist in Paris, not a Confederate minister of the South, not an orator, not a newspaper, not a public man anywhere suggests or ever has suggested that the election of McClellan and Pendleton would even tend to produce a return of the South to the Union—they each and all reject the proposition with scorn. Even Stephens, the mildest of their number, announces that it is "recognized sovereignty" and not Union which they are determined to have, and that the only ray of hope which the nomination at Chicago gives, is a faint possible hope of an earlier independence; never a suggestion that re-union can, by any possibility, come of the election of McClellan.

Did you ever ask a friend of Vallandigham and Pendleton and of the second resolution of the Chicago Platform, what effect the victory of our arms was likely to have upon the election of McClellan? If so, they have confessed to you that victory in the field was their defeat at the polls. What! great victories won by our heroic armies in the field, over traitors to our Government, tend to defeat a Major-General of that army, still drawing his pay from that Government!!! Does this need a commentary? How does it strike the people? What do they say to this? They send their brothers and their sons to battle and to death; they at the cost of life win bright victories in defense of our cherished Government, and every such victory, it is acknowledged by all, tends to defeat the Major-General McClellan! Can those who wish him elected, rejoice at such victories? I trust he has no friend so base as to pretend to such false rejoicing. The private character of a candidate for public honors is not a proper subject for discussion. But when a man comes before the people and asks them to vote him into the Presidency, it is just that we should, with honest fairness, consider his claims to that exalted office. I believe that the private character of Gen. McClellan is without reproach; I cheerfully accord to him all the purity and every kindly virtue which his admirers claim; I think him a Christian gentleman who would not willingly see the Union destroyed;—I shall only speak of his public career as it appears in the record of our time.

McClellan is thirty-seven years old: what has the young man done for his country to entitle him to this high place? The convention which nominated him "does explicitly declare" that the war is "a failure"; so then, it is not for success in war, that he claims our votes. Two years ago, he was removed from his command for alleged incompetency. During those two years, our country has passed through the direst trials and bloodiest wars of modern times; thousands of his brave comrades in arms have died on the battle-field; three hundred thousand of our youth have perished in this struggle for the Nation's life! What has McClellan done at his country's call during these two long years of her greatest peril? What has he done? He is said to be very popular, and to have much influence over that class of men who make soldiers in the field—the army has been in greatest need of men—was his heart full of zeal for the cause, and did he go from city to city, using all his powers to rouse the people for the war, to put down the wicked rebellion and to save his bleeding and beloved land? Had he done so, he would have received the holiest benedictions of the people; he would have been made lieutenant-general of all the armies, and the heaving of the Nation's heart would have lifted him to the Presidential chair, easy as the swell of the ocean lifts a little barque upon the shore! What has he done during these two eventful years? Nothing—but write out excuses for doing nothing before. You can't deceive the people long—they have an instinct, a just perception of truth wiser than logic. Old Blair told McClellan that he would surely fail if he run for the Presidency. After election, McClellan will find that old Blair was right. But he can then very justly make the same excuse for the failure which he so often made for his failures in the war, namely—the want of men.

What then are the pretensions of this young man to this great office? Before the war he had done nothing; in the war, it is explicitly declared "that all has been failure." Since he left the army, it is plain that he has done nothing whatever.

But we are told that Jeff. Davis, Mason, Slidell, Toombs and Judah Benjamin are men of such lofty pride that they will not treat with Mr. LINCOLN, whose manners they don't like; but that McClellan is an educated, courteous, amiable, Christian gentleman, whom they formerly knew well, and that they would be more willing to treat with him for peace. We have many cultured, amiable, Christian gentlemen in the North, and we justly prize their virtues. But, during this grim time of war, I think it safer to let Grant, Sherman and Sheridan; Farragut, Dupont, Porter and Winslow treat with these arch-rebels.

The Hon. Robert C. Winthrop made a speech the other day at New London, in which he gave reasons why McClellan ought to be elected, which I had never seen advanced before. He says:

"Let me not forget, however, to remind you, my friends, that he has in his veins, in common with so many of you, and in common, as I am glad to remember, with myself, too, a little good old Connecticut blood, coming down from an ancestor who settled here a century ago. I am sure you will not think any the worse of him for that."

I believe it is true, as Mr. Winthrop says, that McClellan is of a Connecticut family, who have lived there for more than a hundred years! When Jeff Davis, Toombs, and Judah Benjamin read Mr. Winthrop's speech, I question whether they will be so ready to "negotiate with General McClellan" as their friends now suppose. They may suspect and hesitate lest they get hold of a wooden nutmeg from Connecticut. The origin of the wooden nutmeg story illustrates the surpassing ignorance of the South rather than the sharpness of the North. Nothing could be more preposterous, since the successful counterfeit must have cost twice as much as the genuine article; nevertheless, that story has had much vogue. Its origin is this:

Many years ago a small trader in the very town where Mr. Winthrop made his speech, together with apples, chestnuts, walnuts, hickory nuts, &c., sent a few nutmegs to Beaufort, in South Carolina. A planter, named Bogert, seeing the nutmegs, bought them at a good price; pleased with his purchase, and being especially vain of having choice delicacies at his table, he produced for his guests those rare and somewhat costly nuts. But the nuts would'nt crack, and when broken open were found to contain no meat, and the honest Connecticut Yankee was cursed by the Carolina chivalry as a cheat for selling nutmegs without meat, and which they therefore supposed was made of wood. When our troops entered Beaufort they still found the same prejudice existing against nutmegs and Yankees.

I have a word to say to the Irish voters, who, from a land of oppression, have sought this home of freedom. You have been my true political friends, and I have been as truly yours. The many of your countrymen, with whom I have had much to do, will each bear witness that they have ever received aid, sympathy, and uniform kindness; that no Irishman has had cause to complain, and that no Irishwoman has ever gone sorrowing from my door. I have neither reviled your religion nor traduced your race. I ask your brief attention: Your oppressors of the Old World are striving with all their might to secure the election of the Chicago nominees. What does it mean? When British gold and British journals combine with English nobles and haters of the Irish race, do you think this comes of new-born love toward Irishmen! Be not deceived. English statesmen are wise in their generation, as Ireland has found to her sorrow. Those far-seeing enemies of your Green Isle know well the bearing of this great contest here. May it be possible—when, planted in this free soil, you have grown a very Sampson in your might, that England can lure you to the lap of Delilah, cut off the strength of your locks, put out your eyes, bind you with fetters of brass, and make you *again* to *grind* in her prison house?

Elect McClellan and she will have done all this; not that he would wish it, but he could not help it. His election will surely dissolve the Union, and the knell of the Union is the death of freedom. Be not deceived! Had I the tongue of an angel, and were my lips touched with the altar fire, I could not too strongly utter my deep convictions on this momentous question.

Let me read what one of your able countrymen, Senator Conness, says upon this subject:

"It is not necessary for me to state now that I feel the deepest interest in the approaching contest. With some opportunities for forming a correct judgment, I declare it to be my conviction and belief that the issue of a united or a divided country, with all the blessings of the one, and all the horrors of the other, are involved. I believe that the election of Mr. Lincoln will secure the former, and that the election of Geo. B. McClellan will result in the latter; Union, Freedom, Liberty and National glory on the one hand; Disunion, continued war, Slavery and wretchedness, make the dreadful abyss of the other."

I also read from a recent letter of that intelligent and able statesman, John Bright, one of the few of eminence in England, who is our real friend:

"All those of my countrymen who have wished well to the rebellion, who have hoped for the break-up of your Union, who have preferred to see a southern slave empire rather than a restored and free republic, so far as I can observe, are now in favor of the election of General McClellan. All those who have deplored the calamities which the leaders of secession have brought upon your country, who believe that slavery weakens your power and tarnishes your good name throughout the world, and who regard the restoration of your Union as a thing to be desired and prayed for by all good men, so far as I can judge, are heartily longing for the re-election of Mr. Lincoln. Every friend of your Union, probably, in Europe, every speaker and writer who has sought to do justice to your cause since the war began, is now hoping, with an intense anxiety that Mr. Lincoln may be placed at the head of your Executive for another term."

Surely it can hurt no pride of mine to see the "Connecticut blood of an hundred years" placed at the head of the nation; but I oppose it, because, I know that it will bring the ruin of my country. All the aristocracy of England earnestly desire the election of McClellan. Do you also desire it? If so, it is the first time that English nobles and free Irishmen have wished the same thing.

Vallandigham has just written a letter to the *New York News*, and says that he, (Mr.

Vallandigham,) " wrote the second, the material resolution of the Chicago platform, and carried it through the Sub-Committee and the General Committee, in spite of the most desperate and persistent opposition on part of Cassidy and his friends, Mr. C. himself, in an adjoining room, laboring to defeat it. But the various substitutes never at any time received more than three votes," and "he moved that the nomination of McClellan be made unanimous."

Jeff. Davis has lately made two speeches in favor of McClellan. At Augusta he said:

"We must beat Sherman, we must march into Tennessee—there we will draw from twenty thousand to thirty thousand to our standard, and so strengthened, we must push the enemy back to the banks of the Ohio, and *thus give the peace party of the North an accretion no puny editorial can give.*"

At Columbus he said:

"Does any one believe that Yankees are to be conciliated by terms of concession? Does any man imagine that we can conquer the Yankees by retreating before them, or *do you not all know that the only way to make spaniels civil is to whip them? And you can whip them.*"

"I believe it is in the power of the men of the Confederacy to plant our banners on the banks of the Ohio, where we may say to the Yankees, 'Be quiet, or we shall teach you another lesson.' Within the next thirty days much is to be done, for upon our success much depends. Within the next thirty days, therefore, let all who are absentees, or who ought to be in the army, go promptly to their ranks. *Let fresh victories crown our arms, and the peace party, if there be such at the North, can elect its candidate.*"

And Boyce, of South Carolina, wrote:

"Your only hope of peace is in the ascendancy of the conservative party North. *Fortify that party if you can, by victories.*"

Does any one think that Davis and his friends are fools; and that they don't know how to adapt means to ends? They openly propose to aid the election of McClellan by the slaughter, in battle, of your brothers and your sons! Read their speeches to your neighbor; ask him if he can aid these contemptuous foes of our country by his vote. If so, then be sure that he *can* do now, and that he *will* do hereafter, whatever Jeff. Davis bids him.

Fellow Citizens! there is no shuffling this question; "there can be no neutrals in this war; only *patriots or traitors!*"

In addition to the claims that the nominee of the Chicago Convention is of old Connecticut blood, and a Christian gentleman, one other have we heard, namely: that he did not take Richmond because his plans were interfered with; and when you ask what is meant by that, you are told that McDowell's army should have followed McClellan down the Peninsula, and that none of it was permitted to go. I believe that no such stupendous falsehood was ever before palmed off upon an intelligent people.

As this is all now a matter of record, there is no chance of mistake.

On the 27th of July, 1861, McClellan assumed command in Washington, and on the 4th of September he appointed Col. Marcy Chief of Staff. Lieut.-Gen. Scott made great complaint of the conduct of McClellan, and on the 4th of October sent the following letter to the Department:

HEAD-QUARTERS OF THE ARMY, WASHINGTON, October 4th, 1861.

HON. S. CAMERON, *Secretary of War*,—

Sir: You are, I believe, aware that I hailed the arrival here of Major General McClellan as an event of happy consequence to the country and the army. Indeed, if I did not call for him, I heartily approved of the suggestion, and gave him the most cordial reception and support.

He, however, had hardly entered upon his new duties, when, encouraged to communicate directly with the President and certain members of the Cabinet, he, in a few days, forgot that he had any intermediate Commander, and has now long prided himself in treating me with uniform neglect—running into disobedience of orders.

Of the smaller matters—neglects—though in themselves grave military offences, I need not speak in the face of the following:

1. To suppress an irregularity more conspicuous in Major General McClellan than in any other officer, I publish the following:

(GENERAL ORDERS No. 17.)

HEAD-QUARTERS OF THE ARMY, WASHINGTON, September 16th, 1861.

There are irregularities in the correspondence of the army which need prompt correction. It is highly important that junior officers on duty be not permitted to correspond with the General-in-Chief or other Commander, on current official business, except through intermediate Commanders; and the same rule applies to correspondence with the President direct, or with him through the Secretary of War, unless it be by the special invitation or request of the President.

By command of Lieutenant General Scott.

E. D. TOWNSEND, *Assistant Adjutant General.*

With this order fresh in his memory, Major General McClellan addressed two important communications to the Secretary of War, on, respectively, the 19th and 20th of the same month, over my head, and how many since to the Secretary, and even to the President, direct, I have not enquired, but many I have no doubt—besides daily oral communications with the same high functionaries—all without my knowledge.

2. To correct another class of gross neglects, I, the same day, caused to be addressed to Major General McClellan, the following order:

HEAD-QUARTERS OF THE ARMY, WASHINGTON, September 16th, 1861.

To Major General McCLELLAN, *U. S. Army, Commanding Department of the Potomac:*

The Commanding General of the Army of the Potomac will cause the positions, State and number of troops under him, to be reported at once to general head-quarters, by divisions, brigades, and independent regiments or detachments, which general report will be followed by reports of new troops as they arrive, with the dispositions made of them, together with all material changes which may take place in the same army.

By command of Lieutenant General Scott.

E. D. TOWNSEND, *Assistant Adjutant General.*

Eighteen days have now elapsed, and not the slightest respect has been shown to either of these orders by

Thus the plan was agreed upon. The troops were speedily moved, and before the 5th of April, 121,500 men were embarked, (see the sworn statement of Hon. John Tucker, Assistant Secretary of War, and who had charge of the transports, Vol. 1., p. 295, of report on conduct of the war,) and, according to Gen. McClellan's report in writing, filed with the Adjutant General, he had left for the defences of Washington, some 75,000 troops. (Vol. 1, p. 341.) On the very next day, Gen. Wadsworth reported in writing, to the Secretary of War, that he had but 19,022 men for duty, and that he was ordered by Gen. McClellan to send away four regiments of this number. (Vol. 1, p. 316.) The matter was forthwith referred to Gen. Hitchcock and Gen. Thomas, who made a full report, which closes in these words:

In view of the opinion expressed by the council of commanders of army corps of the force necessary for the defense of the capital, though not numerically stated, and of the force represented by General McClellan as left for that purpose, we are of opinion that the requirements of the President that the city shall be left "entirely secure," not only in the opinion of the general-in-chief, but those of the "commanders of the army corps" also, has not been complied with. All of which is respectfully submitted.

L. THOMAS, *Adjutant General.*
E. A. HITCHCOCK, *Major General Volunteers, United States Army.*

(Vol. 1, p. 318.) The President then ordered that McDowell's corps, "remain in front of Washington until further orders, to operate in the direction of Manassas." (Vol. 1, p. 319.) And this is the interference about which so much has been vaguely said. It may surprise some of you to learn that by far the greater part of this same army of McDowell's were soon after sent to McClellan.

McDowell's corps was composed of three divisions:

Franklin's .... 12,889 men.
McCall's .... 11,151 "
King's .... 10,953 "

Franklin's and McCall's divisions were both sent to McClellan, and only the small division of King was left with McDowell; but because he did not go himself, the false impression still remains that none of his army was sent.

On the 10th of April, McClellan telegraphed to the Secretary of War these words:

"I will run the risk and hold myself responsible for the result, if you will give me Franklin's division."— (Vol. 1, p. 322.)

Franklin was sent to him forthwith, to wit, April 11.

On the next day McClellan telegraphed—

HEADQUARTERS ARMY OF THE POTOMAC,
Near Yorktown, April 12—12 M.

Your dispatch received. I thank you most sincerely for the reinforcements sent to me. Franklin will attack on the other side. The moment I hear from him I will state point of rendezvous. I am confident as to results now.
G. B. McCLELLAN, *Major-General.*
Hon. E. M. STANTON, *Secretary of War.*

And on the day following—

HEADQUARTERS ARMY OF THE POTOMAC. April 13—9 A. M.

Dispatch received. Arrangement proposed by Franklin would assist me much. Our work progressing well. We shall soon be at them, and I am sure of the result. They are working hard on the Gloucester side, and the navy cannot reach them.
G. B. McCLELLAN, *Major-General.*
Hon. EDWIN M. STANTON, *Secretary of War.* (Vol. 1, p. 323.)

Not long after McClellan wanted McCall's division also, and that was promptly sent to him, and so determined was the Government to leave nothing undone which the General wanted, that the following was sent:

WAR DEPARTMENT, WASHINGTON CITY, D. C., June 7, 1862.

Four regiments were embarked yesterday from Washington, and one from here. One more goes to-day from Baltimore and one from here, making seven in all. McCall is ready to move as soon as transportation arrives at Fredericksburg.

Please state whether you feel sufficiently strong for your final movement when this reaches you.

Major-General MCCLELLAN.
EDWIN M. STANTON, *Secretary of War.*

On the same day McClellan replied in these words: "*I shall be in perfect readiness to move forward to take Richmond the moment that McCall reaches here,* and the ground will admit the passage of artillery." (Vol. 1, p. 334.)

On the 11th he telegraphed—

"McCall's troops have commenced arriving at White House. I have sent instructions. Weather good to-day."

On the next day he telegraphed:

"Weather now good. Roads and grounds rapidly drying." (Vol. 1, p. 335.)

And on the same day he writes—

"In your telegrams respecting reinforcements you inform me that Gen. McDowell, with the *residue* of his command, will proceed overland to join me before Richmond." (Vol. 1, p. 335.)

On the 18th he telegraphed that not less than 10,000 men had left Richmond to reinforce Jackson who was North. On the same day the President replied—

WAR DEPARTMENT, WASHINGTON, D. C., June 18, 1862.

Yours of to-day, making it probable that Jackson has been reinforced by about ten thousand from Richmond, is corroborated by a dispatch from Gen. King at Fredericksburg, saying a Frenchman, just arrived from Richmond by way of Gordonsville, met ten to fifteen thousand passing through the latter place to join Jackson.

If this is true, it is as good as a reinforcement to you of an equal force. I could better dispose of things if I could know about what day you can attack Richmond, and would be glad to be informed if you think you can inform me with safety   A. LINCOLN.

Major-General McClellan.

To this McClellan answered: "If ten or fifteen thousand men have left Richmond to reinforce Jackson, *it illustrates their strength and confidence !!"* (Vol. 1, p. 337.)

And yet McClellan's peninsular army, during the month of June, numbered 159,500 men. (Vol. 1, p. 295.)

All this together seems to *"illustrate"* something besides the strength and confidence of the enemy. I think it is the first time in the history of war that weakening an army by sending 15,000 men on other service made the remainder of that army all the more terrific to the opposing General? But I don't understand war; I only claim to know something about evidence of facts.

But for the timely order of the President retaining McDowell, Washington would undoubtedly have fallen, and the Confederacy would have been recognized.

I concede to Gen. McClellan all the private virtues. I dare say he has read all the books on war. I doubt not he understands the science well; he certainly *writes* excellently about it. He has capacity for organizing an army, and possesses many qualities which are pleasing; but of high abilities on the great field of action he has none; the very thing which weakened his enemy struck him with alarm, and he telegraphed to the President that the removal of 15,000 troops of the enemy from Richmond towards Washington "only illustrates their strength and their confidence."

Mr. Winthrop may prove him of Connecticut blood, thrice a hundred years old, but these facts prove him not of the blood of a Cæsar, Hannibal, or Napoleon. He was not made to rule over this great nation in the iron time of war.

The South will surely fail in this Rebellion. I base this confidence not upon our strength or their weakness. I concede that in a righteous cause they would prevail. Men are slow to see how weak is earthly might and human power, when in conflict with the omnipotent Spirit of Justice! The South had no grievance from this Government; they were never wronged or oppressed in the least—they are not of different language, race, or religion; no natural boundaries divide us. They made this wicked war from a mere thirst for power—they were dethroned of their absolute dominion by the natural growth of the free North. They rebelled as Satan rebelled, because "they would rather reign in Hell than serve in Heaven!" They are now in the full enjoyment of that kind of sovereignty.

The Rebellion rests on *no principle*—it envelopes no grand idea even; it has no support but the mere wicked love of absolute power. It will surely fail.

It is said, however, that every people is to be the judge of its own wrongs. Nothing can be more true. But all other peoples will also judge; and the combined judgment of the enlightened world, acting upon the human will, is resistless as the fiat of the Almighty.

The force of this idea is already apparent. In the beginning of this Rebellion, all Europe was against us; her entire sympathy was with the South—with the wronged and weaker party, as they supposed. Recognition was almost certain; was *sure*, if the South could hold out a reasonable time. Where is the hope of recognition now? Let me read from Jeff. Davis' speech at Augusta, delivered a few days ago:

"Who now looks for intervention? Who does not know that our friends abroad depend upon our strength at home! That the balance is in our favor with victory, and turns against us with defeat, and that when our victory is unquestioned, we will be recognized, and not till then."

The waves of human thought go on electric air over the world. Europe is just beginning to look into this question; by-and-by she will understand it; and finally she will say: the South are *all wrong;* and will withhold her sympathy. Then, the arm of Rebellion will drop, paralyzed in its socket. The rebels may still feebly say, we have a right to judge of our own wrongs. Civilized Europe will answer, yes; but when you bring your complaints to us, we have a right to judge also.

I do not expect peace very soon, though their armies be broken up. I will do the South the justice to say that her statesmen and her warriors are true to their Confederacy. Not one of them has uttered a word which looked in the slightest degree towards a return to the Union. They, at all times, and everywhere, declare that on no terms will they ever consent to a union with the North. They are earnest about it. They are as brave and high spirited as we are. They are in terrible straights; they cry out for troops; they say: "Send Lee troops *from anywhere.*" But "anywhere" is a vague place, and the troops do not come from thence at their call. Davis, by the great weight of cares and the mortifications of defeat, has lost all prudence and composure. He tells us, in his very despair, that his troops are absent in large numbers without leave, and he implores the women to send them to the army. He threatens like a man without power; and yet neither he nor any one in the South talks of submission or of a return to the Union under any President, whether that President be Lincoln or McClellan.

Davis' army is nearly exhausted. When the war began there were less than four hundred thousand fighting men in the Confederacy, according to the census. That number must be very small now, yet they have no thought of returning to the Union. Before this war ends they will free and arm the slaves. Of that I have no doubt. Then the end draweth nigh; then the bitter questions about which we have puzzled so much will be solved; then will *begin* the faint, slow dawn upon this long night of gloom. Slow, very slow, the dawn will open, feeble in its first gleam; only the eye of faith can discern it, but it will surely, finally expand into the heavenly day of Union and of peace. I have reason to believe that soon after the election propositions will be made to the Southern States to lay down their arms and return to the Union, with assurances that they shall have every right which the Constitution and the laws can give them. But as I read their destiny they will not return; they will spurn the offer; they will arm the slaves and fight on, "dragging their slow length along." From the seaports taken, and the military posts fortified, will radiate lines of trade and increasing communication. Mexico will be an outlet for many rebels; Europe and the Isles of the West Indies will receive some, and by slow degrees peace will be restored—a peace worth all it will now cost—a peace which no son of ours will ever see broken.

There is nothing personal in this coming election; it is not a contest between Lincoln and McClellan. It is a conflict between two great contending principles—between free and despotic government; and clearly presents the question whether the prosperity, the happiness, and the greatness of our country shall be preserved or forever destroyed!

No mortal issue was ever so vast and grand as ours to-day. No people ever had such a trust to try their faith and their fidelity. Mere selfish politicians will never believe that a higher power rules the destinies of men; that the people can be trusted; that they cannot long be deceived; that in trying times, when the mind is awake, and exalted by great events, the earnest people, seeking only for the truth, will have their light from Heaven; and that, "THE VOICE OF THE PEOPLE WILL BE THE VOICE OF GOD."

Printed at the Daily Era Office, No. 9 Spruce Street, New York.

SPEECH

OF THE

HON. EDWARDS PIERREPONT

IN FAVOR OF THE

ELECTION OF GEN. GRANT,

DELIVERED AT THE GREAT MEETING OF THE

GRANT DEMOCRACY,

HELD AT COOPER'S INSTITUTE,

Wednesday, Oct. 21, 1868.

New York:
WM. C. BRYANT & CO., PRINTERS, 41 NASSAU ST., COR. LIBERTY.

1868.

SPEECH OF HON. EDWARDS PIERREPONT.

Mr. President:

Four years ago, you and I, and many patriotic men, assembled in this Hall to aid our Country in her day of peril.

We asked no honors and no office;—*and we received none.*

Four eventful years have passed since then,—and now a new danger threatens.

Supported by all who were with us then, by our unfaltering friend Gen. Dix, who speaks to us so well from over the seas, and strengthened by many new and noble men, we meet again upon this platform.

You have been steadfast even unto the end, and it is a bright presage for the future that you preside here to night.

Then, we invoked the God of Battles, and we helped to win the bloody fight : Now, we invoke the Prince of Peace, and, we hope, a far more glorious victory.

Friends and Fellow-Citizens :

Old party politics are dead; the war made new issues. When Lee surrendered his army to General Grant, we thought that the Rebellion was ended : But Treason has a new birth ;— not yet hath it put its armor on ;—not yet does it dare to proclaim its fellest purpose—the seizure of the Government, and the restoration of Slavery ! Now, it seeks by diplomatic arts to win what it lost by war ;—to make treason honorable, and fidelity odious ;—and, as Wade Hampton expresses it, " To restore the Lost Cause !"

By some strange fatuity, our Northern people will never take warning until it is too late.

They never would believe, until Fort Sumpter fell, that the South meant war. They will not now believe that the crushed Rebellion is reviving!

Have not the enemy murdered enough of your children, to quicken your senses to approaching danger?

The Convention which met at Tammany Hall on the 4th of July, ballotted twenty-two times, running into the 10th day of the month, before Hotatio Seymour was nominated as its candidate for President.

In the same Convention, a Rebel General stepped forward and nominated Frank P. Blair for Vice-President. No ballot was needed;—one wild yell of wild enthusiasm filled the Hall;— Blair had the full heart and soul of the Convention. He fairly represented its spirit.

Why did the Convention hesitate so long to nominate Seymour, and why, with such eager unanimity did they hasten to nominate Blair?

Read the list of leading names in that Assembly, and read the speeches of Seymour and the letter of Blair, published just prior to the Convention, and you shall see the reason for this striking difference.

In this list I find one hundred and five men who were Confederate Generals, Colonels, Majors, Captains, Governors, Senators, or Members of the Rebel Congress.

Among them are Wade Hampton, Buckner, Ransom, Vance, Bocock, Hill, Preston, Clingman, Rhett, and the petted General Forrest, remembered for his cruel and inhuman massacre of Union Soldiers, after their surrender, at Fort Pillow.

In that Convention were many good and true men of the North, but they held no sway, and their voice was not regarded.

Mr. Seymour, in his recent speeches, had denounced every form of repudiation. In his Cooper Institute Speech of June 25th, he says:

"If we make our paper money good by a harsh system of con-
" traction, we shall cripple the energies of the country, and make
" bankruptcy and ruin. If, on the other hand, we debase the cur-
" rency by unwise issues, we equally perplex business, and destroy
" sober industry, and make all prices mere matters of gambling
" tricks and chances. This will end as it did in the Southern Con-
" federacy. At the outset, the citizens of Richmond went to market
" with their money in their vest pockets, and brought back their
" dinners in their baskets; in the end, they took their money in
" their baskets, and brought home their dinners in their vest
" pockets."

In his Albany speech of March 11th, he says:

"The bonds so unwisely and so wastefully issued have gone into
" the hands of innocent holders, who, to a vast extent, are compul-
" sory owners."

"It is a mistake to suppose that they are mostly held by capital-
" ists. Large sums belonging to children and widows, under the
" order of Courts or the action of Trustees, have been invested in
" Government bonds. The vast amounts held by Life and Fire In-
" surance Companies and Savings Banks are, in fact, held in trust
" for and are the reliance of the great body of active business and
" laboring men or women, or of widows and orphans. The Savings
" Banks of this State, which are the depositories of the poor, or of
" persons of limited means, hold about $60,000,000 of Government
" bonds. The whole amount held in the State of New York, in the
" forms of trust, will not fall below $200,000,000. If we look into
" other States we shall see that only a small share of these bonds
" are held by men known as capitalists, but they belong, in fact if
" not in form, to the business, the active and the laboring men of
" society. The destruction of these securities would make a wide-
" spread ruin and distress, which would reach into every workshop
" and every home, however humble. * * * * * *
" It is a mistake to suppose that the interests of the bondholder and
" the tax-payer are antagonistic. The fact is overlooked, that in
" order to make any saving by giving the bondholder a debased or
" worthless paper, we must bring upon ourselves *disaster and dis-
" honor* which will cost a hundred fold what we can save. It means
" that we are to give to the laborer for his toil a base currency; it
" means that the honor of our country shall be stained; it means

" that our business shall be kept in uncertainty and confusion; it
" means that the laboring man shall suffer by the increased cost of
" the comforts of life; it means that the tax-payer shall be burdened
" by a Government proved to be corrupt and imbecile by this very
" depreciation of its money, We cannot afford to speculate upon
" the Nation's honor at so *fearful a cost.*"

Such might be the words of a sagacious statesman with sound financial views; such might be the words of a patriot jealous of his country's honor.

Wade Hampton, and the other Rebel generals who dominated over that Convention, had read these speeches.

They knew Seymour to be the son of a New England sire, and they doubted his readiness to sell his birth-right.

Wonder not that they delayed his nomination so long—but wonder and be sad, that a gentleman of the North, whose ideas upon the great question of the day were so just, should be humbled to the earth and bend down before these Rebel generals, all fresh from the slaughter of his countrymen, and take back the noble words he had uttered before they would consent to his nomination!

Seymour assures us that he did not wish to be nominated, but that he was " caught up in a whirlwind " and couldn't help it. A whirlwind is an unsafe thing for Seymour to ride upon. The Prophet " Elijah was taken up by a whirlwind into *heaven*"— and Seymour fancied that he was going to be taken up by the same vehicle, into *the Presidency;* but he will find it whirling down the other way with terrific speed—about November.

Three days before the Convention met Blair published *his* declaration of principles, using these words:

" There is no possibility of changing the political character of the
" Senate, even if the Democrats should elect their President, and
" a majority of the popular branch of Congress. We cannot, there-
" fore, undo the Radical plan of Reconstruction by Congressional
" action; the Senate will continue a bar to its repeal. *Must we*
" *submit to it? How can it be overthrown?*

" There is but one way to restore the Government and the Con-
" stitution, and that is for the President elect to declare these acts

" null and void, compel the army to undo its usurpations at the
" South, disperse the Carpet Bag State Governments, allow the
" white people to re-organize their own Governments, and elect
" Senators and Representatives.

" We must restore the Constitution before we can restore the
" finances, and to do this we must have a President who will exe-
" cute the will of the people, *by trampling into dust* the usurpations
" of Congress, known as the Reconstruction Acts. I wish to stand
" before the Convention upon this issue."—There let him stand—
there he will stand.

This was purely revolutionary; this promised lawless violence
and war. The letter suited the Convention exactly. Blair
knew it would. No ballot was needed for Blair. Blair was the
son of a Southern slaveholder. Blair could be trusted. A Rebel
General rose and nominated Blair; and with loud acclaim, 'mid
wildest enthusiasm, he was selected.

Seymour bowed down his intellectual head before the Rebel
power, accepted a platform which repudiated every just sentiment of his recent speech, and, as friends report—went away
sorrowful!

Hear him in reply to the tender of his nomination:

" I have been caught by the great tide that is swelling our party
" on to victory, and I am unable to resist the pressure."

This is the tide which swept over Pennsylvania and Ohio the
other day; Seymour foresaw it dimly, but he mistook its character; he thought it was one of those old Democratic tides, which
ante-date the war; his blinded eyes couldn't see that it swelled
out from millions of loyal hearts, heaving with honest love and
solicitude for the safety of their country!

Old Democratic leaders for the last ten years, have had no just
sense of public opinion. The same kind of Democratic leaders
lived eighteen hundred and forty years ago;—Christ said, they
were "fools, and blind, that could discern the signs of the times."

SEYMOUR, continues:

" You have also communicated to me the resolution adopted by

"that Convention. As its Charman I am familiar with its language
"and as a member of that Convention I am a party to its terms
"I accord with its views; I stand upon its position in this
"contest, and I shall strive hereafter, whether in public or private
"life, to carry them into effect."

These resolutions demand repudiation of the Nation's faith, and declare the solemn acts of Congress unconstitutional and void.

This is the first time in our history that a political convention has undertaken to declare what laws of Congress are unconstitutional and void: and the first time that a candidate for the Vice-Presidency has proposed to "TRAMPLE INTO DUST" the Statutes of Congress, which he admits that he could not get repealed.

This platform had the Rebel General Wade Hampton as its chief builder; with defiant boldness he gives us its whole hisstory.

The Charleston *Journal*, informs us, that—

"General Wade Hampton was welcomed by the people of that
"city, on Friday night, upon his return from the Tammany Con-
"vention. He was received by a long procession, and having been
"conducted to a four-horse carriage, was escorted, like a conquer-
"ing hero, amid the shouts of the multitude, to his temporary stop-
"ping place in the city."

He said:

"More than four years—years which have seen a Nation's death,
"which have brought to us sorrow, humiliation and ruin,—have
"passed since I last stood in your noble and battle-scarred old city.
"Then proudly erect, flushed with victory and devotion in her
"patriotism, she held in her heroic hands the key of our State,
"defying with indomitable courage, the assaults of her enemies.
"While a portion of her sons here guarded so bravely the portals
"of the State, others were following the glorious Southern Cross,
"wherever it was waving in triumph, or were sleeping their last
"sleep on the fields, which their valor had contributed to win. *All
"were doing their duty as Carolinians,* and the great historic names
"of the Revolution were gilded with a new lustre as the descend-
"ants of Moultrie, of Rutledge, of Lowndes, of Hayne, of Pinckney
"and Huger, fought as did their fathers for this dear old Carolina

" of ours." * * * "So long as patriotism, constancy and valor are
" esteemed, the wondrous story of her defence will stir the hearts of
" brave men, and noble women will teach their children to lisp the
" name of Beauregard."

Beauregard you will remember, was an officer in the regular army, was educated at West Point, at the expense of the Government which he had sworn to defend and whose flag he betrayed.

The speech continues—

" I hope and believe that the blessed day of our deliverance is
" drawing near. The signs in the political skies are full of hope,
" and we bring back to you from the united Democracy of the
" North, tidings of great glee."

" After a free and full consultation with delegates in the Conven-
" tion, representing all the Northern States, I am thoroughly con-
" vinced that the great heart of Democracy is fully aroused ; that it
" beats in profound sympathy with the suffering South ; that it is
" fully alive to the dangers which threaten to destroy the Constitu-
" tion and the Government, and that it is unalterably fixed in its
" purpose to rescue that Constitution from destruction, to restore
" that Government to its legitimate functions, and to bring back
" the Southern States to their place in the Union, with all their
" rights, dignity and equality unimpaired. These are the objects
" for which the Democractic party are fighting ; and, planting them-
" selves on the Appian way of the Constitution, grasping once more
" in friendship the hands of their brethren of the South, setting up
" again the broken altars of the country, they have sworn never to
" cease fighting until their objects are accomplished.

Thus talks this Rebel General about the Constitution, which he had betrayed, and the Government he fought so long to destroy.

Listen further :

"*I yield to none in devotion to that ' Lost Cause ' for which we
" fought. Never shall I admit that the cause itself failed, and that
" the principles which gave it life were therefore wrong. Never shall
" I brand the men who upheld it so nobly as ' rebels ' or ' traitors.'*"

* * * * * * *

"As it was my good fortune to be on the Committee which framed this
" instrument, it may be interesting to you, perhaps, to learn the detail
" by which it was perfected, and the views of those who made it. As
' you are aware, the Committee on Resolutions consisted of one member
" from each State."

"Gentlemen were here from the North, South, East and West, and by
" all we were met with extreme cordiality. They said they were willing
" to give us everything we desired; but we of the South must remember
" that they had a great fight to make, and it would not be policy to
" place upon that platform that which would endanger *prejudice* at the
" North."

Wade Hampton must have been a little vexed, at these foolish prejudices of the North against rebellion, against re-enslavement and repudiation of the honest debt. But Northern prejudice did not stand long in the way.

"They, however, pledged themselves to do all in their power to relieve
" the Southern States, and restore to us the Constitution as it had existed.
" As we were met in such a kindly spirit, I could not but reciprocate
" it. I knew that I was representing the feelings of my people when I
" did so."

(After this apology, we hope that the Rebels will not be *too* hard on Wade Hampton for treating Northern Democrats with common decency.)

"I told them that I could withdraw all the resolutions I have offered,
" and no doubt other Southern delegates would do the same, and would ac-
" cept the resolutions offered by Hon. Mr. Bayard, the Senator from Dela-
" ware, which declared that the right of suffrage belonged to the States. I
" said I take the resolutions if they would allow me to add but three words,
" which you will find embodied in the platform. *I added this : And we
" declare that the Reconstruction Acts are revolutionary, unconstitutional
" and void.* When I proposed that every single member of the Com-
" mittee—and the warmest men in it were the men of the North, came
" forward and said they would carry it out to the end."

Hear him further :

"Victory will bring even more than this to us, for it will give us, along
" with constitutional liberty, the right to manage and control our own

" State Government in accordance with the time honored provisions of the
" Constitutions of the United States. When may we hope to see the res-
" toration of honor and decency in the conduct of affairs; we may hope to
" see our rulers as of old, intelligent, patriotic NATIVE BORN—and white.
" In that blessed day of deliverance, we shall have no carpet-bag or mili-
" tary Governors."

Yes, in that blessed day of the election of Seymour and Blair, " NATIVE BORN " rulers alone are to have peace. Our adopted fellow-citizens are all to be excluded. " NATIVE BORN " is the watchword!

Ho! Rally to the standard of Seymour and of Blair, ye foreign-born who have adopted our country as your home; in their day of glorious victory none but the *native-born* shall hold a single office.

The Charleston *News*, in concluding its report, says:

" On leaving the stage an attempt was made to secure General
" Hampton and raise him on the shoulders of the crowd,"

Governor Sharkey, of Mississippi, says:

" The Democratic party has put a platform that ought to be ac-
" ceptable to all North and South. Its foundation is laid in the
" Constitution. It demands immediate restoration of all the States
" to their equal rights in the Union—it declares the Union to be
" indissoluble—and it *declares the whole Congressional system of re-*
" *construction void, and, as a consequence, everything which has been*
" *done under it void also.* On this platform we of the South can
" stand; it will restore us to our rights—to our position of 1865—
" *and blot out all that has been done under the arbitrary and un-*
" *warrantable demands of Congress."*

He says of Seymour and Blair:

" They cannot falter now, they are committed. They cannot un-
" dertake to administer a Government part valid, part void."

And the Mobile *Tribune* adds:

" The great Democratic party will rise in its might, and the dag-

" ger of Brutus may aid in accomplishing our redemption from
" Radical rule, ruin and usurpation."

" If we are successful in the approaching contest we shall gain
" all that we lost in the 'Lost Cause.'"

" By the election of Seymour and Blair," says Governor Vance, of North Carolina, " all that the Confederacy fought for will be " won."

And it is asserted by the Mobile *Register:*

" That the counter-revolution will not be complete without more
" blood-letting."

And the Richmond *Enquirer* adds:

" The white men of the Southern States have seen the day when
" they could use the bullet, and, if God in his anger permit the
" necessity to arrive, they will use it again."

The Georgia Democratic Convention declared:

" There might once have been a necessity for the Rebels of Georgia
" to submit to the military authorities, but there is none now. The
" Democratic chivalry of the North are marching to our rescue."

Says Governor Wise:

" Secession is not dead, it is more alive to-day than ever. I sup-
" port Blair because he promises Revolution."

J. M. Ramsey, of Georgia, declares:

" That the true men of the South are ready to rally once more
" under the Rebel flag and try the issue of the cartridge box."

Toombs bid defiance in these words:

" The Reconstruction Acts are null and void, and shall not stand.
" The grinning skeletons that have been set up in our midst as leg-
" islators shall be ousted by Frank Blair, whom our party has ex-
" pressly appointed for that purpose."

Capt. Semmes, who robbed and burned your unarmed merchan ships, in a ratification speech at Mobile, said:

"I drew my sword against the old flag, * * * * " I have come here to-night, from the country, to ratify and rejoice with you in the nomination of Seymour and Blair."

Col. Herndon, following him, said:

"If there were any omissions in the platform, the brave and magnanimous speeches of Seymour and Blair supplied them all."

Then reading the letter of Blair, which promised "to trample into dust," by military power, the laws of Congress, he exclaimed:

" Who but a brave, true, generous heart could utter such a sentiment as this?"

The Rebel *Judge Jones* said: "He asked for no better platform than the letter of Gen. Blair."

Mr. Chas. Gibson, in his speech, said:

"Mr. Blair, in this letter, tells us that if he be elected President of the United States, or become President—he tells you that if he become President of the United States, *he will use the necessary measures to remove the State Governments of the South.*"

The Rebel *Judge Churchill* used the following language:

"Thank God! the people have been ahead of their leaders, *and have never believed that their sacred cause was wholly lost. Their faith is now rewarded. A great party is now ours, and we should all press on to victory.*"

When a Law of Congress is distasteful, the Rebels declare that it is unconstitutional, and Blair proposes to "trample it into dust" by military power. "The President-Elect" he tell us, must do this, he cannot even wait for the inauguration. But if the Constitution itself stands in the way, what do you think is to be done then? Why, declare it *unconstitutional*, to be sure!

The Fourteenth Amendment was long since adopted, and has in due form been declared a part of the Constitution; and yet ex-Senator Pugh, of Ohio, says:

"I would not give them a three cent. postage stamp for their Fourteenth Amendment. It is not part of the Constitution, and it never will be. It is a base fraud, *and I say, as Frank Blair said, these Carpet-bag Governments must be overthrown.*"

This Fourteenth Amendment provides against the repudiation of our national debt, against any recognition of the Rebel claims, and against any payment for the loss of their slaves. You see why this part of the Constitution is so odious, and why Blair, with military feet, means "to trample it into dust."

I have given you the views of leading Seymour and Blair men in their own words. Why should we not expect these views? Vallandingham moved the nomination of Seymour. The Rebel General Preston nominated Blair, and four confederate Generals, with Vallandingham added, made the Ratification Speeches in New York. These speeches, these journals, and these letters, which I have read, tell us that the election of Seymour and Blair will restore the "Lost cause," will justify the Rebellion, and re-instate the South in every right which she had before the revolt. They are right; no honest man can doubt it.

Does any sane man, for one moment, imagine that, if Blair is elected, the South will ever consent to pay a dollar of the debt incurred in putting down their Rebellion?

This cry about the burden of the public debt, is a false cry, raised by the enemies of the Government. The debt grows less, the means of payment grow greater every month: when peace is fairly restored, and the industry of the whole country revives, the debt will not be felt: and before Grant's administration is over, people will wonder that they were ever frighted by this phantom.

Even during the most costly years of the war, when the Southern States were in actual revolt, and, of course, contributed nothing to the revenue; the taxes of the North were easily borne, and the material prosperity of our people was never greater. When hostilities ceased, the expenses of the Government were *forthwith* vastly diminished, and the productive industry of the country was greatly increased. Millions of the war debt have already been paid, and the income tax has been reduced one-half.

With the opening of the Pacific Railroad—with the inconceivable increase of wealth which will follow the completion of that work ; with the new dawning trade of the East ; with the countless emigrants from China whose willing hands will reveal the hidden riches of our soil ; with the numberless laborers from Europe now weekly landing upon our shores ; with the increasing population and stimulated enterprise of the ever-robust and progrssive North, and with all this unite the whole vast resources of the regained and regenerated South ; and while the hollow cant, about national bankruptcy and ruin, is droning in our ears, New York will become the monetary centre of the world, gold will be our currency, and the public debt will have ceased to be a burden.

The two great contending principles, which now divide the country, are fairly represented by two Generals :

The one by General Grant, the other by General Blair. No one can doubt upon which side General Grant stands ; and General Blair has taken especial pains that no one shall doubt upon which side he stands. The people are going to vote. They will vote for General Grant or for General Blair. Many Democrats now think they will not vote at all ; but when the time arrives they will surely vote—all will vote ; it will be far the largest vote ever cast ; it will be a decisive, an overwelming vote.

Which of these two Generals shall be your Chief Ruler for the next four years ? Which can you most safely trust with this great office, in these unsettled times of much confusion and great distrust ?

You want peace, order, security ; a rivival of our varied industry and a restoration of our whole Union upon terms which are fair and just. To whom will you turn as the safer man ?

It will occur to our people, that if Seymour were elected President, he may die, and give place to Blair. Within a few short years three Presidents, just entering upon their term of office, have died ; and the Vice Presidents have reigned in their stead. What these Vice Presidents would do, no one could tell,—but each *did*, just exactly what the party which elected him did not wish. Seymour might perish under the weight of office; and if he did not please the Rebels, some Southern patriot, like Wilkes Booth, might dispose of him. If Seymour were out of the way no one can doubt what Blair would do, he has told us that.

I have known General Grant since the time when he came from the West to take command of the Army of the Potomac. He has impressed me as one of the most remarkable of men. He has always been a Democrat. To the great principles of the Democratic party (which began to perish with the war,) I have always been attached. I believe in coined gold and not in stamped paper; I believe in liberty protected by law; I believe that the foreign-born, who have adopted our country, and sworn allegience to our Government, should have the same rights, and the same protection, (under the Constitution,) as the native-born; I believe that the Government should act with even justice upon the rich and the poor; that it should allow the utmost freedom of trade consistent with its absolute necessities for moderate revenue; that it should not trammel enterprise by legislative monopolies; that as a Government, it should aim at no paltry imitation of Royal or Imperial splendor; but be a simple, economical, stern and just Protecting Power, leaving the individual to whatever of luxury and extravagant display his folly may suggest; that it should relieve its citizens from harrassing taxes, by levying the tax upon few articles, in such manner as to compel every man to pay his just share in accordance with his means; that it should have no costly army in time of peace, and that the people should, by "eternal vigilance" guard against the absorption of the rights of the States by the Central Power.

Conversations with Gen. Grant had led me to believe that such was the substance of his own views, and I was very desirous that he should be the Democratic candidate. One day at his house in Washington, while he was Secretary of War, I told him that I thought he would make a good Democratic candidate if he was right on the question of negro suffrage. He replied that he had no wish for the Presidency, that he had now a much higher office than he had ever expected,—that General Sherman would make a good President, and that he would gladly give the half that he was worth to make Sherman, or any other fit man, President; that his feelings and sentiments were entirely opposed to negro suffrage; but that he did not wish to be restrained by any pledges from the right to change his opinions in future if new exigences convinced him that he was wrong; for, said he, you will remember that early in the war, when I was in command at the west I publicly stated that if the negroes had an insurrection I would hold my army in check until it was put down. But long before the war was over I should have been glad of a negro insurrection, and would have moved my army all the faster. What I want is the Union—the whole country returned to peace and submission to the laws. I do not like universal negro suffrage now, but the freedmen ought to be protected, and if the only way to protect them in their helpless condition is, to give them the suffrage, then I shall be in favor of letting them vote. I want the Union restored, and to have the South come back, obey the laws, and submit as good citizens, and if the future proves that they will not do it without negro suffrage, then I would give them negro suffrage.

Washington never thought more wisely or talked more justly.

That General Grant fairly represents the patriot sentiment of the North, no man can doubt. From the beginning of the war to its close, he was at his post of duty; always ready, uncomplaining, patient, vigilant and just; trusting in God, in a righteous cause, and in his own brave men, he never knew a failure. Poor—without a rich friend—with no reputation, and no political influence,—he rose to the head of the army, conducted the greatest war in the annals of time to successful end, and within five short years, from his humble start, his was the foremost name in the civilized world.

His detractors say, that he has no experience in affairs of State; nor had he experience in war until he commenced it. It is also said that his success in war was owing to good fortune.

So let his success in peace be.

Good fortune is a powerful goddess, and he whom she favors is certain of success.

Washington was first a great General, and then he was a great statesman.

Grant has proved himself a great General, and the same high gifts of firmness, determined purpose, unswerving fidelity, calmness of judgment, justice, moderation and wonderful aptness in the employment of the ability of others, added to a clear common sense approaching to genius, assure us that he will make a President whom we can safety trust.

Seymour has had no experience in the administration of Federal affairs, and has always been noted, as "infirm of purpose, "letting I *dare not*, wait upon I *would*." In July 1863, he made a public speech, very discouraging to every friend of the Government and tending to impair the success of the war. On the same day,—Grant made no speech,—but marched his brave soldiers into Vicksburg, and 30,000 enemies of your country surrendered.

This is the last great issue of our time; the most momentous ever presented for your verdict. You cannot mistake the issue. The dying words of the brave Douglas in our last conflict were, "There can be no neutrals in this war—Only patriots or traitors."

The same issue passed upon by the American People in 1864, is again presented, with added features, more odious and revolting. Then the proposition was, that the "war was a "failure," and ought to cease. Now it is boldly claimed that the Rebellion was right, and that Davis and Lee and Beauregard, and all the other Rebels, educated at public expense, and who turned traitors to the Government, which they had sworn to defend,—whose hands are yet dripping with the blood of Northern men, who went down to death to save the nation's life, —are men of high honor; of whom Blair in his speech of acceptance, with irrepressible enthusiasm, exclaims:

"What civilized people on earth would refuse to associate with "themselves under all the rights, honors and dignities of their "country such men as Lee and Johnston?

"What civilized country on earth would fail to do honor to those "who, fighting for an erroneous cause, yet distinguished themselves "by a gallantry never surpassed, in that contest for which they are "sought to be disfranchised and exiled from their homes; in that "contest they proved themselves worthy to be our peers."

He should have added—AND WE WISH THEM TO BE OUR MASTERS?

Montgomery Blair, in Alexandria, made his public confession and recantation in these words:

"Many who like myself have opposed secession and rebellion, and "fancied ourselves wiser than the Rebels, if not more partriotic, "will have to confess our mistake. In the present aspect of affairs, "I have to confess that it is yet to be decided whether those who "fought for the Union have not blundered."

In affairs of State, you know that a blunder is a crime. You see why the name of Blair was hailed with such shouts in a Convention where Rebels ruled. Will any but a Rebel vote for him?

Much surprise is felt that the colored freedmen are voting with their late masters. Why be surprised? When these same masters can come to New York, and rule a Convention of Northern white men, why should they not control their recent negro slaves?

Now, we hear that perjured oaths and broken vows of fidelity to the Government are no dishonor, that the war against the revolt was a blunder, that the Emancipation Proclamation of the President, and the deliberate Acts of Congress, are void, and that by force of arms, they are to be swept away at the beck of the South, in order to restore them to their ancient rights.

The Supreme Court of the United States have decided, that by war the Rebels lost all their rights under the Constitution, and that all they can have, is of favor. But of what avail are the Laws of Congress and the decisions of the Supreme Court? Blair promises "*to trample them into dust;*" and next will severely follow a claim that the Rebels shall be paid for the loss of their slaves.

Let us here pause, and ask why they should not be paid? They lost much by the war, and by the Proclamation of Freedom. If the war was unconstitutional and wrong, then surely the Emancipation Proclamation was void, and the laws by which money was raised to prosecute that war, are void also.

I have presented this issue as the leading Seymour and Blair men have framed it. It is a fair issue—clear, open and bold—there is no dodging this issue.

And now, I ask upon this issue, who will vote against Grant? Will Mr. John Q. Adams, after his recent letter and speech of just rebuke to the South, vote against Grant?

Every Rebel hater of our free Government will vote against Grant.

Every cruel jailor who exposed, starved and robbed our prisoned soldiers, will vote against Grant.

Every aider in those crimes against humanity and against civilization, perpetrated at the Libby and at Andersonville, will vote against Grant.

Every contemner of our flag, despires of our Government and violator of its benign laws, will vote against Grant.

Every Rebel raider from Canada, who robbed and murdered the defenceless people of St. Albans. Every inhuman wretch who plotted to poison your waters, burn your cities, and introduced pestilence into all the North, will vote against Gran

Every traitor, every conspirator who aided in the murder of President Lincoln, and the assassination of Secretary Seward, will vote against Grant.

And some good men, blinded by party prejudice or held in bondage by party fears, may vote against Grant.

But tell me, will any father, the blood of whose only son was shed in his country's cause, vote against Grant?

Will the surviving soldier, who endured the perils, and now shares the glories of successful war, vote against Grant?

Will the trustees of the widow and the orphan and the humble laborer, whose little all is in some savings Institution, dependent wholly upon income derived from Government Bonds, vote against Grant?

Will any Father in the Roman Catholic Church, looking to the welfare of the children of that Church, whose earnings are deposited for safety, and drawing interest from United States securities, vote against Grant?

Will our adopted fellow citizens, upon whose advice millions of foreign capital have been invested here, vote against Grant?

Will any intelligent man of business, merchant, banker, manufacturer, salaried clerk, or day-laborer, who wishes stability, security and prosperity for himself and his children, vote against Grant?

Will any man who does not wish the Nation humbled, treason honored, and patriotism insulted, vote against Grant?

Consider it well fellow-citizens,— vote deliberately,— vote conscientiously,—vote down the patriot,— vote up the Rebel if you will!!—vote Grant a failure, and Lee, the Hero of the War:—But,—before you thus vote,—tear down these mocking monuments erected to your patriot dead; demolish every memorial stone at Gettysburgh, and in every place where a grateful nation has reared a soldier's tomb!

Level three hundred thousand little hillocks, under which sleep three hundred thousand young men of the country, they died to save; the grass is very green, so watered by mothers' tears, and the roses bloom well, which mourning sisters and bereaved wives have planted on those graves!—Trample them in the earth—they are all a mockery—the sleepers died in an ignoble cause, and well deserved their doom—and the rotting prisoners of the Libby, and the starving, tortured soldiers at Andersonville, had but their just deserts!

Vote against Grant; and when you see the Rebels, all red with the blood of your mothers' sons, holding high revelry in the Capitol—and confusion, dismay and anarchy in the land—go tell your children:—WE VOTED FOR THAT!

I would have the South treated justly;—yea, very generously; I would take no step for vengeance;—but I would not restore them to power, with their present mad views, and audacious purpose, to subvert the laws, and destroy the liberties of my country.

The vote will soon be cast; when the ballot has decided an issue in America, the decision conquers even the will:—all submit as to the fiat of God.

As this is the last, so will it be the bitterest contest. In it the son shall be divided against the father, and the father against the son, and a man's foes shall be they of his own household.

It is a war of the mind, a war of ideas—of the will, and of all the evil passions.

THE RESULT IS CERTAIN.

The storm will rage with great blackness, but as the sun rolls down on the 3d of November next, and stamps with the ink of night, the eternal record of that day, you shall see One, calm, serene and well worthy of your trust, rising above the storm, and you shall hear his voice, saying:

"LET US HAVE PEACE!"

SPEECH

OF THE

HON. EDWARDS PIERREPONT,

Delivered at the Great Ratification Meeting

OF THE

REPUBLICANS,

HELD AT COOPER INSTITUTE,

Thursday, Nov. 3, 1870.

NEW YORK:
EVENING POST STEAM PRESSES, 41 NASSAU STREET, COR. LIBERTY.
1870.

SPEECH

OF THE

HON. EDWARDS PIERREPONT.

You, my fellow citizens—the busiest, the intensest people upon the face of the earth—whose pressing avocations of to-day crowd out the memories of yesterday—need often to be reminded of what "you yourselves do know."

In 1824, the great Henry Clay of Kentucky was Speaker of the House of Representatives. He was the ablest orator in the Democratic party. In that year the people failed to elect a President—Adams, Clay, Crawford and Jackson were all candidates. Neither one had a majority of the electoral vote, and it fell upon the House of Representatives to choose the President. In a caucus of the dominant party, Wm. H. Crawford of Georgia was nominated, but Mr. Clay, with his powerful influence, went over to Mr. Adams who was thereby elected, and Mr. Clay became the Secretary of State.

From that time onward through a period of twenty-eight years, the great Whig party flourished. Clay and Webster were its giant leaders.

In 1852, the mission of that party was ended; its work was done, its fight was over and its army was disbanded. Out of the fragments of the Whig party—out of the Free-soil party, out of the Liberty party, out of Democrats who opposed the arrogant pretensions of the slave power, out of deeply religious men of all parties, who resisted the spread of inhuman slavery—arose the Republican party, which took shape and name in 1854, and whose first great success in 1860, was the election of Abraham Lincoln to the Presidency.

But ten years of rule, and half those years of civil commotion or terrible war! Years full of sorrows, which pressed the life from many hearts, and sent to untimely graves so many of your kindred. Years in which through faith and toil and prayer and suffering, the nation was saved, and the foulest crimes that ever cursed a christian people, were "burned and purged away."

Has the party which did this Herculean work performed its full mission? is it ready to disband its forces,—to turn over the glorious fruits of all its labors, to be enjoyed, wasted, or destroyed by those whose hands are yet stained with the blood of your own sons!

The Saviour tells us, that, when the unclean spirit is gone out of a man, he wanders about seeking rest, and finding none he returns unto the house from whence he came out; and if he finds it all empty, swept and garnished, he takes with him other spirits more wicked than himself, and they enter in and dwell there; and the last state of that man is worse than the first.

This foul spirit of slavery and rebellion, you have driven from your house; and you have washed out his loathsome foul stains, with much blood. He has wandered through many places, seeking rest; but finding none, he will surely return to the house from which you drove him; and if he finds it all swept and garnished and we stand uncovered in the hall, ready to receive him, he will enter in with others more wicked than himself, and dwell there, and our last state will be worse than the first.

The spirit which has found no rest, and now proposes to return and take possession of your well-garnished house, has begun in earnest; its minions are numerous, bold and active. It can find no rest :—it never will rest. It begins with high determination, zeal and energy, and desperation, but in success; it will leave no art untried, no labor neglected; it will succeed if it finds none but faithless servants, or jealous inmates, or greedy plunderers, or disappointed seekers, or craven cowards at the gates.

Pardon me while I turn you to the history of the past, that you may read the future. "That which hath been, will be again." For more than forty years the Congress which was elected two years before the presidental contest, has determined that contest. And now, a new House is to be elected. Within a few days we shall know whether the Congress which continues through the term of General Grant, is Republican or not. If it is Republican, then you may be reasonably sure that the next President will be a Republican ; if it is anti-Republican, then you may reasonably fear that the next President will be the humble tool of the Rebel Power, swift to do its bidding, ready as they have promised, to set at naught the amendments to the constitution which favor liberty, and ready to recompense the slave-holder for his liberated slaves.

Do you think that the members of the late convention which was governed by rebel chieftains, have radically changed since then? Not at all. The same men generally, and the same spirit precisely, which ruled the last, will rule the next Democratic Convention.

Let us look at this question in the light of common sense, and of recent events.

Last week the State Agricultural Society of Georgia held a great fair at Atlanta. When Hon. Benjamin Yancey, President of the society came, he found the old star-spangled banner waving over the congregated people, and he ordered the hated flag to be pulled down ; and nothing but fear of future consequences, it is said, kept their dusty feet from trampling the abhorred ensign in the mire. Last week in this very hall, eulogiums of unmingled praise were pronounced over the Rebel dead; and our younger children are puzzled to know whether Lee or Lincoln was the worthier patriot. Last week, at Alexandria, close by the capitol of the nation, a public reception was given to one called the " *Great Ex-President Davis.*"

These are but a few of the many indications of what has already begun.

Just now, there is dissatisfaction felt by a few Republicans, I dare say. It is always so. Two years before the re-election of Mr. Lincoln, Seymour carried New York ; but in 1864, when the people had to face the real question, they forgot their differences, and redeemed the State.

It is not given us to know the future ; a kind Providence has veiled it from our eyes, and no wise man would lift the curtain, if he could, which God's hand has drawn over the stage of our destiny. But, through reason, and the history of the past, we may fairly predict what is likely to happen.

We can plainly foresee that the Congress now about to be elected will be Republican; not in the ratio of two to one, but by a fair working number, which makes a far stronger administration than a two-thirds majority.

When the legislative branch of the government is so numerous that it can pass laws over the veto of the Executive, the selfishness and vanity of abounding power is sure to cause disturbance in the harmony, and thus weaken the vigor, of administration. We can foresee that the Republican party, chastened and consolidated, will grow wiser in some respects; will more carefully consider the internal revenue, the tariff, and the navigation laws, and adapt them to the intelligent wants and the real interests of the whole country. But we can also see that success does not spring up from the ground, and that without the use of means, our desired ends will not be accomplished.

You are soon to elect not only a Governor, Lieutenant-Governor, and other State officers, but you are also to elect an entire Congressional delegation. This, therefore, is a very important canvas; it bears directly upon national issues; it may determine the next Presidential election. Your candidates are all good men. Gen. Woodford as Governor, and Mr. Kaufman as Lieutenant-Governor, would secure the best administration to the State. One had an excellent record in the war: both have an unsullied reputation in civil life. No honest man can doubt that, if elected, they would faithfully carry out the principles and the wishes of the Republican party. No honest or dishonest man can doubt that the opposing candidates, if elected, would, to the fullest extent, carry out the principles and the wishes of their party. To which of the two parties can you most safely entrust the government of the State?—to that which has proved true to the Union; or to that which is to-day in close alliance with the enemies of the Union?

We judge a tree by its fruits. None but poison fruits ever grew upon the old slave-tree; and fruit from any branch engrafted on that stock, will smell of death and taste of blood for many years to come!

The Republican party, during its short career, has done collossal work; but its labor is not ended. It is now in its prime of power; its greater work is yet to be done. It has torn down the decayed old fever-breeding tenement, and cleared away the rubbish. It has laid the new corner stones upon the rock of humanity, justice and equal liberty; and now the building of the structure requires more skillful hands, more wise forecasting minds, than it required to tear down the ruined edifice, which, incongruous and falsely reared, was tumbling to its fall. The soldier nobly did his work; he will have the undying gratitude of patriots of his own time, and " the thanks of millions yet to be!" But the work of the Republican statesman has but just begun, and the Republican mission will not end, until the statesman's work is finished.

Expect some blundering in the beginning, which a generous people will forgive, to a party which is honest in its main purpose, and which has such a record of great deeds, and heroic success in the saving of the nation. Be quite sure, that the Republican mission is not ended. It is the Democratic party, which untrue to its earliesr history, and to the honest convictions of its best men, has lost the confidence of the people, and must perish as a national power. The only chance which it has of electing the one it nominates, is to nominate a Republican. But I don't think they will nominate a Republican. I think they will only nominate from the *Republican State of Ohio*, its present Democratic Senator—an able man—not destined to be elected.

Let me give you some of the elements of my confidence.

And, first of all, the people as a whole, desire what is best and right; and their instinct is wonderfully true in the discernment of what is best and right; and when they come soberly to consider the effect of restoring to power the old slaveholder, the rebel, the opposer of the war and the hater of the Union, and those who would a thousand fold, have preferred the rebel General Lee to the patriot General Grant, they will not hesitate to vote again for the great general who won heroic victories over the enemies of the Union, and saved the nation in its day of peril!

Next, the entire emancipated vote will be given for those who proved the negro's friend. During the entire war, not an instance can be named, where fear, or hope, or gain, or danger, could ever make the bondsman swerve from his fidelity, or betray a soldier of the North; and it is all folly to suppose, that the freed slave will vote for his old oppressor.

Next, the country will gratefully remember what the Republican party has done; that through weariness and every discouragement; through difficulties vast; through long and desolating war; through dangers and dissensions at home, it overcame all; it saved the country entire, made liberty real and universal, preserved our glorious heritage of freedom; prepared the way for our rapid development in wealth and greatness—gave a safe and uniform currency to the whole nation, and equal rights and equal laws to all; destroyed the inhuman monster, so long our reproach, our blight, our terror and our curse; and ushered in the day, when it was no longer statutory crime to teach a poor benighted soul to read the word of God! and made it no longer possible, under the Union flag, and under the very dome of the capital, for brutal ruffian to tear the child from its mother's arms and sell it to eternal slavery!

Next, the country will remember at the fitting time what the opposing party has done; it will remember its opposition to the war, its sympathy with our enemies, its readiness to receive with open arms the chiefest leaders of the rebellion; allies of those whose cruelties to our prisoned soldiers shocked humanity; allies of those who planned and executed those cold atrocities unknown to christian war; they will remember ANDERSONVILLE and the LIBBY!

The country will remember that when the rebel General Lee died, every anti-Republican Journal, from the Pacific coast to the furthermost corner of Maine, deplored his loss, as that of a pure patriot, and a christian hero, whose memory should be cherished, and whose name should be handed down to our children as one most honored in our history; and they will remember that Secretary Boutwell was assailed through those journals, because he did not wish to have raised in mourning for Lee, the flag of the Union, which that general had dishonored and betrayed; every hater of that flag was a sincere admirer of Lee,—his memory is sacred in their love; and his virtues have been exalted through the party press, as far above those of the martyred Lincoln, or the great Union General Geo. H. Thomas, who was from the same State as Lee, and who was Lee's superior in every virtue, and every heroic quality that can ennoble man! Turn me to a Democratic Journal, even in the loyal states, which spoke of the dying Thomas, with one ten-thousandth part of the love and admiration with which the same journal spoke of Lee. The two generals were both from Virginia ; both were educated at West Point at the national expense ; both had registered a solemn oath to defend the Union, its flag and its laws; one, before the war, was of high rank in the armies of the Union, petted and trusted by General Scott; great in place, and influence; able, if determined, to have averted this fratricidal war. He violated his solemn oath, deserted his old friend Scott, betrayed the Union which had fostered, educated and made him ; trampled in the dust the old flag which had waved so gloriously over him in Mexico, and bathed his recreant sword in the blood of his countrymen.

Thomas, also from the South, a much younger man, and under far greater temptations, was true to his country, to his flag and to his oath. Thomas dies, having lived true to honor, to patriotism, to every christian virtue! No half-mast flag was raised for him over Democratic journals ! No parading of his great virtues and lofty patriotism appeared in Democratic prints. There is deep meaning in this, and it will not be forgotten.

" Tell me where thou dwellest and whom thou lovest, and I will tell thee who thou art." All this will be remembered when the soldiers' graves are decorated, and on election day, for one generation at least.

This ovation to the shade of Lee was a "*got up*" affair : It was a cold political contrivance ; there was no grief in it ; a circular letter was sent round to many respectable and to some eminent men, to get them to join in the demonstration ; their patriotic refusals, which will appear some day, upset the plan, and changed the whole programme. All men respect heartfelt sorrow ; but the mother who mourned for her children, and the old father, who wept for his son whom the treason and the sword of Lee had slain,.did not come to Cooper Institute to parade their grief. A public demonstration of this kind is made to honor the acts of the hero's life, and the principles for which he contended. In this case, it was to honor the acts and the principles of Jefferson Davis and of Robert E. Lee.

Every man well informed in public affairs knows that the entire Rebel element of the South will heartily join in electing *any* Northern Democrat who may be nominated; confident, as they are, that he who may thus be elected, will be under the absolute sway of the same confederates who dominated over Tammany Hall in their late convention. I do not say that if a Northern Democrat were elected President, he would wish to disturb the peace of the Union by violating the amended Constitution, and the re-construction laws ; I dare say he would earnestly desire the prosperity of his country; but he would be utterly powerless for good, in the hands of those who elected him. The great party which puts the President in power is stronger than the man; so must it always be, in a government like ours. Careless observers mistake the public mind ; they meet with criticising men who are not personally satisfied ; who want something different; who always do want something different ; who are never content, unless all goes as they direct, nor even then. I heard all, and much more of this talk, in 1862, about Mr. Lincoln; and yet he was triumphantly re-elected in 1864. I hear much less of it in 1870, and I predict that General Grant's election in 1872 will be equally triumphant. I know that the confidence of the people is strong and increasing; they believe in his honesty, his foresight, his firm purpose, his real sympathy with the people ; in his silent, latent forces, equal to any emergency ; and in his luck and unfailing good fortune ; they will vote for him again, as will all the more intelligent men who wish well for their country. It is of the utmost interest to the Republican party that this question of the succession be settled; only a year from next May, and you make a new nomination. Nothing so much distracts and weakens the party in power, as to be casting about for the next Presidential candidate. I regard the question as already settled ; your enemies are trying to make you think that it is not settled. But it is settled. If General Grant is not the man, who is he? Name me any six, out of whom one can possibly be selected, as against General Grant. You cannot name them; and a President of the United States does not spring up in a day; he must have made a record. The people know that Grant was a great general in our war; that he led our brave soldiers to difficult and to glorious victory; that by his great qualities he preserved the unity of this proud nation; they know that his latent powers appeared when most needed, and that they will again appear in all their determined vigor, when necessity demands; they know that he was inexperienced in politics when he came into power; they know that he means to do right, and that he grows wiser by time; they believe in him; they trust him; they are determined that he shall have a fair chance; and if everything does not go *exactly* as they could wish, they wisely prefer "to bear the little ills they have, than fly to others that they know not of;" and if God spares the life of General Grant, he will be the next President of the United States!

Let us look straight into the face of this business, my countrymen: the most tempting place of power now upon the earth, is that held by the President of the United States, brief in its tenure, to be sure, but dazzling exceedingly, in the distance.

In too eager chase after this receding rainbow, many of our best Statesmen have stumbled to their ruin.

No Southern Rebel can soon hope to be President :—No Northern Democrat can ever hope to be President, save through the aid of Southern votes. The confederate vote will be given to the Northern Democrat only upon one condition; the condition is, that the South stand behind the recovered throne, and wield the sceptre as they will. If that day comes, your new amendments, your new guarantees of Freedom, your re-construction acts, and your vast financial system, will be trampled into dust, and the debt incurred in subjugating the very men thus restored to power will be scoffed and repudiated. Be not *again deceived*, ye who did not believe that civil war could come! The brave men, the great judges, who gave liberty and glory to England by condemning a traitor-king and a corrupt nobility, (on the return of the Stuarts,) died upon the scaffold, or fled to this country, where they dragged out a wretched life in dens and caves of the earth. No one believed that such could be their fate, when the great Cromwell died: Don't you think it will be *safer* at least to keep confederate generals out of the goverment during the present generation ?

The southern demands upon the northern Democracy have always been absolute; when these demands were *reluctantly* conceded, the south threatened secession ;—when not *wholly* granted, they made war.

The price of southern aid, is abject submission. Uninformed men think that the South must have changed,—that they must have learned something by their defeat in 1868.

Not a bit of it. They had nothing to learn. They *prefer* the rule of General Grant, to any Democratic rule which is not entirely subservient. They say now, as they said to Northern Democrats at the Charleston convention ; ahoy; or we leave you to your fate. They despise the northern dough-face ; they respect, while they hate, the northern Radical, who *fights* for his principles.

I have said thus much, because I wish now, at this stage of our history, to call the attention of the great party which destroyed slavery and baptised " Liberty and Union " with their blood, to the evils of distracting counsels, to the sin of wandering after strange gods, and of thereby permitting the cast-out spirits to return into possession of your re-constructed government, and thus to make its last state worse than before the war ! And one other word let me say : In politics as in war, there must be a leader, whose decision is final ; without it, there can be no success. The President is that leader ; he is patient in listening to suggestions—ready to take advice—but when he decides upon a course, all true men will cheerfully acquiesce ; this is the only way to success. With many commanders, and no general, victory was never won. Here lies the greatest danger against which I warn the Republican Party.

In the vast diversity of interests, the President has a most perplexing task.—Ten thousand men press him with almost as many different views. He must decide ;—he cannot satisfy all. He will do he tbest he can. Sustain him ; and he will prove as wise in peace, as he was great in war.

The candidates whom your conventions have nominated, are all good men ; vote for them, if you would retain your power ; elect them by honest votes ; neglect no honest means for success; show that you still mean fidelity to that great party which une~~bound~~ the hands of four million slaves, and saved the nation from dissolution and eternal disgrace.

SPEECH

OF THE

HON. EDWARDS PIERREPONT,

DELIVERED BEFORE

The Republican Mass Meeting, at Cooper Institute,

September 25, 1872.

NEW YORK:
EVENING POST STEAM PRESSES, 41 NASSAU STREET, CORNER LIBERTY.

1872.

FELLOW CITIZENS :—I have not come to defend Gen. Grant. I point you to the record he has made, which is eternal ; in the blaze of whose increasing splendor foul slanders will shrivel as a scroll, and base revilers perish as stubble.

Nor have I come to defame Horace Greeley. The good which he has done will live after him; the evil—let it be interred with his old clothes and his vain and foolish aspirations for the presidency.

I have come to talk with you on public affairs, that we may reason together, and see what is, on the whole, best in this epoch of our history.

A great nation, about to commit its destinies for years to the guidance of one man, will pause and consider well before it casts its vote,

When the deed is done, regrets, however deep and sincere, will not avail. Let us look fairly at this question of the candidates, and see which, under all the circumstances, ought to receive your suffrage.

A few months ago Horace Greeley published to the world his views of the Democratic Party in these words:

" It is rebel at the core to-day—hardly able to reconcile the defeats of Lee, Johnston, Bragg, Hood and Price, and the consequent downfall of its beloved Confederacy, with its traditional faith in Divine Providence. It would hail the election of a Democratic President in 1872 as a virtual reversal of the Appomattox surrender. It would come into power with the hate, the chagrin, the wrath, the mortification of ten bitter years to impel and guide its steps. It would devote itself to taking off or reducing tax after tax, until the Treasury was deprived of the means of paying interest on the national debt, and would hail the tidings of national bankruptcy with unalloyed gladness and unconcealed exultation. Whatever chastisement may be deserved for our national sins, we must hope that this disgrace and humiliation will be spared us."

Mr. Greeley has uttered many brave words in the cause of truth, but none more true than these.

A northern doughface, slopping over with the lukewarm milk of human kindness, may believe that the late rebels are sorry, repentant and honestly accept the situation with intent to abide by it. But no man with an intellect above good-natured idiocy, at all informed of the past conduct and present sentiment of the late Confederates, can doubt that they mean to gain by intrigue what they lost by war; that to a man they are sorry that they failed in their wicked plot to subvert the Government, and that they would to-day dig a deeper chasm and fill it full with blood, if they did not fear that brave patriots from the North, seizing their old guns, would row over it.

Fellow-citizens, let me read a page of our past history. As early as 1818 the South proposed to allow the Territory of Missouri to become a State. The North opposed this proposition unless slavery were excluded. Maine was not then admitted to the Union, and the advocates of slavery were determined that Maine should not be admitted without slavery unless Missouri was at the same time admitted with it. In 1820 a compromise was effected, and the bill which allowed Missouri to come in with slavery provided that human bondage should forever thereafter be excluded from all territory north of the parallel 36° 30', which was the southern boundary of Missouri. This solemn compact, which the trusting North believed to be "forever," as it expressly promised, was trampled down in 1854, at the behest of the South, and then, for the first time, the North awoke to the fact that slaveholders kept no faith, but, corrupting one Northern man after another, by seductive promises of the Presidency, they grew emboldened and threw off disguises, violated every pledge, and trampled down justice and humanity, with shameless perfidy, repealed the sacred compact, and set up the hellish fiend of slavery to be a worshiped god throughout this land of freedom!

But that was not enough. The worshipers of this demon saw that martyr-fires were burning in the North, and that from their ashes dangerous converts to freedom were springing fast, and the devotees of the "peculiar institution" plotted the overthrow of our government to preserve this great abomination. Democratic Conventions, the Peace Congress, Union-saving speeches of timid old politicians, the prostration of

Northern divines, citing texts from Holy Writ, and trying with Heaven's livery to conceal their devil-worship, were all of no avail. The Union must be rent, the old flag insulted, and war, with its unnumbered woes, must come. You know the rest. Weeks, months and years passed on in war. Save to the eye of faith and to the heart trusting in a righteous God, success seemed doubtful. Mr. Greeley wanted to let the rebels go; and now, in turn, the rebels want to make Mr. Greeley President of the United States.

In those dark days, when our generals, one after another, failed, there was *one who did not fail.* He took the sword of Lee, and the accursed rebellion writhed over and seemed to die. There is some life yet in its rotting remains, and it will show lively signs if Mr. Greeley is elected. And hence you see why the late Governor of Virginia, in his speech the other day, exclaimed, "Give me Jew or Gentile, dog or devil, I care not which, so we beat Grant."

Yes, anything to beat Gen. Grant; traduce him, vilify him, put him out of the way. They know full well that while Gen. Grant is at the head, the amendments to the Constitution and the Reconstruction laws will be respected. With keenest instinct, they preceive that Grant, with his dogged obstinacy, his iron will and his immovable courage, is the deadliest foe to any violation of the nation's rights as settled by the war.

Are these rights in any danger by the election of the secession candidate?

Let us see. The foremost of the Greeley men, the late Democratic candidate for Vice-President, the present Senator from Missouri, the fearless, outspoken Frank Blair, who scorns to conceal his real sentiments, declares that he stands by his Roadhead letter, which says:

"We must have a President who will execute the will of the people *by trampling into dust* the usurpations of Congress known as the Reconstruction acts."

And the *Caucasian,* a journal of Blair's own State, gives its platform thus:

"State sovereignty, *white supremacy,* and REPUDIATION! This is liberty!

"Our platform : *The Constitution of* 1860, and the rights of the States!

"DOWN WITH THE FIFTEENTH AMENDMENT!

"Direct taxation and the rightful representation of all the States, or ANOTHER REBELLION!"

On the 26th of May last, Jefferson Davis, addressing the people of Georgia, at Augusta, said :

"It is not a tribute to me individually, but *because you feel that I am one of yourselves that you come to do me honor.* You *know me only as the representative of your cause. That cause is dear to me—more precious even than life* [applause], *and I glory in its remembrance.* My simplest words may work you harm. If I say, 'Good night, my friends, go to your homes,' and a Congressional investigating committee happened to be within hearing, its members would swear that I directed you to go off and join the *Ku-Klux.* [Laughter and applause.] *Filled with that jealousy which springs from the knowledge of their inferiority, and of the justice of your pretensions,* and conscious of broken covenants and a violated constitution, they mistrust every movement, and tremble with fear when they think that right may again prevail."

Two days later he addressed the people of Atlanta as follows :

"I am not of those who accept the situation. I accept nothing."

"These cant phrases that we hear so much about of 'accepting the situation,' and about our rights having been submitted to the ' arbitrament of the sword,' are but the excuses of cowards. And, then, my friends, about the much talked of subject of 'accepting the situation.' You are not called upon to acknowledge that you have done wrong unless you feel it. I don't believe I did any wrong, and, therefore, I don't acknowledge it. Wait patiently until the tide turns—as sooner or later turn it will—and the day is not far distant when the sun will shine upon you a free, independent and sovereign State."

With utterances like this the Southern journals literally abound.

But we have fresher expressions upon this subject. I read from the *World's* reports of Mr. Greeley's speech made at Pittsburg, last Thursday. He says :

"I was one of those who said, 'No, there is no such alternative; I deny that the Southern people, the great majority of them, are against the Union. I demand that there shall be a fair, open, free discussion before all that Southern people, of an honest, unterrified, unconstrained vote, and if they approve, if the people of the South say they want disunion, I will consent to it. [Cheers.] I know they will not.' I knew that the Southern people, that the great majority, must have voted as they actually did that winter, not for secession but for clinging to the Union. [Cheers.] And now, to-day, if the nation was to be imperilled, and there were just two modes of saving it—to trust to the chances of civil war, or to the chances of a free vote of the Southern people—I would very greatly prefer to take the latter chance rather than the former."

A few days before this speech was made there was a convention of the soldiers and sailors of the war at Pittsburg. In the *Evening Post* and *New York Times* of the 16th inst. you will find the following :

"BALTIMORE, Sept. 15.—The rebellious spirit which animated the people of this city during the late war, and which was exhibited in positive acts of violence whenever they could be indulged in with impunity, was shown this evening to be as strong as ever. The Washington veterans, in passing through the city on the way to Pittsburg to the Soldiers' and Sailors' Convention, were attacked, at 7 o'clock, by ruffians concealed behind railway cars, at the Calvert street depot.

"The scenes of 1861 were repeated in their main features, and one soldier was seriously injured, having been struck by a brick, which smashed his face in a shocking manner."

The Massachusetts Sixth met with the same reception in 1861.

Mr. Greeley says "let us shake hands over the bloody bodies." "It is all wrong for the *North* to keep up these feelings."

In the same speech Mr. Greeley gives his views about the soldiers and sailors who convened at Pittsburg, thus :

"The party that meets here and shouts for Grant and Wilson: No other party requires that any human being should stand proscribed on our soil for a rebellion that ceased seven and a half years ago. No party, no man of any party but this, *the very party that held a great military parade* this week in order to further separate and divide the hearts of the American people from each other. [Cheers.] They hold essential to their triumph that hatred should continue ; that distress, suspicion, and alienation should continue. Do what you will, do what you may, they are determined not to be satisfied."

How unreasonable these northern soldiers are, not "*to be satisfied*" with being murdered on their way to save the capital from traitors, and with having their "faces smashed in" on their way to meet their brave comrades who had survived the war.

Mr. Greeley says these men are all of the "Grant and Wilson Party;" so they are ; and if he will take an elevation where he can look over into the 5th of November next, he will see an interminable throng—some with armless sleeves, some with artificial legs, some pale from the sufferings of the war, leaning on their old fathers for support, some with the port of health and military mien, some with the sailor's swing—all moving on, with no arms in their hands, but little paper billets in their stead. That, Mr. Greeley, is what you called at Pittsburg "the military parade, the Grant and Wilson Party." Including their kindred and their grateful countrymen, a formidable array ! You are right, they are for Grant and Wilson ; *shame* sits forever upon the *soldier* who votes for Horace Greeley !

Why did the Democratic Party nominate Mr. Greeley ? On what bargain was it done ? Just before this unnatural alliance was made public, the *World*, the ablest journal in the Democratic ranks, said : Mr. Greeley's sole hope of an election depends upon his receiving the unanimous support of the Democratic Party. * * * If he is nominated by the Democratic Convention and elected by Democratic votes, he cannot ignore the Democratc Party in organizing his administration. * * * If Democratis are to vote for Mr. Greeley, it must be *under such circumstances* that he will be *compelled* to acknowledge his obligations to the party, and will *make* him *dependent* on it for the success of his administration." The *circumstances* were all arranged to mutual satisfaction, and Horace Greeley received the unanimous nomination of that party which he had lately pronounced so utterly disloyal and rebel at the core.

We know where we stand. We have two great parties in the field : The old Bourbon Democratic Party, with its ancient bigotries, it secession sympathies, its rebel supporters; "with the hate, the chagrin, the wrath, the mortification of ten bitter years to impel and guide its steps." On the other hand, we have the Republican Party; with no hate or chagrin or wrath, but with a record of more than ten years of patriotic devotion and glorious deeds of imperishable renown.

Past experience proves that the Southern politicians never mistook their man; they never accepted a Northern President unless sure of his Southern principles, and they have not changed; they do no even pretend to have changed; they boldly say that the advocate of secession and the bailer of Jeff. Davis is reliable, and that he will surely see that they are paid for their liberated slaves—the four hundred million which he once proposed. Everywhere throughout the South, you shall hear that they expect to be paid for their human chattels, if Mr. Greeley is elected. Let us see what Gov. Aiken, the great slave-holder of South Carolina, said upon this subject. I read from the speech of Senator Morton, delivered in this hall a few months since : "I met a very distinguished Southern gentlemen at West Point, last summer—a man that you all know by reputation ; and I will give you his name, because it was not said in confidence to me, but was said in the presence of others; one of the noblest and purest men of the South, and a loyal man throughout the war, and of the largest slave-holders throughout the South—Gov. Aiken, of South Carolina. He believed slavery to have been unlawfully abolished, and he said : 'I have made out an inventory of my slaves and laid it aside, because I believe that a sense of returning justice will yet compel this nation to pay for the slaves.' And so far as I know, this has been done by almost the entire body of the former slave-owners of the Southern States. When the Democratic party comes into power, they will come forward with that claim, and they will say to the Democracy, and say truly : 'You are committed in favor of paying us for our slaves.'"

But some one says that the Fourteenth Amendment to the Constitution forbids such payment. So it does; but the Fourteenth Amendment will go where the Missouri Compromise went, and be "*trampled in the dust*" with the other reconstruction measures, if Mr. Greeley is elected.

You will then see troubled times in our financial affairs, and general distrust. Four hundred million is a large corruption fund, and the Fourteenth Amendment would be as a spider's web. Remember the Missouri Compromise.

Gen. Grant or Horace Greeley in the Presidency! A momentous trust! A nation's prosperity hangs upon this issue. We have tried Gen. Grant; Mr. Greeley we have not tried. Grant holds aloft the Republican banner—its inscriptions you have all read.

Greeley holds up the Democratic standard; to it is tied the rebel flag—yes, and Horace Greeley bears it! and if elected, its folds will cover over his face, and blind his eyes, and his masters, hating and despising him, will tie him with fetters of brass, and take him down to Washington, and make him grind in their prison-house. He cannot help it. Even the strongest man is not so strong as the party which elects him.

Senator Sumner says in his letter: "Horace Greeley stood forth a Reformer and Abolitionist; President Grant enlisted as a Pro-slavery Democrat, and at the election of Buchanan, fortified by his vote all the pretensions of slavery."

Well, what if we concede all that? Is Gen. Grant now the less an earnest Republican? If Judas, an original disciple, had reproached St. Paul with having been once a persecutor of the Church, that would not have helped Judas or hurt St. Paul.

There happens to be another man on your ticket whom Mr. Sumner would call a pro-slavery Democrat, voting for Buchanan. He not only voted for Buchanan, but was in Buchanan's Cabinet. He is the same man who, while there as Secretary of the Treasury, gave the memorable order: "If any man attempts to haul down the American flag, shoot him on the spot."

Don't you think the old flag will be safe in the hands of Gen. Dix? And when he is Governor, do you think the thieves will dare break into the public treasury and steal?

Gen. Dix has held some place of trust from the time he was eighteen years old. He has discharged the duties of all these offices with ability, fidelity, untarnished and unsuspected virtue.

Your city, your county and your State have long been plundered. Even your Reform Legislature could not alone protect us, and the people call Gen. Dix to the rescue. And here the tried old faithful veteran comes. The people know that they can trust *him*, and the great swelling wave will lift this honest man to the highest office in the State—the last, just, crowning reward of an honest life.

But there was another "Pro-slavery Democrat" in Mr. Buchanan's Cabinet, who, when he found that slave-holders were enemies of the Union, turned like a lion in his lair, and with energy unparalleled, with indignation unmatched, and with a directness and devotion which could not be surpassed, took the side of liberty, and by night and by day, gave his great mind, and his very life, in its noblest prime, to save his country; and when the lightning wires told that Edwin M. Stanton had been called to his great reward, did Charles Sumner reproachfully say: "He was a Pro-slavery Democrat, and in the election of Buchanan fortified, by his vote, all the pretensions of slavery."

Mr. Sumner also delivered an elaborate oration in the Senate of the United States, with intent to degrade the President in the eyes of the civilized world; carefully revised and printed before it was pronounced; part of the material used was a dead man's words, claimed to have been whispered in the confidence-chamber of the dying Secretary. I forbear considering at length the propriety of ever repeating such conversations for any purpose, and especially for the purpose of defaming the Chief Magistrate of your country, with whom you have disagreed. But I cannot waive considering the probable truth of the statement which Mr. Sumner makes.

He says that Mr. Stanton, just before he died, told him this:

"'I know General Grant better than any other person in the country can know him. It was my duty to study him, and I did so night and day—when I saw him and when I did not see him—and now I tell you what I know: he cannot govern this country.' The intensity of his manner and the positiveness of his judgment surprised me; for though I was aware that the late Secretary of War did not place the President very high in general capacity, I was not prepared for a judgment so strongly couched. At last, after some delay, occupied in meditating his remarkable words, I observed, 'What you say is very broad.' 'It is as true as it is broad,' he replied promptly. I added, 'You are tardy; you tell this late; why did you not say it before his nomination?' He answered that he was not consulted about the nomination, and had no opportunity of expressing his opinion upon it, besides being much occupied at the time by his duties as Secretary of War and his contest with the President. I followed by saying, 'But you took part in the Presidential election, and made a succession of speeches for him in Ohio and Pennsylvania.' 'I spoke,' said he, 'but I never introduced the name of Gen. Grant. I spoke for the Republican Party and the Republican cause.' This was the last time I saw Mr. Stanton. A few days later I followed him to the grave where he now rests."

I have before me the speeches to which Mr. Sumner alludes, and I find the name of Gen. Grant mentioned twenty-one times in a single speech, and in each of them that name is spoken with the greatest respect. In his speech at Philadelphia occurs the following;

"In Grant we behold the leader of our armies in the path of victory. In Grant we behold the great General, who, under Divine Providence, led our armies, supported, as they were, by some of these who are before you to-night. * * * *

"The mistakes mentioned are, Seymour says, 'the mistakes of the Republican Party.'" What, then, has Gen. Grant got to do with them? [Cheers for Grant.] While Congress may have made mistakes, if you please, without number—day by day made mistakes—Grant was before the enemy's face fighting him; he was taking no surrender, except that it was 'Unconditional!' No terms left his lips but 'Unconditional surrender' of the enemy of his country."

I might detain you long with extracts of similar tone; but these suffice to show how inaccurate was Mr. Sumner where absolute verity was so easy to be obtained. The other part of the statement depends upon Mr. Sumner's memory of words from lips which speak no more; that kind of evidence, in courts of justice, is received with exceeding caution, and, if inconsistent with established facts, it is not believed at all.

It is known to some of you that for many years I was very intimate with the great Secretary, and was one of the friends who bore him to his grave. I saw him often during his last illness, and have a large number of letters from him, several of which relate to Gen. Grant, and one to Gen. Dix ; their testimony will be more convincing than uncertain words repeated long after their alleged utterance, and by one whose mind and imagination had grown morbid and diseased by brooding over grievances of a personal kind.

His letter about Gen. Dix, alike honorable to Mr. Stanton and just to Gen. Dix, I will read first :

WASHINGTON, April 16, 1862.

Hon. EDWARDS PIERREPONT:

My Dear Sir—This morning my son called my attention to a paragraph in the New York *Ledger* of Saturday, April 5, on page 4, ascribing to me the authorship of Gen. Dix's telegram to New Orleans, and saying that it has high authority that I wrote it. Will you be so good as to call on Mr. Bonner and inform him, from me, that I did *not* write that order, that its author was Gen. Dix, and request him to correct the *Ledger's* mistake, in order that credit may be given to whom it justly belongs.

The correction might be made in some such way as the following : " We are requested to state, on the authority of Mr. Stanton, that the famous telegram sent by Gen. Dix to a naval officer in New Orleans in these words—'*The first man that attempts to haul down the American flag, shoot him on the spot !*'— was written by Gen. Dix—that the credit of that order belongs to Gen. Dix, and not to Mr. Stanton."

You may perhaps suppose the correction of this mistake is a small matter, and not worthy of attention in times like these.

But that order was a historic fact of much significance in a very dark hour. I admired it at the time it was made ; would be proud of it if it belonged to me ; and desire to see its merit acknowledged and awarded to him who alone is entitled to it —Gen. Dix. How it could ever be ascribed to me I cannot conceive, and would be glad if you would ask Mr. Bonner upon whose authority the statement was made, in order that the erroneous impression may be corrected to its fullest extent.

Yours truly,
EDWIN M. STANTON.

Soon after the November election, he wrote as follows :

WASHINGTON, Nov. 13, 1868.

Hon. EDWARDS PIERREPONT:

My Dear Sir—Your letter reached me here on my return home from Baltimore, where I had been making a visit for rest and change of air. For your kind appreciation of my political exertions, made under much debility and suffering, please accept my thanks. * * * During my absence, Gen. Grant returned home; but, confined to my house, I have not seen him. Divine Providence seems to have furnished us with a fit President as well as a great General.

On the 1st of December, 1868, he wrote again, expressing the like confidence.

It will be remembered that the date of this conversation, as fixed by Mr. Sumner, was after the President had called in person upon Mr. Stanton, and tendered him the office of Judge of the Supreme Court, which Mr. Stanton accepted, and about which he had often spoken in warm eulogy of Gen. Grant. May we not safely conclude that Mr. Sumner's wearied brain needs rest?

We will consider the fitness of Gen. Grant and Horace Greeley for the great office. I know them both pretty well; I shall try to present them to you fairly. Remember that it is the chief ruler of a great people, after a great civil war, whom you are about to select. The abilities which we seek are those of a great governor; not those of an artist, a poet or man of letters; men of science, writers, orators and literary men, from Cicero to Lamartine, have always failed as rulers of the State. No man of sense believes that Juvenal, Raphael, Shakespeare, Milton, Newton or La Place could ever have governed the nations whose history they adorned; whereas, Julius Cæsar, Charlemagne, Frederick the Great, Napoleon, William of Orange, and more than all, the great Cromwell, were able rulers, each of whom was first a great soldier, and then a statesman of imperishable fame. Come down in history to our own country. Our first great ruler was the immortal Washington, the great Captain of his age.

The next marked ruler was Gen. Jackson, whose military fame preceded his civil reputation. The greatest rulers in every age have been the greatest soldiers of their time. Painters, sculptors, scholars, writers and journalists of other men's deeds, have always failed at the helm of State. They have not that combination of faculties and of will which the position requires. Upon this subject the instincts of mankind have generally guided them aright. Horace Greeley is a man of eminent abilities, but as unsuited to the Presidential office as was the poet Horace for an Emperor of Rome. It is one of the weaknesses of our people, to imagine for the moment, that the man who has achieved great success in anything, is fitted for the Presidency; and hence we have had successful steamboat men, express men, railroad men, telegraph men, explorers, pathfinders, writers and journalists talked of as candidates for the chief executive office.

Rosa Bonheur can paint a horse better than any living artist, but she can't shoe one.

I would not detract from Mr. Greeley's justly-earned reputation—he has immense industry and a powerful pen which he has always used on the side of humanity. He is a true hater of oppression and of privileged class—very placable and of kindly nature. In money matters, honest; in politics, more far-sighted than is generally supposed, and shrewd even to cunning; with large love of approbation, the spring of his great ambition. Able as a journalist, vigorous as a writer, and always in sympathy with liberal principals; he never keeps an even course, and often startles his friends by crotchets the more dangerous because sincere. He is liable to influences of whose evil he is not conscious. His best friends would never select him to lead an army, to preside over a turbulent assembly, to control a bank or run a railroad. He has never shown any of the qualities of a great leader, and we have no right to suppose that he can now make an able ruler over a great nation. A noted letter, which Mr. Greeley has been careful to republish, written to Gov. Seward when he quarreled with the Governor and Thurlow Weed, will throw light upon the temper, the ambition and real character of this Liberal candidate for the Presidency. We read from it as follows:

"You were Governor, dispensing patronage worth $3,000 to $20,000 per year to your friends and compatriots, and I returned to my garret and my crust. I believe it did not then occur to me that *some one of these abundant places might have been offered to me without injustice;* I now think it should have occurred to *you.*

* * * * * *

"In the Harrison campaign of 1840, I was again designated to edit a campaign paper. I published it as well, and ought to have made something by it, in spite of its extremely low price; my extreme poverty was the main reason why I did not. *

"Now came the great scramble of the swell-mob of coon-minstrels and cider-suckers at Washington—*I not being counted in.* Several regiments of them went on from this City, but no one of the whole crowd—though I say it, who should not—had done so much toward Gen. Harrison's nomination and election as yours respectfully. I asked nothing, expected nothing; *but you, Gov. Seward, ought to have asked that I be Postmaster of New York.*" * * * *

"But this last Spring, after the Nebraska question had created a new state of things at the North, one or two personal friends, of no political consideration, suggested my name as a candidate for Governor, and I did not discourage them. * * *

"I suspect it is true that I could not have been elected Governor as a Whig. But had he and you been favorable, there *would* have been a party in the State, ere this, which could and would have elected me to any post, without injuring myself or endangering your re-election. * * * *

"I should have hated to serve as Lieutenant-Governor, but I should have gloried in running for the post. I want to have my enemies all upon me at once—I am tired of fighting them piecemeal. And, although I should have been beaten in the canvass, I know that my running would have helped the ticket and HELPED MY PAPER." * * * *

Are these the breathings of a lofty patriotism, or do you distinguish the vengeful odor of a bitterly disappointed personal ambition?

When Richard, the usurping king, asked his trusted page whom he could call to aid in his most wicked and ambitious scheme against the safety of the State, the page replied: "I know a discontented gentleman, whose humble means match not his haughty mind."

Gen. Grant, for the public, never talks or writes or speaks; he is inarticulate—silent. He does not impress men generally. He seems inert, and in mixed society draws into his shell. To this nation of ceaseless talkers he seems a kind of Sphynx. But he has *done* some things. He is younger than Horace Greeley by more than eleven years; he has done things for this people which Horace Greeley could not do—which no other man could do.

The danger is over now, and almost forgot; but there was a time, a gloomy time, when this nation's life was in peril; when ten thousand Horace Greelyes could not save it, and Gen. Grant did. We tried many other Generals, all well placed in the social scale, supported by all the upper influences in the land; all failed. An obscure man from Galena, poor, of no reputation or family influence, led the Union armies from victory to victory, and *never failed* ; and when the sword of Lee was surrenderd to his younger victor, the nation offered up heartfelt thanksgivings to God, and Grant was almost worshiped as the savior of our liberties! Are you going to *crucify* him now? Why, what evil hath he done? My brave and honest countrymen, you do not mean to be unjust. Gen. Grant don't seek this office. He never did seek it. He don't want to be driven from it in disgrace by the enemies of the country which his brave comrades died to save. Let us look over the record of the past four years, and see what evil he hath done. You called this soldier, forty-six years old, to take the helm of State in the perplexing troubled days which followed a great civil war. Four millions of ignorant slaves had been freed, a powerful confederation of States in war had been subdued by arms. Wholly unused to public affairs and to political tricks, this inexperienced man was placed in the Presidential chair. Did you deem him so far from human that he could make no blunders? and is that his crime that you thought him so perfect that you pardon no mistake? I read his modest words in accepting the re-nomination:

"If elected in November, and protected by a kind Providence in health and strength to perform the duties of the high trust conferred, I promise the same zeal and devotion to the good of the whole people for the future of my official life as shown in the past. Past experience may guide me in avoiding mistakes inevitable with novices in all professions and in all occupations."

Modest, as he is always modest. I have known him since long before the surrender of Lee, and never did I hear him tell of any of his victories ; never heard him even allude to them ;

never heard him utter a word that would indicate that he had achieved anything. Who ever heard of a boast or vain word from his quiet lips? All who know him will bear witness to the same unpretentious, simple ways of this remarkable man.

Can you tell me why this great effort to drive him from the office which he has so worthily filled? I think I can tell.

General Grant had proved himself so great a man that the nation expected too much—more than was reasonable; they expected *perfection*, and would tolerate nothing less in their idol: and, true to our English blood, we began to think that he had been overpraised—a crime which the Anglo-Saxon race never allows to go unpunished. In a republic, where office is open to all, each office had a thousand aspirants. Each office filled made many enemies and sometimes an ingrate. The vanity and pretension of official aspirants is amazing. Grant had no skill to flatter, and no wish to excite false hopes. When all the offices were filled the disappointed became sour, and talked about patriotism, and hinted at the incapacity and possible corruption of the Executive. Many concealed their grief, hoping that something might turn up, until the Presidential term was drawing to its close, and the time came for new combinations through which new hopes were excited in the thousands of expectants for place; and in looking about they saw better chances in a new deal, and hence the noisy *outs*, vastly outnumbering the quiet *ins*, got up a din to drown every voice which tried to speak in refutation of the foul slanders with which the President was assailed. Many were restless and wanted a change for the sake of change, thinking little of what a change might involve. Some honest people were made to believe that the President was growing rich, while every well-informed person knew that his income did not meet his necessary expenses. Jealousy of his position; jealousy which plays so vile a part in public affairs, came in, and vague distrust, fomented by envy and disappointment, and rebel hate of him who crushed their treason, all joined in general plan to oust the President from his seat, and out of the grand jumble came a result, unexpected, unwished, and which amazed every leader of the movement, and for a time paralyzed their action. They had sown the wind, they did not expect the whirlwind would force Horace Greely upon them; and when the clouds cleared away and they saw that ghost appear, they stared aghast, like the murderous Thane at the ghost of Banquo!

The great God has his own mysterious way to bring about results; through fiery trials He sends all men destined for exalted deeds. Grant is as sure to be the next President as is the continued motion of the planetary spheres, and the terrible ordeal through which he is to pass presages great events in the next five years. When the people have seen him walk through the fires and come out with his mantle unsinged they will reproach themselves for the cruelties which they have allowed him to suffer; but he will be purified and strengthened for the great work which lies before him.

Alex. H. Stephens, by far the most philosophic and appreciative intellect in the Southern States, has recorded, in an elaborate history of the war, his opinion of General Grant. Mr. Stephens says:

"I was instantly struck with the great simplicity and perfect naturalness of his manners, and the entire absence of everything like affectation, show, or even the usual military air or mien of men in his position. He was plainly attired, sitting in a log-cabin, busily writing on a small table by a kerosene-lamp. It was night when we arrived. There was nothing in his appearance or surroundings which indicated his official rank. There were neither guards nor aids about him. Upon Colonel Babcock's rapping at his door, the response 'Come in' was given by himself in a tone of voice and with a cadence which I can never forget.

"His conversation was easy and fluent, without the least effort or restraint. In this nothing was so closely noticed by me as the point and terseness with which he expressed whatever he said. He did not seem either to court or avoid conversation, but, whenever he did speak, what he said was to the point, and covered the whole matter in a few words. I saw before being with him long that he was exceedingly quick in perception and direct in purpose, with a vast deal more of brains than tongue, as ready as that was at his command.

"We were here with General Grant two days. * * * He furnished us with comfortable quarters on board one of his dispatch-boats. The more I became acquainted with him the more I became thoroughly impressed with the very extraordinary combination of rare elements of character which he exhibited. During the time he met us frequently and conversed freely upon various subjects, not much upon our mission. I saw, however, very clearly, that he was very anxious for the proposed conference to take place, and, from all that was said, I inferred—whether correctly or not I do not know—that he was fully apprised of its proposed object.

" Upon the whole, the result of this first acquaintance with General Grant, beginning with our going to and ending with our return from Hampton Roads, was the conviction on my mind that, taken all in all, he was one of the most remarkable men I had ever met with, and that his career in life, if his days should be prolonged, was hardly entered upon; that his character was not yet fully developed; that he himself was not aware of his own power, and that, if he lived, he would in the future exert a controlling influence in shaping the destinies of this country, either for good or evil. Which it would be, time and circumstances alone could disclose. That was the opinion of him then formed, and it is the same which has been uniformly expressed by me ever since."

The career of Grant has been a marvel from the beginning—not to be explained upon the ordinary principles of judging men. With reverent voice, I say that I believe he is raised up by Providence for greater deeds than he has yet performed. I find nothing in history which he resembles except the great Cromwell, and I find no such self-poised head as his since Cromwell died. I am an earnest advocate for the re-election of Gen. Grant because I believe in him—because I think it, under the circumstances, the only safety for the country. I am not an office-holder, and, as we are talking rather confidentially to-night, I will tell you that I do not intend to be. I have taken the full measure of that matter. I intend to remain your fellow-citizen with unsealed lips, free to criticize any man who holds the people's trust and to denounce any man who betrays it.

I have given some study to the system of our government, and tried to learn the source of its power and its real dangers. It differs radically from all others. No feudal seed was ever planted in our soil, and the feeble attempts to engraft feudal scions on our stock failed, as they will always fail. No reverence for great families or historic names has any hold here. In theory and in fact the power lies down in the hearts of the people, and their will gets expressed through public opinion, from which there is no appeal. Office, being open to all, until within a few years, was generally sought for the advancement of social position, to gratify personal pride and love of eminent consideration for public service, or to perform a useful duty to the State. As wealth increased and corrupting luxury came in, bad, cunning men discovered that they could use official trusts to steal the earnings of the people under the cover of deceiving laws; and the cheated citizens were made to believe that the fraudulent taxes all came out of the rich; though they were puzzled to see how it was that the rich grew richer and the poor poorer, while no taxes were levied upon the poor. They are just now beginning to learn that all taxes really come out of the labor and industry of the people, and that the idea that capital pays the taxes is a covert fraud—the great cost of rent which the laboring poor and the industrious mechanic or clerk has to pay is chiefly caused by the fraudulent tax which the tenement pays.

No honest men but the rich can ever grow rich in a government where your officials are robbers and levy taxes for plunder. If we cannot preserve our government from official corruption our liberties are near their end. Come up and face this question, fellow-citizens; do you believe that the election of Horace Greeley will work reform? Do you not know that his election will throw a pall over every cheerful hope of rescuing our city and State from robbers? Do you not know that the thieves will run under his skirts for shelter, and tell him that they are sorry, and "eager to clasp hands across the bloody chasm," and only want to be let alone, until they can work back through plausible device into their former places.

Reformers, you know very well that the election of Horace Greeley does not mean reform. You cannot face an honest audience and tell them that you think so. If you do they will not believe you. A desire for reform swept this State like a whirlwind last Autumn, and it will do it again. I know that we shall have reform or despotism. I do not believe that the election of Horace Greeley tends to reform, but to confusion and anarchy; and you all know what follows anarchy. I shall do what I can to elect Gen. Grant, and then I shall do what I can to aid in placing able and honest men around him, and if he proves recreant to his trust and corrupted by continued power, uses his great office for unholy purposes, I will be free and as earnest and as public in denunciation as I am now in my advocacy. I have chosen my path in life, and I intend to walk in it, fearless of thieves and scoundrels, and bad men in high places. Life has no value without liberty, and where you dare not speak the truth, there is no liberty.

Mr. Greeley very fairly said that Gen. Grant had made a better President than he had expected, and that he would do better the second time than the first. I shall not be found abusing Mr. Greeley; I venerate the much good he has done; in a few short weeks no living man will excite so much of our condolence. The dishonest men who have been deluding him, cheating him, will desert him, revile him, and with lusty oaths declare that they never knew him; swear that it was all a joke, that they never expected to elect him, and that the whole fantastic trick was a juggling fraud. The discussion of this question, and the universal intelligence circulated through the priceless services of the Press, have awakened the people. They begin to see how unjustly the President has been slandered, how difficult has been his task, and how well, upon the whole, he has performed it. Men of business, men of substance, men of families whom you love, come face to face with this question, and you will shudder at the peril which you have escaped. I know that you will not support this nomination, conceived in fraud, against the peace and prosperity of your country. You will vote for Gen. Grant, and thank God that the good sense of the people tells them how wiser it is to "let well enough alone," "to bear the little ills we have than fly to others that we know not of." Security, confidence, development and unexampled prosperity will surely follow the election of Grant.

No one who has had opportunity can fail to notice how carefully the bankers, merchants and business men of other countries watch our political action. They care nothing for our candidates, but only regard the matter as affecting our credit and the safety of our bonds. Men of business in Europe cannot believe it possible that a sober nation like ours is going to upset its policy, radically change its Administration—disturb all, just as it is beginning to be settled, and thus discredit and drive back our securities, stop all negotiations, and put an end to the vast enterprises now starting to develop and enrich our country. The answer to these apprehensions is: *The people are not going to do it.* Every man I meet, Democrat or Republican, makes some halting excuse when he says that he is for Greeley—talks about "the lesser of two evils," "the surroundings of Grant" and other apologetic trifles, showing that his heart is not in it, and that his conscience revolts at this violence to common sense. When the time comes to count the vote, the party will be amazed at the feeble show, and awake to the fact that a straight-out Democrat would have polled a *much larger vote.* And the sagacious *World* will point to its issues of last spring and justly say: "*I told you so.*"

A word about Gen. Grant's oppression of the South, and I have done. Last February I went through most of the Southern States and tried to learn their real condition: They were not very prosperous—they were nearly all for Greeley, even then; I mean the rebel whites, not the loyal blacks. Since the war the South has suffered a good deal from bad government—no doubt of that—but much of it was incident to the situation, and more was due to their own sullen pride and obstinate will. Had they frankly accepted the inevitable, and returned to their allegiance, and honestly tried to aid the Government in reconstruction, they would have suffered little from misrule; the victorious North would have been over-generous to the fallen foe, and would have readily removed every disability. I sincerely believe that, before another year has passed, the South itself will rejoice in the re-election of Gen. Grant. And now, when we are at peace with all the world, when our prosperity is great and our industries are fast reviving, we are asked to make a change, to try something new, "to clasp our eager hands across the bloody chasm" (the South has shown no haste to shake hands). Govern justly, generously; protect the freedman in his rights; but do not, in blind fatuity, surrender the very ark of your liberties to those, who in peace, were so faithless, who in war could perpetrate or permit the inhuman cruelties of Andersonville and the Libby.

SPEECH

OF THE

HON. EDWARDS PIERREPONT,

DELIVERED BEFORE

The Republican Mass Meeting, at Wilgus Hall,

ITHICA, N. Y.,

October 11th, 1872.

NEW YORK:
EVENING POST STEAM PRESSES, 41 NASSAU STREET, CORNER LIBERTY.

1872.

SPEECH

OF THE

HON. EDWARDS PIERREPONT,

DELIVERED BEFORE

The Republican Mass Meeting, at Wilgus Hall,

ITHICA, N. Y.,

October 11th, 1872.

NEW YORK:
EVENING POST STEAM PRESSES, 41 NASSAU STREET, CORNER LIBERTY.

1872.

Fellow-Citizens :

LEARNED naturalists tell us that the animals which came out of the ark were the same in kind as those which now exist, and that each, after his kind, from the lion to the kid, had the same appetites, the same instincts, the same *animal nature* as now. *Human nature* was the same before the flood as it is to-day. That Cain murdered his brother, you all know; but did you ever think what he killed him for?—Jealousy—that was all—jealousy, because his younger brother's offering was more acceptable to the Lord. Inspired by the same jealousy, Joseph's brethren determined to murder him, but at the suggestion of one less cruel, they mingled a little avarice with their envy, and sold their brother as a slave. Murderers of the life, for jealousy, are a little out of date, but in their stead, we have assassins of the reputation.

Formerly those who differed in opinion were put to the rack; now they are put to the public newspapers and to public speakers; the torture is more refined, and wrings the deep anguish from the soul, runs through the household nerves, from wife to prattling child, and fiends have new delight.

In our Saviour's time they brought to him a woman who had done a wrong, and wanted to stone her to death. The Saviour said, "Well, stone her to death, as you claim to have the law, only do it in this way : gather the stones, form the ring, put her in the midst, and let him that is without sin among you, cast the first stone." These virtuous hypocrites, so eager to vindicate the law, looked one on the other, and every arm was palsied, and not a stone was thrown, and they went out one after another, and the poor woman was left unhurt, alone.

But now men's consciences have grown so blunted, or they themselves have grown so free from fault, that they cloud the noonday-sun with stones, which they throw so thickly at their fellow-men; and of all, the President of the United States is the one most assailed. His ordeal, severe as that of ancient martyr, he has stood. He has walked with unshodden feet over the burning plowshares, and through the crackling flames, and the innumerable voters of Nebraska and of Maine, of Vermont, Ohio and Pennsylvania looked on, and when they saw him issue from the fires without a blister upon his feet or a singe upon his garment, in loud and overwhelming numbers they gave him their vote; and all the people say: AMEN!

The election of Grant is secure; but we must redeem our great State, out of which four years ago, Gen. Grant was defrauded by false counting.

The news which we have just received is sure to make the Greeley men abandon the national contest and cause them to concentrate all their energies upon this State. If they can secure New York, then they have a good nucleus for future plot against the union of the States and the success of free government.

The late war was not an accident. It grew out of the two great contending principles which have ever, from time to time, convulsed the world. The contest between good and evil, between freedom and slavery, between liberty of conscience and tyranny of the soul, between God and the Devil; and this warfare will continue, until HE, whose right it is to reign, shall have put all enemies under his feet.

This new plot against the Union and the liberties of the country was hatched of secession brains. It began before Mr. Greeley made his memorable tour through Texas and the South, in the Spring of 1871. After his return he made and published a speech in the city of New York, on the 12th of June: in it several passages occur which we did not then understand, the meaning of which the Baltimore Convention made clear. As a specimen of those passages, then obscure, but since so plain, we cite the following:

"But, gentlemen, the past is past. Let the dead bury their dead. *I am perfectly willing to pass receipts with the* REPUBLICAN PARTY, *and say that our accounts are now settled and closed.*"

This was uttered by Mr. Greeley to a large assembly in the city of New York, while fresh from his meeting with Jeff. Davis and other leading rebels of the South. We did not then imagine that they were going to make him the Democratic candidate in 1872. But *he* did; and hence his notice, that he was ready to close accounts and pass receipts with the Republican party. The account is closed—no receipts are needed—what profits he will reap from the new partnership, next November will disclose. Secession Georgia has gone for him by an overwhelming vote; the Grant men were driven from the polls. I dare say that Texas and Tennessee and other rebel States will follow this example. We can "forgive them, only because they know not what they do." This Southern plot to get control of the government by the seduction of an ambitious, able Northern man, and a lifelong enemy, is not new. Reference to the past will throw light upon the present. It was well known in the early winter of 1850, that Mr. Webster had partly prepared a speech in harmony with the sentiments of his life on the subject of slavery. On the 14th of February he wrote to his friend, Peter Harvey, as follows:

"WASHINGTON, Feb. 14, 1850.

"My dear Sir,—I do not partake, *in any degree*, in those apprehensions which you say some of our friends entertain of the dissolution of the Union, or the breaking up of the government * * *

"I have, thus far, upon a good deal of reflection, thought it advisable to hold my peace. If a moment shall come that any temperate, rational and practical *speech* which I can make would be useful, I shall do the best I can. One purpose I wish to execute—and that is, to call on Mr. Berrien, and other Southern gentlemen, to state distinctly *what are these acts of the North, which, it is said, constitute a series of aggressions by the North on the South.*

"This matter ought to be looked into a little more carefully than it has been. *Let the North keep cool.*"

And to give a little foretaste of what that "*speech*" was to be, he wrote the very next day to Rev. Mr. Furness, of Philadelphia, as follows:

"WASHINGTON, February, 15, 1850.
"My dear sir,—I was a good deal moved, I confess, by reading your letter of the 9th January. Having regard for your talents and character, I could not feel indifferent to what you said, when you intimated that there was, or might be, in me, a power to do good, not yet exercised or devoloped. It may be so; but I fear, my dear sir, that you overrate, not my desire, but my power, to be useful in my day and generation. *From my earliest youth* I have regarded slavery as a great moral and political evil.

"I think it unjust, repugnant to the natural equity of mankind, founded only on superior power; a standing and permanent conquest by the stronger over the weaker. All pretence of defending it on the ground of different races, I have ever condemned. I have ever said that if the black man is weaker, that is a reason against—not for, his subjugation and oppression. In a religious point of view, I have ever regarded it, and ever spoken of it, not as subject to any express denunciations, either in the Old Testament or the New, but as opposed *to the whole spirit of the Gospel, and to the teachings of Jesus Christ.*

"The religion of Jesus Christ is a religion of kindness, justice and brotherly love. But slavery is not kindly affectioned; it does not *let the oppressed go free.* It is, as I have said, but a continued act of oppression."

How incredible, that "*the speech*" which was expected to call Mr. Berrien and the other Southern gentlemen to account for their arrogant charges against the North, and in favor of "letting the oppressed go free," should, in *three short weeks*, have been turned into an argument in support of the most infamous law to oppress the slave, and in scorn and mockery of the "higher law," as taught by the religion of Christ!

A crashing thunder-clap from a cloudless sky could not have more startled the astonished North! A Southern senator had suggested, that there was an able statesman in the North who, if his mind expanded to embrace the views and interests of the whole country, would be made the next President of the United States. All knew to whom the allusion pointed. Webster was then sixty-eight years old. His dream of years had been the presidency. He fancied that oft repeated dream was now to be reality; and he suppressed his honest spech, which was in harmony with the teachings of his youth, the record of his life, the convictions of his conscience, and the holiest sentiments of every enlightened friend in the civilized world; and perverting his great intellect to the unholy use of trying to make his trusting countrymen believe that right was wrong, and wrong was right; to make them "conquer their prejudices," violate their conciences, abandon the worship of God, and prostrate themselves before the Devil, who had, from a high mountain, promised him, what he valued more than all the kingdoms of the world, —the Presidency,—if he would fall down and worship him, Webster fell before the tempter, and rose to make his memorable speech of March the 7th, 1850. A speech which shocked the moral sense of the Christian world—made mourning in ten thousand honest hearts that loved him, and had trusted him so long, and threw into painful perplexing doubt ten times ten thousand more. But the deed was done. A conscientious wave of murmur rolled deeply down towards Washington, and the "Godlike Daniel" heard it; but his tempters flattered him, and soon after made him Secretary of State, and told him that the presidency was near. The accursed law was passed, and to show their contempt and unutterable scorn of what they called "the dough-faced, mean and mercenary North," they inserted a provision in the bill, that if the evidence induced the commissioner to surrrender the hunted slave to the claimant master, then the commissioner should be paid by the *United States* $10 for the service, but only *half* that sum if the evidence showed the man was free.

Webster had helped the slave-hunters to all they asked, but the slave-hunters had not yet given the promised presidency in return; but, being men of boasted honor and chivalry extreme, they will surely keep their word—of course they will; they would challenge you, stab you, or beat you after the style of Brooks, if you suggest that they will not keep their promise to Webster. But the Convention is hard by, and in June, 1852, it met. They balotted many times; and how many Southern votes did Mr. Webster get?—Not a vote! Two known and trusted slaveholders had their votes.

A Virginian was nominated for President, and a North-Carolinian for Vice-President. But Webster had not one Southern vote—not one.

He did not wait for the election, but went home to die.

At Marshfield, beside the sounding sea, he looked through those solemn eyes out upon the vast ocean :—all was gloom ; he looked within ; and memories of his young days upon New Hampshire's hills came back ; his early trust, his honest youth, his religious teachings, his manly faith in God and truth, the faces he had loved, the numbers in his adopted State who had trusted him almost as a savior, and given their consciences to his keeping ; and now they loved him sadly, but trusted him no more—the panorama of his whole life unrolled, and he saw it all—his great heart turned within him, and of no disease, he died. There prone he lay,—the grandest, saddest wreck, that ever stranded on ambition's shore.

But "his works do follow him." Northern gentlemen were made slave-hunters for the South ; and Commissioners, sitting as Judges on human liberty, generally earned the ten dollars, and found evidence that the victim was a slave. Some fathers killed themselves, and some mothers killed their children, to escape the horrors of slavery.

The higher law was scoffed, and Northern pulpits furnished their full quota of subservient tools, and wittily laughed about the "higher law." Two years passed on, and then in obedience to the slave-owners' mandate, that sacred compact with the North, known as the Missouri compromise, which excluded slavery "*forever*" from all territory north of 36° 30' was repealed, and a boastful senator said in his place, that he would "call the roll of his slaves on Bunker Hill." When this base deed of perfidy was done, then rose the mighty North, and the great Republican party sprang to life. In its first campaign it was defeated by Buchanan, but showed such strength that the South saw that the awakened conscience of the North could not be hushed by threats or bribes, and that slavery was doomed.

Then the plot to subvert our government earnestly began ; then followed the election of Lincoln in 1860, which the slaveholders desired as the pretext for the overthrow of free government in the states. Buchanan was timid and infirm of purpose ; Breckenridge was a bold, ambitious slave-holder from Kentucky. The first plan, in the winter before the inauguration of Mr.

Lincoln, was to force Mr. Buchanan to resign, and leave the government in the hands of Breckenridge, whom the plotters could trust. Delaware, Maryland, Virginia and Kentucky were to join; march thirty thousand troops into Washington, declare the Union dissolved, and form a new union with these four States surrounding the District of Columbia, and Breckenridge legitimately at the head; the Southern States were all to join this new confederacy; the north-west were to be invited in; the middle States, it was supposed, would follow from commercial interests, and thus " a bloodless revolution," as the traitors called it, was to be accomplished, and New England, with her twelve senators and her troublesome conscience, was to be left out.

This plan, written by one of the conspirators, is now in the city of New York, with comments reflecting severely upon Gov. Hicks, of Maryland, because he refused to join in the treason. I mentioned the substance of this to Gen. Scott, at West Point, during the war. "True, sir," said he—"true, sir, every word of it; I was consulted about it—they did not ask me to join in it, but to remain quiescent; I prevented it; Gov. Hicks was shivering in the wind, sir, shivering in the wind, and I stiffened him up—I prevented it."

This plot failing, secession followed, and the terrible war came. These men whom slavery had made tyrants could brook no interference with their absolute power. They frankly said, that they would rather "reign in hell than serve in heaven," and during four full years they enjoyed the luxury of that kind of sovereignty, until Jeff. Davis fled in the disguise of a woman's petticoats before the soldiers' of Grant. From that hour they have plotted to regain their power and restore their "lost cause;" not by war—they had tried that—but by diplomacy; not out of the Union, but in it. They have never for one moment repented—never admitted that they were wrong, but have always insisted that they were right. Jeff. Davis, in his triumphal progress through the South, in May last, denounces all as "*cowards*" who "accept the situation" and who admit that the arbitrament of the sword has decided their condition. They nowhere accept the situation, but only yield to might, which they all say is not right, but only a temporary condition of necessity. They remembered the great Daniel Webster, and they knew that Horace Greeley was from the same granite State, but of less granite stuff, of a more restless and equally unsatisfied ambition, and they singled him out as their man. Mr. Greeley was not the choice of the Liberal Republicans, but was forced upon them by the intrigues of the secessionists of the South, allied with the copperheads of the North.

The same breed of men which tempted Daniel Webster from his allegiance to the North and to freedom, have now seduced Mr. Greeley to abandon his convictions of a lifetime for the hope of the Presidency. This is a secession plot, an unnatural alliance, a coalition, in which every hater of the Union joins. It will surely fail. The forces will be routed and scattered in disgrace, and thousands who are now in the combination will be ashamed of it and conceal it as a crime. It is based upon no principle. It is neither natural or honest, and it must come to grief.

Do the Democratic party think that Mr. Greeley is *fit* to be President? Does Mr. Greeley think that the Democratic Party are fit to *make* a president? Hear what each says of the other!

So recently as the 6th of last June, the *World* cited a large number of extracts from the *Tribune*, to prove that no Democrat with the slightest self-respect, could support Mr. Greeley. Out of a large number of these extracts from the *Tribune*, I read a few:

" If there were not a newspaper nor a common school in the country, the democratic party would be far stronger than it is. Neither elementary instruction nor knowledge of transpiring events, is necessary to teach the essential articles of the democratic creed: 'Love rum and have niggers.' The less one learns and knows, the more certain he is to 'vote the larger ticket, from A to Izzard.'"

"If democracy has concocted or borrowed an 'interference theory,' which justifies such meddling, it is a worse theory than even we had supposed. All do know that there are several hundred thousand mulattoes in this country; and we presume no one has any serious doubt that the fathers of at least nine-tenths of them, are white democrats."

" The *World* recently gave a graphic account of the dens and denizens which give character to the Five Points, and other 'slums' of our city—a class, perhaps, lower in the scale of being than can be found in any heathen city on earth."

"We thereupon asked our contemporary to state frankly whether the pugilists, black-legs, thieves, burglars, keepers of dens of prostitution, &c., &c., who make up so large a share of our city's inhabitants, were not almost unanimously democrats."

"For the last thirty years, every American slave-holder on the African coast, has accounted himself in politics a democrat. So, every one who chooses to live by pugilism, or gambling, or harlotry, with nearly every keeper of a tippling-house, is politically a democrat."

Speaking of the Democratic party, he said :

" It is rebel at the core to-day—hardly able to reconcile the defeats of Lee, Johnston, Bragg, Hood and Price, and the consequent downfall of its beloved Confederacy, with its traditional faith in Divine Providence. It would hail the election of a Democratic President in 1872 as a virtual reversal of the Appomattox surrender. It would come into power with the hate, the chagrin, the wrath, the mortification of ten bitter years to impel and guide its steps. It would devote itself to taking off or reducing tax after tax, until the Treasury was deprived of the means of paying interest on the national debt, and would hail the tidings of national bankruptcy with unalloyed gladness and unconcealed exultation. Whatever chastisement may be deserved for our national sins, we must hope that this disgrace and humiliation will be spared us."

And the *World*, commenting upon these extracts, said :

" If he does still think that all the vilest classes, all the scum and dregs of the community, are drawn to the Democratic Party by a sympathetic chord, he disgraces himself in asking for democratic suffrages ; and if these incessant charges of thirty years are wanton calumnies, it would be an indescribable baseness on the part of Democrats to adopt him as their candidate. If the party is infected with such a loathsome moral leprosy as he has so perpetually asserted, how utterly *vile and sordid must be his hankering for office to ' come also among them !'* He wound up one of his *foul* tirades against the Democracy by saying : ' *May it be written on my grave that I was never its follower, and lived and died in nothing its debtor.*' And let the people say, *Amen !*"

And on the 25th of last May, this same *World* newspaper said :

"We have demonstrated, over and over again, that Mr. Greeley is an unfair disputant; that he *is perverse, ignorant, wrong-headed, sophistical and argumentatively dishonest; that his views are at all points opposite to those of the Democratic Party; that his judgment is as unsound as his impulses are wayward.*" *

* * *

It estimates Mr. Greeley now, as itself and all Democrats estimated him up to the moment of his unexpected nomination; and because it keeps right on in maintaining its long-settled opinion of a man whom it has always regarded *as a fanatic and a charlatan*, it is—'erratic.' Which is much the same thing as saying that a line of undeviating straightness runs zig-zag.

"Mr. Greeley is a very antithesis of a Democrat. He has strenuously fought the Democratic Party all his life. *There is no one question, either of principle or policy, on which he agrees with us except the transient question of amnesty. By nominating him we should stultify ourselves as Free Traders; stultify ourselves as opponents of the paternal theory of government; stultify ourselves as the champions of State Rights; stultify ourselves as antagonists of the Ku-Klux law, the odious bayonet election law, martial law in the Southern States, and the whole series of subjugating measures which Mr. Greeley has championed, and the Democratic Party has unanimously opposed, within the last two or three years.* We have not altered our opinion of these detestable laws, and Mr. Greeley has not changed his. For either to change now, or rather to profess a change, in order to help on the proposed coalition, would have such an air of insincerity that the self-respect of both parties should forbid them to publish so *hollow* a renunciation."

On the 5th of last June, the *World* further said:

"The truth is, that Mr. Greeley has next to no Republican strength, and that his most active Democratic support comes from the *trading element of the party and the followers which that element controls*. It was, therefore, a cunning piece of strategy to hold the ratification meeting in this city, the seat of the shivered Tammany Ring. If the sheep were fairly separated from the goats it would be found that Mr. Greeley's supporters in this city consist almost entirely *of that class* of Democrats whom he has been accustomed to denounce in the *Tribune* as the dregs and offscouring of creation."

Mr. O'Conor, in a letter to Judge Lyon, of Richmond, dated September 30th, 1872, speaking of the Southern men and of Mr. Greeley, says:

"The desolation of which they complain is attributable to him. The long and disastrous war that filled his "bloody chasm" with fratricidal slaughter, and involved the whole country in debt and demoralization is due to the "unequaled energy," combined with the folly, of this one exceedingly able, exceedingly amiable and exceedingly mischievous man. I regard the possibility of his election with inexpressible aversion. If the ideas of heathen times prevailed, I would cheerfully surrender my person as a sacrifice on the altar of that deity whose controlling events might thus be propitiated and induced to save my country from the impending evil."

These extracts abundantly show how hollow, how false, dishonest and unnatural is this coalition of the Greeley men with the Democratic Party.

The people have never distrusted Gen. Grant, and he has never distrusted them; in our darkest hour he did not doubt for one moment that the people would vote right; we are apt to trust those who trust us, and to like those who like us. When the first news of the North Carolina election came and looked so gloomy for our cause, the President said to an old life-long friend, "General, don't be disturbed, you and I have camped out upon the plains, and heard the wolves howl at night; you would think from the noise that there were a thousand, but we know that there were not more than three." The false howling from North Carolina did not disturb the President at all.

The news which we have just received from Pennsylvania and Ohio assures the success of Gen. Grant. His election means peace, continued, and vastly increased prosperity. All business-men feel that, and many a democrat will deposit a silent vote for Gen. Grant, rather than risk the commercial disturbance and financial distrust which would follow the election of Mr. Greeley.

I concede that to a capitalist of collossal means, general prosperity is not always the most profitable. Disturbance and financial distress vastly increases the opportunity of such men to double their wealth. They take advantage of the depressed market, and make heavy purchases of stocks, of bonds, of goods of various kinds, and when the market turns, they sell at enormous profit. The beginning of the war caused great commercial distress, and soon the great fortunes were largely increased, while many of the smaller ones perished utterly. The relative distance between the *rich*, and those of moderate means has widened immensely within a few years. A great millionaire can truly say that *he* does not fear any financial difficulty from the election of Horace Greeley; I dare say, he would profit by it. In depressed times the rich grow richer, and the poor, poorer; I speak not for the very few of enormous wealth, but for the men of business generally.

Our people are awake to this new coalition of rebels, copperheads, disappointed republicans and ambitious politicians, and they will scatter it like chaff by the overwhelming re-election of General Grant.

We hear much about the North keeping up hostile feelings, and refusing to " clasp hands aross the bloody chasm." Who dug the chasm and filled it up with blood? Who prevents the green-sward from growing over it? Who imposed the carpetbaggers upon the South?—themselves have done it all, and they alone are responsible. It is time to stop this senseless cant about the way the South have been treated. Badly governed they are, I grant, but it is their own mad fault. Let them accept the situation, return allegiance to the Union, and honestly aid the government in restoring peace, good will, harmony, and just government to all, and there is not an imagined right which the generous North would not too cheerfully give. But while they *allow* scourgings and torture, and murder of innocent men, for opinon sake, or applaud to the echo the sentiments of their rebel chief, who tells them that all "*are cowards* who accept the situation," they cannot expect peace, influx of capital and new population, or any great prosperity.

The troubles in the south are the fruits of their own doings, and they are not chargeable to the north. When justice and good sense take the place of sullen pride and revengeful passions, they can have liberal treatment and prosperity without a parallel. Their bad rulers are chosen by their own voters, and the North are no more to blame for their dishonest governors than are the South for the official thieves who have stolen our substance. Away with these false charges against the North, and the administration of Gen. Grant, in relation to the South. They are not made in the interests of the Union and the good government of the United States—they are the offspring of rebel hate, and the disappointed malice of ambitious men.

Mr. Greeley's coalition cannot capture this State. It is *sure* for Gen. Grant for the following reasons :

First.—It was really carried for Grant four years ago, when the democratic party was in the height of its power, united, and in the most perfect discipline.

Second.—Mr. Greeley cannot poll the vote which Gov. Seymour polled, by more than twenty thousand.

Third.—Gen. Grant will get a colored vote of full seventeen thousand, which he did not get in 1868.

Fourth.—The Tammany ring is broken up, all their power is gone, and there will be no false counting this year.

Fifth.—The Ring cannot rob the public treasury and debauch petty leaders by stolen money.

Sixth.—The honest Democrats have no heart in voting for Greeley—they think his nomination by the party a blunder and a fraud, and most of them will not vote for him.

Seventh.—The Republicans carried the State last fall by a large majority, and most of the reformers will now vote for Grant. It is safe to predict that he will carry the State by more than twenty thousand.

I shall rejoice when the vote is cast, and the election settled, for more reasons than one. It will leave the way clear for the consideration of the great questions which are sure to arise within the next five years. The question of Mexico, the question of tariff, the question of taxes, the question of finance, the question of acquisition of new territory, and the labor question. These questions will force themselves upon us, and they will get considered. I went two days ago to the office of the Board of Health, in the city of

New York, and asked for a report of the deaths in the city. I hold the report in my hand. Two thousand eight hundred and twenty-six children under five years old died in a single month this summer. Their little dying plaint will come up some day, and ask us why we let so many die? The doctors say unwholesome food and polluted air was the chief cause. Is there no relief from unwholesome food and polluted air in this *rich*, sea-washed city of ours? I have no time to night for these discussions; they will intrude themselves upon the stage before long, and you will hear about them.

I ask no better evidence of the hopeless condition of our opponents than the wild and desperate measures to which they resort. This is the first time that I have seen religion made prominent in politics; the first time that I have known eminent men invoke religious prejudices in favor of one and against the other candidate; and may it be the last. Let Jew or Greek, Protestant or Catholic, worship God as his conscience dictates, but do not bring his religious faith into political strife. Vote for the man who is right on the great questions affecting the union of the States and the safety of our country. Vote for him who is capable and honest, who was right on the war, and who has continued right on the questions involved in that war, and never ask whether he be Protestant, Episcopal or Roman Catholic.

On the next day after Mr. Kernan was nominated for Governor, the *Tribune* told us in a very significant article that he was " a *sincere* and *earnest* Roman Catholic." What was that paraded for? Every one knows. Did any Republican paper say that Gen. Dix was "a sincere and earnest" member of the Protestant Episcopal church? No; nothing of the kind would have been tolerated. But we have another man—Governor Seymour—a more adroit and skillful politician, seizing in desperation upon the religious question, and trying by cunning phrase to set voters against Gen. Dix because he is a Protestant, and in favor of Mr. Kernan because he is " a *sincere* and *earnest* Roman Catholic!" Hear him. I read from his Oneida speech, published in the Albany *Argus*, Sept. 23d, as follows:

" In looking over the history of my State I found that we

ave never had a Catholic Governor, though Catholics constitute about one-third of the population *and a very large share of the voters.* One thing I cannot bear to have said, they have been voting for Protestants for nearly a hundred years, and I *cannot bear* to have it said that Protestants are more bigoted than Catholics, and I *cannot vote once for a Catholic* in return. Every public man in the State has asked Catholics for their votes. I ask them if they cannot reciprocate the favor."

Vote against General Dix—speak against him if you will, Governor Seymour, but do not invoke religious prejudice to your aid; do not bring the crosier, and the vestments, and St. Peter's key and the triple crown from the mouldering Vatican and the old ills of Rome, and insist that free Americans shall bow down to these baubles. Don't raise such issues here; you may light a fire which you cannot extinguish, and you will bring the spirits of your New England sires from their forgotten graves to chide their recreant son, and tell him, that to the manly soul, there is one *thing* more dear than houses, or lands, or political success, or wife, or child, or life itself, and that is—" *the liberty of enlightened conscience.*"

I ask you to vote for General Dix, not because he is a Protestant and a good, religious man, but because he is an honest man, because he was right on the war, because he has continued right, he has always been right, and he always will be right. He took the side of the Union from the start, he has been devoted to the end. There is not a tarnish upon his long life of devoted service to his country, and we know that in his hands the government of our State will be administered with wisdom, ability, justice and unswerving integrity.

Daniel Webster and Horace Greeley were born amidst the hills of New Hampshire. In the morning of life they breathed the same inspiring air—the air of liberty and of religion. In manly life, they each moved to the great city of their adopted State. Each sought the Presidency through the same unworthy means, and each will share the like fate as sure as there is a God in Heaven. The great Creator rules by laws—unerring and inexorable laws,—and he who resists great moral laws will be as surely crushed as though a planet rolled over him.

Horace Greeley will not be the next President of the United States.

REMARKS

OF

Hon. EDWARDS PIERREPONT,

AT A MEETING OF THE BAR IN NEW YORK, JANUARY 17, 1873, UPON THE RETIREMENT OF JUDGE NELSON FROM THE BENCH.

Judge PIERREPONT, in moving the adoption of the address presented by Mr. STOUGHTON, said:

Mr. Chairman: When eminent men have died, it has been the custom among civilized nations to take some public notice of the event. But the number of those who have *voluntarily* retired from a great office are so few, that it can hardly be said that any custom touching such retirement has been established; the rarity of this occasion makes it the more noted, and for every reason it was most fit that you, Mr. Chairman, should have been selected to preside at this unusual meeting of the bar.

When a man, in his early prime, resigns a high office to enter some broader field of ambition, or to seek new gratification in the pursuit of wealth, he neither deserves nor receives any special marks of approbation from his fellow-men.

But when one has spent a long life in the public service, and has so borne himself in his great office as to command the respect of every honest citizen, and at the call of duty lets go his hold on power, while all his faculties remain, he is a man so rare as to attract more than a passing notice; and we have met to say something of this GRAND OLD MAN, who was 80 years old the 8th of November last, and who, by continuing three months longer, would have had an uninterrupted career of judicial life full 50 years. We search in vain for a career like his! How nobler is it than to have clung feebly to his place till death pulled him reluctant from his seat.

How like the man; how in harmony with his high sense of duty was his retirement from an office in which he, sooner than others, felt that the burden of his years might possibly diminish his usefulness. No pride, no love of power, no vanity stood for a moment in his way; a lofty sense of duty governed him in the end as at the beginning, and as all through his life.

It was well known, if Judge Nelson retained his office until April next, that the half century of his judicial life would then be complete, and many supposed that the natural desire to fill up the fifty years would prolong his stay upon the bench; but those well acquainted with Judge Nelson, knew that the high tone of his character would not allow him to retain the office, one day after he became satisfied that he could not fully discharge its duties.

Lord Mansfield, the Chief-Justice of the King's Bench, resigned at the age of eighty-three. He had been upon the bench thirty-two years. Between Judge Nelson and the Lord Chief-Justice there were some striking points of resemblance. So noted was Lord Mansfield for preferring substantial justice to musty precedent, and so firmly did he believe in the flexibility of the Common Law, and that its rigid rules should bend to new exigencies in the advancement of commerce, of science, of civilization and humanity, that it was a common thing for the old lawyers to sneer at what they called "Lord Mansfield's Equity Judgments;" and Junius, in a letter addressed to the Lord Chief-Justice, November 14th, 1770, says:

"Even in matters of private property we see the same bias and inclination to depart from the decisions of your predecessors, which you certainly ought to receive as evidence of the Common Law. Instead of those certain positive rules by which the judgment of a court of law should invariably be determined, you have fondly introduced your own unsettled notions of equity and substantial justice. Decisions given upon such principles do not alarm the public so much as they ought."

The *public* were not alarmed; the public saw that Lord Mansfield was right, and that "equity and substantial justice" was what good men desired, and not inequity and injustice, in deference to worn-out precedents unsuited to the advancing times.

In earlier years we heard the same criticisms, from old lawyers, about the rulings of Judge Nelson, and almost in the same language: but the names of those who censured Lord Mansfield and Judge Nelson for their adherence to "equity and substantial justice" are already forgotten, while both of these great jurists will be held in reverence so long as the common law continues to be administered.

In the construction of Statutes of the United States, subtle and unsubstantial technicalities interposed to defeat justice had small chance of success where Judge Nelson was presiding.

At the trial of the great frauds of Kohnstamm I was employed by the Government to conduct the prosecution; several of the eminent lawyers here present were engaged for the defence, and one, now no more—the lamented and much beloved James T. Brady, whose great legal abilities would have made him distinguished without the aid of his more brilliant and unparalleled rhetorical powers. Mr. Brady, with his usual eloquence and skill, summed up the case for the accused; but the jury found the defendant guilty, and upon remarking to Mr. Brady that the jury were prompt, and that I had feared a disagreement—" I had *hoped* it," said Brady, " until the charge, but what could I do against that old lion there?"— turning towards the Judge as he sat kingly upon the bench, and looking like a veritable old lion, as he was.

Nature did much to make Judge Nelson what he has been. Nature gave him a commanding presence; a strong constitution, an even balance of the passions and the intellectual faculties; a genial soul and great vital forces; a natural love of right and substantial justice; a resolute will and an honest heart; a mind, body and a moral tone healthy, manly and robust. Culture did greatly aid him; but his natural endowments were vast. He did not deserve much credit for being a great, just man; he could not help it very well. It was natural and easy; and his life flowed on as the strong current of a river. It would be interesting and instructive to have his brother Judges of the Supreme Court give their estimate of Judge Nelson's characteristics and judicial abilities. I have frequently heard several of them speak of their eminent associate, and quite recently the Chief-Justice has expressed unmeasured admiration of the easy facility, wisdom, ability and remarkable character of him whose retirement from the bench the Chief-Justice considers an irreparable loss to himself personally, and to the public service generally.

The influence of Judge Nelson upon the New York Bar has been very great. The tone and manners of the Bar will always depend upon the tone and manners of the Bench. Good temper, courteous manners, and dignity of deportment are very importent, *if not essential*, in the administration of justice.

The Bar and the Bench will ever go hand in hand and quite abreast in every respect, and the community are quick to discover the fact, and great merchants and men of business will not entrust their important interests to a Bench and a Bar composed of inferior men; and so sure as you degrade the Bench, you degrade the Bar; and with equal certainty you thus drive the important business from the lawyers and the courts, and other means of adjusting differences of magnitude will be found.

Judge Nelson took no active part in politics; but no man was a more close or more interested observer of public affairs. In the distracted times of 1860, when the Democratic Party looked around for a candidate who could unite the North and the South, and command the confidence of the entire country, Judge Nelson seemed to be the only man; the sole difficulty in the way was the fact that he was a member of the Supreme Court; and the sentiment of the people seemed then, as now, to be, that when a man enters that Temple of Justice, and puts on the robes of office, he shall never make the sacred seat a stepping-stone from which to ascend to any political place.

When the governments of Great Britain and of the United States undertook a negotiation which resulted in the Treaty of Washington, our sagacious Secretary of State, with that good judgment for which he is distinguished (by the approval of the President). selected Judge Nelson as one of the High Commissioners; and the crowning act of a great career in the public service was the prominent part he took in concluding that treaty, by which enduring peace between these two great nations, speaking the same language, governed by similar laws, and worshipping the same God through the same religious forms, was secured.

The Lord Chief-Justice Mansfield lived five years after resignation of his office. May our equally great and equally respected Judge, live many times those years, if he so wishes and God wills; "and when old time shall lead him to his end, goodness and he fill up one monument."

HISTORICAL DISCOURSE

BY

THEODORE D. WOOLSEY,

AND

ORATION

ON

THE INFLUENCE OF LAWYERS UPON FREE GOVERNMENTS, AND THE INFLUENCE OF MORAL FORCES UPON THE PROSPERITY OF GOVERNMENTS.

BY

Hon. EDWARDS PIERREPONT, LL.D.,

PRONOUNCED BEFORE

THE ALUMNI OF THE LAW DEPARTMENT

OF

YALE COLLEGE,

AT THE

FIFTIETH ANNIVERSARY OF THE FOUNDATION OF THE DEPARTMENT, IN THE CENTRE CHURCH AT NEW HAVEN,

June 24th, 1874.

PUBLISHED BY THE LAW DEPARTMENT OF YALE COLLEGE

1874.

HISTORICAL DISCOURSE

BY

THEODORE D. WOOLSEY,

AND

ORATION

ON

THE INFLUENCE OF LAWYERS UPON FREE GOVERNMENTS, AND THE INFLUENCE OF MORAL FORCES UPON THE PROSPERITY OF GOVERNMENTS,

BY

Hon. EDWARDS PIERREPONT, LL.D.,

PRONOUNCED BEFORE

THE ALUMNI OF THE LAW DEPARTMENT

OF

YALE COLLEGE

AT THE

FIFTIETH ANNIVERSARY OF THE FOUNDATION OF THE DEPARTMENT, IN THE CENTRE CHURCH AT NEW HAVEN,

June 24th, 1874.

———•●•———

PUBLISHED BY THE LAW DEPARTMENT OF YALE COLLEGE.

1874.

PREFATORY NOTE.

The celebration of the Semi-centennial Anniversary of the Yale Law School, on Wednesday, June 24th, 1874, was attended by a large number of its alumni from all parts of the country. The public exercises of the occasion took place at the Centre Chuch in New Haven, on Wednesday afternoon, Hon. MORRISON R. WAITE, LL.D., Chief Justice of the Supreme Court of the United States, presiding, when the following discourse and oration were pronounced. After the adjournment of this meeting, the Alumni of the School proceeded to its new apartments, occupying one floor of the new Court House building, for an informal and social reunion. Short addresses were made by Chief Justice WAITE, Hon. JOHN BOYD, of the Class of 1826; Hon. THOMAS H. BOND and HENRY WHITE, Esq., of the Class of 1827; Rev. O. E. DAGGETT, D.D., of the Class of 1830; Hon. CORNELIUS VAN SANTVOORD, of the Class of 1835; Hon. EDWARDS PIERREPONT, of the Class of 1839; Hon. WILLIAM G. BATES, of Westfield, Mass.; Hon. ALPHONSO TAFT, of Cincinnati; Prof. CYRUS NORTHROP, of the Class of 1859, and Prof. WM. C. ROBINSON. Later in the evening the doors were thrown open for a more general reception, which was attended by the President and Fellows of the College, the Faculties of the other Departments, the Governor and Lieutenant-Governor of Connecticut, with the principal State officers, and other invited guests, gentlemen and ladies, numbering in all about five hundred.

An Alumni Association was organized by the graduates of the Law Department in 1872, which meets annually on Wednesday of Commencement-week, at the Law School Lecture-room. That day will hereafter be devoted to the Anniversary Exercises of the Department, which will hold its commencement in the afternoon, when members of the graduating class will read theses or deliver orations on legal topics, and a prize of $100, established by Hon. JAMES M. TOWNSEND, of East Haven, Conn., will be awarded to the best writer and speaker on the occasion.

The staff of instructors in the Department during the past year has been as follows : REV. NOAH PORTER, D.D., *President*, FRANCIS WAYLAND, M.A., Professor of *Mercantile Law and Evidence*, and Lecturer on *English Constitutional History;* WILLIAM C. ROBINSON, M.A., Professor of *Elementary and Criminal Law and the Law of Real Property;* SIMEON E. BALDWIN, M.A., Professor of *Constitutional Law and the Law of Contracts and Wills*, and Lecturer on *Roman Law and Comparative Jurisprudence;* JOHNSON T. PLATT, M.A., Professor of *Pleading and Equity Jurisprudence;* CHARLES J. MCCURDY, LL.D., Lecturer on *Life Insurance;* Rev. THEODORE D. WOOLSEY, D.D., LL.D., Lecturer on the *Law of Nations;* Rev. LEONARD BACON, D.D., LL.D., Lecturer on *Ecclesiastical Law;* Rev. JAMES M. HOPPIN, D.D., LL.B., Lecturer on *Forensic Composition;* MARK BAILEY, M.A., Instructor in *Elocution;* FRANCIS BACON, M.D., Lecturer on *Medical Jurisprudence*, and FREDERICK H. BETTS, M.A., Lecturer on *Patent Law;* DAVID D. BALDWIN, M.A., *Librarian*.

HISTORICAL ADDRESS

BY

THEODORE D WOOLSEY.

---o---

When Roman law was reaching its mature form, distinguished lawyers, like Q. and P. Mucius Scævola, were wont to receive students into their houses, in order to give them some kind of informal instruction in jurisprudence. This was done not for pay—for an aristocratic Roman gentleman would have scorned getting a reward from pupils—but in order to benefit young friends, who had no law books nor law schools to aid them in learning the science. Cicero, thus, although never a professed jurist, was put by his father with Q. Mucius Scævola, that he might draw instruction from his lips. But when Roman law became a complicated system under the emperors, schools arose for its study. Thus in the time of Justinian there were three great law schools, one at Rome in the West, and two in the East, at Constantinople and at Berytus or Beirout, together with some others of less note. The Eastern schools were represented in the preparation of the Digest by as many as four professors.

The modern university system began with the revived study of law at Bologna in the twelfth century, and this, as much as any other cause, overthrew feudalism by substituting new and better law for that of the feudal period. At another great centre of university life, the University of Paris, civil law was not studied until late in the seventeenth century, owing to the management of the popes, who were afraid that Paris, as a law school, would eclipse Bologna. In our mother country, London, rather than the universities, was the centre of law study, where the inns of court provided societies, into which young men desiring to become lawyers and pleaders could be admitted, and could for a time obtain instruction.

Sir William Blackstone, as many of my hearers will remember, cites from old Fortescue this question, Why the laws of England were not taught in the universities, as the civil and canon laws were? Whatever may have been the reason, whether it was that the Latin of the lecture-rooms there was not suited for the proper treatment of the law of England, or that law students would go where cases on appeal were tried and a body of lawyers dwelt, in order to learn forms and principles at the place of chief resort,—I say, whatever may have been the reason, the fact seems to be admitted that there was no formal instruction given at either university in common law, until Mr. Viner founded at Oxford the professorship of that science, of which, in 1758, Blackstone was appointed the first incumbent.

In our country, for a long time after it became independent, the three learned professions were all alike in trusting for their new supplies to private instruction. Now and then a minister of eminence, like Dr. Bellamy of Bethlem, in this State, gathered about him quite a number of young men who had devoted themselves to the ministerial profession. The pupils heard lectures, read sermons or subjects of sermons or theological essays, and their influence on one another must have been very stimulating. Probably the same thing was true of eminent physicians. It certainly was of eminent lawyers.

It is worthy of notice that the first law school in the country of any considerable note was founded in the town of Litchfield, next to Bethlem, where Dr. Bellamy lived. Bellamy's school was begun at least twenty-five years before the revolutionary war. The law school at Litchfield owed its origin to Tapping Reeve, a native of Long Island, a graduate at Nassau Hall, a son-in-law of President Burr, and so a brother-in-law of Aaron Burr, Vice-President of the United States, and was begun in 1784, just after the revolution was over. Some time before the end of the century Judge Reeve invited James Gould, a lawyer in Litchfield, a graduate of Yale College, of 1791, to take part in the instruction. They continued partners in the school until 1820, when, Judge Reeve having retired, Judge Gould became the head of the school and ere long associated with himself for a time Jabez W. Huntington, afterwards Senator of the United States and Judge of the Supreme Court of Connecticut. Down to 1833, when Judge Gould, about five years before his death, discontinued his lectures, there had been educated at Litchfield, according to Mr. Hollister (Hist. of Conn., Vol. 2, p. 597), 1,024 lawyers from all parts of the United States, of whom 183 were from the Southern States. In this number are included fifteen United States Senators, five cabinet officers in the general government, ten governors of States, fifty members of Congress, forty judges of the highest State Courts, and two judges of the Supreme Court of the United States.

In the latter part of the eighteenth century and in the early years of the present, a school was set up in the city of New Haven by Charles Chauncey, a lawyer of extensive practice. Of this school I know but little. Judge Samuel Hubbard, of the Supreme Court of Massachusetts, and Judge Wayne, of the Supreme Court of the United States, studied under Judge Chauncey.

Mr. Seth P. Staples, a graduate of Yale College, of 1797, who soon attained to a large practice and a high reputation, and who, early in his professional life, seems to have collected a large library of unusual value for those times in this part of the country, gathered around him a number of young men, whose law studies he superintended. This school, from which the existing law school of Yale College is a direct descendant, must have begun in the first decade of this century. One of the scholars in it was Samuel J. Hitchcock (Yale, 1809), a tutor in Yale College from 1811 to 1815, who fitted himself for the bar during his official connection with his alma mater, and afterwards settled in New Haven in the legal profession. In a few years Mr. Staples invited Mr. Hitchcock to assist him in the instruction of his pupils, and in 1824 removed to New York, leaving the school in the hands of Judge Daggett and Mr. Hitchcock. Mr. Staples' great repute as a lawyer did not desert him on his removal to a larger sphere of professional labors. He stood in the front rank of his profession, especially in commercial and patent law ; he gave, at one time, lectures on the first of these branches with great success ; he lived to a good old age and died at the age of eighty-six, honored and deserving of honor for his private and professional life, in 1861.

Of Mr. Staples, one of his pupils in 1823–1824, the last years of his instruction in New Haven, thus speaks : " Those who only saw him in the conflicts of the bar and heard his bitter sarcasms, could form no true estimate of his character. They saw nothing of his kindlier nature and social qualities, as exhibited in the office and the recitation room. As a teacher he exerted a magnetism over his students unsurpassed by any man I ever knew—a magnetism that drew his pupils into thorough study of first principles. No greater contrast could well exist than that presented by comparison of the formal law lectures of the Litchfield school and the off-hand comments and illustrations of Mr. Staples' class-room : Judge Gould read his able and finished lectures with a cold dignity to his students, each seated at his separate desk, intent on copying from his lips the principles laid down and the authorities referred to, embodying a system of law for future reference and use. In the New Haven school, at the time it was made a department of the college, the class recitations superseded in great measure the formal lecture. The student in his study drew the principles from the text book. In the recitation they were sifted, tested and illustrated. It was here that Mr. Staples was perhaps unrivaled as a teacher. His practice at the bar enabled him to illustrate principles and decisions from his own experience and observation, in such a manner as to fix them in the mind in a manner very different from the mere entry of them in a note book. Mr. Staples read few lectures, and they were not of a high order. It was as an offhand commentator that he impressed *himself* as well as *the law* on the minds of his students."

In 1824 the school thus bequeathed by Mr. Staples to two of his brethren of the bar, had, through the publication of the students names on the annual catalogue, a sort of vague connection with Yale College, of which most of them could be called resident graduates. In 1826 the connection became closer, since, in that year Judge Daggett was appointed Professor of Law on the foundation provided by a number of Chancellor Kent's friends for his Alma Mater, and called by his honored name. It was not, however, until 1843 that the degree of Bachelor in Law on examination began to be conferred, which placed the law faculty and department on a level with the others. Thus, one may say, that fifty years ago the school was acknowledged by the college as in some measure belonging to it; forty-eight years ago it began to be a part of the university; and thirty-one years ago it reached its majority by acquiring the privilege of having its students, after a certain term of study and a successful examination, promoted to academical honors. In this way a fourth faculty of instruction was added to the college.

Considered in relation to its instructors, the school has had three stages, and is now in the third. The first includes the years from 1824 to 1847, when Judge Daggett was at its head assisted by Mr. Hitchcock, until the death of the latter, in 1845, and by Mr. Isaac H. Townsend from 1842 until his death, in 1847. Nearly two years before Mr. Townsend's death, Judge Wm. L. Storrs was appointed one of the instructors of the school, but resigned his position in 1847, finding that the duty of instruction called him away too much from the preparation of opinions on cases of appeal in the Supreme Court. Our honored townsman, Henry White, Esq., gave his assistance to the instructors during nearly two years, from February, 1846, to October, 1847. Thus at the end of the college year in 1847, as Judge Daggett also, owing to his advanced age, had retired from instruction, it became necessary for the college authorities to put a new corps of officers into the school, and so a *second* stage commenced. The choice fell on Hon. Clark Bissell, who had been a judge of the Supreme Court of Errors, from 1829 to 1839, and was, at the time of his appointment, governor of the State; and on Henry Dutton, a lawyer, residing in Bridgeport, who had been a tutor in the college, and was now in the full practice of his profession. Governor Bissell continued his connection with the school until the autumn of 1855, when, at a ripe old age, he retired from active employments to his home in Norwalk, where he closed an honored and useful life two years afterwards. Mr. Dutton was elected governor of the State in 1854, and in 1861 was chosen one of the judges of the Supreme Court of Errors, which office he filled until his superannuation, at the age of seventy, in 1866. He continued to be the head of the school until 1869, when he died. In the year 1855, Hon. Thomas B. Osborne, who had been a member of Congress, was appointed to be an associate in the school with Governor Dutton, and continued to give instruction until 1865, when he resigned, four years before his death. From that time until Professor Dutton's death, he had the sole charge of the school, and being often called away by his private or professional business, was not able to give the due degree of attention to his professorial charge. The school, therefore, in the last years of his life and of his office, greatly declined, until there appeared a meagre list of sixteen or seventeen students on the catalogues of 1867 and 1868, of whom a considerable part could scarcely be called students. This second stage continued for twenty-two years—about the same number of years with the first.

At this point of greatest depression, when it seemed doubtful whether the study of law as a department of instruction in Yale College ought not to be abandoned altogether, the services of three gentlemen of the legal profession, in New Haven, Messrs. Baldwin, Platt and Robinson, were engaged to carry on the instruction in law for another year. It was at first rather an experiment than a permanent plan, both on their part and on that of the college authorities. They began with seventeen students. In 1871, Hon. Francis Wayland, who had been Lieutenant-Governor of the State, was associated with them. The school recovered, by degrees, its old numbers, and at least its old reputation. The present year has brought with it more students than have ever appeared on the catalogue before.

This increase is due to several causes besides the zeal and ability of the four professors, " whose works praise them in the gates."

One of these causes is that the new professors have been able to enlarge and broaden the system of law training, by calling in the aid of auxiliary lecturers to a greater degree than before. Thus the late Professor Hadley delivered here his clear and beautiful lectures introductory to Roman Law, which have been given to the public since his death. Dr. Leonard Bacon has lectured on Ecclesiastical Law ; Dr. Francis Bacon on Medical Jurisprudence ; Judge Chales J. McCurdy on Insuance; other gentlemen on International Law, on the Law of Patents, and on the Style and the Elocution of the Forum. It is believed that nowhere in the United States these subsidiary branches of knowledge, of which, perhaps, the special pleader or the drawer of legal formulas can afford to be ignorant, but which, when known, broaden and elevate legal study, bringing it out of the dull routine and dryness of common practice, as well as supplying food for thought—I say that nowhere in the United States are these handmaids to a finished legal education brought more effectively into the service of legal studies and made more useful than in the Yale Law School, in the latest stage of its development. And by the carrying out of this plan, it is made apparent how much more comprehensive and finished a legal education ought to be, when it is pursued as a department of a university, than when it stands alone.

The *second* cause of prosperity and ground of hope for the future lies in the apartments which have been secured for the school by the action of the New Haven County Bar and the County Commissioners. A court house had been projected, to be placed by the side of the town house, built a few years since, when it was suggested that room could be afforded for the law lectures and the library within the walls. The third story was planned with this in view, it being understood that the books of the library should be open for consultation for the judges of the Supreme and other courts held within the building, as well for the lawyers, who were to have the privilege of taking them into the neighboring court-rooms when they had cases before the tribunals. The plan has been so carried out that, at the expense of the county, a large and commodious lecture-room, an elegantly finished library, with an adjoining chamber, ready to receive books whenever the overflow shall make it necessary, a private apartment for the Dean of the Faculty, and other rooms, suitable for the purposes of "quiz-clubs" and moot-courts, have been provided. Perhaps in no place, where a law faculty has not a building of its own, could better arrangements have been made. The bench, the bar, the school are brought not only into proximity but into harmony; the books are made available both for the student, the lawyer and the judge; and the liberality of the county which has furnished all this, free of charge or rent, receives back what, I understand, is universally agreed to be a full equivalent for what it has expended, the use of the intellectual instruments of law, no adequate collection of which had previously existed nearer than Hartford or New York.

This is the best possible arrangement that could be made for the supply of present wants; but I must avow the opinion, that, if the school should be greatly enlarged and be put upon a permanent basis of strength, increased accommodation, somewhere in a central spot, not far from the courts, would be found essential. If, for instance, the number of students should grow to two hundred, or even a hundred and fifty, instead of fifty-four, more lecture-rooms would be wanted, unless the best hours of the day should be monopolized by one or two out of a number of professors. And if the library, instead of confining itself mainly to reports of English and American courts, to the text-writers of our system of law, and to collections of statutes, should aim successfully at exhaustive comprehension, so as to include civil law with its best expounders in every language, ecclesiastical law, the digests, codes, reports and systems of all the leading European nations, with whatever is valuable on the theory of legislation, on the doctrine of rights and the State, on the history of governments and institutions, apartments many times the size of the present ones would be found necessary.* Meanwhile, it behooves us to

* It will be gratifying to the friends of the school to learn that something has already been done in this direction. Within the past two years about a hundred volumes of English, French and German works upon the Roman Law, as many upon different branches of political science, and over twelve hundred relating to American and English constitutional history, have been added to the Library.

accept, in all thankfulness, the chambers so liberally provided for us, and to congratulate ourselves that the books can be of general service to the profession.

The *third* cause from which we may hope for success is the enlargement of the library itself. So far as I am informed, before about 1845 there was no library pertaining to the school. Those who needed to consult authorities had to go to Judge Hitchcock's private collection, which, indeed, for that day, was quite large. In the year mentioned, and soon after the death of Judge Hitchcock, a subscription was taken up for the purchase of his library, and a considerable sum was raised for this purpose, but not enough to procure it without the intervention of the College to make up the deficiency. It was agreed upon at the same time that a certain small part of the annual receipts of the school should be devoted to the preservation and increase of the library. But in process of time, when the receipts dwindled, and the purchasing power of money became reduced, it was found not easy to keep the library in good condition, still less by additions to make it represent the progress of legal science. In 1869, therefore, when the present instructors took the school into their hands, it was found that many sets had become mutilated, that quite a number of books had disappeared, and that others were hardly fit to be used. A beginning was now made of supplying the deficiencies, but the principal movement for this purpose took place in 1873, when, chiefly by the efforts of Prof. Wayland, nearly twenty thousand dollars were collected, for the most part in New Haven and New York, to be used in the immediate purchase of additions to the library. The books procured by these new funds bring, as far as possible, the law-learning, including the laws, the text-writers, and the reports of judicial decisions, of both England and of the United States, within the reach of the students, down to the present time. The labor of purchasing these volumes, and of seeing them properly arranged in the library, fell chiefly to the share of Prof. Platt, to whom the school and all who use the books owe great thanks. While the collection was thus expanding, Governor English, by his munificent gift of ten thousand dollars to serve as a permanent fund for the increase and preservation of the library, provided for the wants of the future. Thus, what may be called the soul of the school is full of life and growth, and it will be a pleasure to all who take an interest in Yale College to associate the name of this benefactor of more than one department of the institution, with a constantly increasing supply of that food, without which neither law nor any other branch of knowledge can have a proper support and vigor. Fifty years hence this fund, if well husbanded and well expended, will largely exceed by its annual harvests all other sources of supply, and the library will hardly fail to keep pace with the times.*

I have spoken thus far of the outward and material side of the law department. In what remains of this address, I will call my hearers' attention to the men who have chiefly directed its affairs. And here, as I cannot well speak of the living or of those who have but just passed away, what I say must be chiefly confined to those who may be regarded as fathers and founders of the institution.

First of all comes before us the imposing form of Judge Daggett, that gentleman of the old school, with his aquiline nose, and other striking features, his white-topped boots, small clothes and silk stockings, his courtesy toward all, and that expectation of respect from others which belonged to the gentlemen of the former time. He was born in Attleborough, Massachusetts, in 1764, and came to Yale College for

---

* It should also be mentioned that, by the liberality of Hon. Marshall Jewell, Hon. James M. Townsend, and E. J. Edwards, Esq., foundations for prizes have been established, by which three hundred dollars are annually awarded to the successful competitors among the students, for excellence in scholarship, forensic composition, and oratory.

his education, probably because his relative from the same place had some time before filled the office of president of the College. He received his legal training in New Haven, after his graduation in 1783, in the office of Charles Chauncey, of whom, as having trained a number of young men in law we have already spoken, and was admitted to the bar in 1786.

Mr. Daggett seems to have early won the confidence and admiration of the people in New Haven and in the State. Starting in active life at the time of the formation of the Constitution, he espoused with warmth the federal side in politics, as against the States' rights or democratic theory; and the State being decidedly under the control of the federalists for a generation, it was not strange that a brilliant young man should be early called into political life. He was sent by the people of New Haven to represent them in the General Assembly, at the age of twenty-seven, in 1791, and for five successive years afterwards, for the last three of which he was speaker of the House of Representatives.

From 1797 until 1804, he was a member of the Supreme Court of Errors. Then he was again sent to the Assembly, and again to the Council, and in 1813 was chosen a senator of the United States. The years after his term as a senator until 1824, when he joined Mr. Hitchcock in the school, were spent in the work of his profession exclusively, without his being called into political life. In 1826 he became an associate judge of the Supreme Court of Connecticut, and was chief judge in 1833–1834, when he became superannuated, at the age of seventy.

At the time when I can first remember him, he was regarded as a great pleader, and especially his speeches in the case when Joshua Stow sued Sherman Converse for a libel produced a powerful impression upon the community. Here the feelings of the advocate were warmly enlisted on the side of his client, in whose newspaper a man of some note in the

State had been charged with malpractice as a collector of taxes, with infidelity, and with other things injurious to his character. The suit grew out of political dislike of one who was obnoxious as a democrat and as an overturner of the old charter of Charles II, under which Connecticut had been governed from 1664 until 1818. Mr. Daggett was here in his glory, and perhaps no plea ever excited a deeper interest in New Haven, expecially among the students, than this. As a learned and scientific lawyer, however, Mr. Daggett did not rank so high as others, who were his juniors, and who confined themselves more closely to the duties of professional life. He had in his busy years little leisure to study the doctrines of law, except in connection with his cases. Political duties absorbed much of his time, and his judicial functions, after he was invested with them, prevented him from elaborating his lectures. He was, moreover, sixty years old when he took charge of the school. But I will let one of his pupils speak of him, who within the last few weeks has kindly communicated to me his recollections.

This gentleman, who belonged to the school near the end of Judge Daggett's connection with it, expresses himself thus:

"He lectured every morning immediately after Judge Hitchcock's recitation, and the lectures on constitutional law (which were also delivered before the seniors in college) were made very interesting, because his experience in the Senate and intimacy with many of the founders of the Republic, supplied him with many anecdotes which he told with much gusto. He had been a decided federalist, and delighted in giving an occasional slap to Mr. Jefferson, whose character and career were at that time the subject of much discussion in the debating societies of the college and the law school."

"His good humor, readiness at repartee and crusty mode of summing up his sentiments in a few words, made him always more interesting in conversation than in the lecture-room. His lectures on the common law, which were read from well-worn manuscripts, were not as interesting. He had been so long out of practice that he had not kept up with the later decisions, and the substance of them was contained in Swift's Digest."

Others of his pupils concur in the estimate here expressed.

Of Judge Hitchcock, the colleague of Judge Daggett until his death, we have spoken as a graduate of Yale of the year 1809, and a tutor there for four years from 1811 to 1815. The accuracy of scholarship which distinguished him at college he carried into the profession of law, and soon acquired the confidence of his professional brethren and of the public. Before 1822, I believe, he began to teach law to the pupils whom Mr. Seth P. Staples gathered around him, and as we have already seen, when that gentleman removed to New York, the school was entrusted in part to him.

The leading work of his life from this time until his death, in 1845, was that of a teacher. He was a dry, exact man, clear in his perceptions, with little geniality or enthusiasm, yet with a great love of truth, and a thoroughly conscientious spirit. He shrunk from no labor, was patient in acquiring and in imparting the principles of his science, and evidently had the good of his pupils at heart. He was, withal, one of the most decidedly religious men to be found in any department of life. He was not fitted to make a deep impression on a jury, nor did he either desire or obtain political honors; but this, I think, may be said of him, that if his professional brethren wanted advice, there were few, if any persons in the city, or in the State, to whom they would sooner go than to him.

One would not suppose from the preciseness and formality of Mr. Hitchcock's general manner that he could interest students, but it would seem as if, in matter of fact, few men have ever taught law in this country with more success than he. One of his pupils expresses his recollections of him in these words: "I was a great admirer of Judge Hitchcock. He was a model teacher. He was so clear, you could not fail to understand him fully; so copious in instruction and illustration, that he seemed to exhaust the subject, and you felt that he was master of the principles of law, and of their application and analogies; and yet so compact in style that he never used a word too much. As I had just come from Harvard, I often compared him with Judge Story, and was at a loss to decide which was the most admirable instructor. We recited to him in Cruise's Digest. It was called a book hard to understand, but under his teaching it was all clear and plain; and we wondered how it had got such a name. Recitations to him were for a full half-hour lectures from him on the subjects we were studying." Another gentleman, who studied law in this school in the years 1838 and 1839, writes of him thus: "The mainstay of the school was Judge Hitchcock. Many of the students had studied one year at Cambridge, where the school was much larger, and where Judge Story was the great ornament; but they all gave the palm to Hitchcock over Greenleaf, able and learned as the latter was admitted to be. The introductory lecture of Judge Hitchcock always made a great impression. He dwelt upon the distinction between *reading* and *study;* upon the fact that they had not come there to win prizes in the shape of degrees; that a man might read law forever, and not be a lawyer; he must study, and he might study much, but it would be to little purpose unless he accustomed himself to feel that he had the responsibility of some future client [in his hands] whose property or rights would depend upon the accuracy with which the books [he had studied] were comprehended. His running comments, as the recitation progressed, were remarkable, not so much for the matter as for the manner of putting them. There was a tinge of cynicism about him which gave much effect and pungency to his utterances. He had an intense horror of shams. The series of questions with which he tested the students' knowledge were what might be described as searching; they gave an interest to the pages of Cruise and Chitty, which the students, on previously reading them, had never suspected to exist."

"The recitations in the first volume of Blackstone's Commentaries had a particular interest for those who did not intend to follow the law as a profession, and many of the theological students were in the habit of coming into the lecture-room at this time."

"You are aware there are some chapters relating to subjects which are obsolete or have no possible application to this country. On that account they are not made the subject of recitation in most law schools; but Judge Hitchcock made us [study] them all, as he said that we should find frequent references to them in our future reading, and would better understand some of the influences which had built up the common law. The chapter on the king's royal title, he thought, should be carefully studied by every one who wished to get a clear idea of English history. It was amazing, indeed, to see what stores of illustrations from history, fiction, poetry and the classics were treasured up in the brain of this man, who appeared to the world as nothing but a dry lawyer."

We add to these communications from his students the passing remark, that a man who has an under-current of enthusiasm for some special science or study, united with conscientious accuracy and clearness, will make the most successful of instructors. As soon as he wins his pupils' confidence and respect for his intellect and acquirements, the enthusiasm will be catching, and the more so, because it is of a simple, undemonstrative kind.

There was another teacher of the law school, an associate of the gentlemen already mentioned, to whose short but honorable career, a few brief words must be devoted. Mr. Townsend entered the school as an instructor when Judge Daggett was seventy-eight years old, and three years before the death of Judge Hitchcock, with the reputation of a well read and learned lawyer. His brief career of five years as a professor of law fulfilled the expectations of those who appointed him. He was a most amiable, simple-hearted man, full of interest in the pursuits to which he had devoted his life.

In 1846 the law department was constituted, by a formal act of the Corporation, one of the co-ordinate branches of Yale College, and Judge Storrs, Mr. Henry White and Mr. Townsend were appointed professors. Mr. White gave instructions, as we have said, for the greater part of two years, but found it incompatible with his professional engagements to continue his labors longer. Judge Storrs' stay in his professorship was equally short, for a reason that has been mentioned already. Mr. Townsend sickened in 1846, and died in January, 1847. With this break in the succession of instructors, I shall bring my notices of its instructors, already too long, perhaps, to a close, for those who succeeded,—especially Governor Dutton and Mr. Osborne,—have too recently passed away, to render sketches of their lives or labors in the law department either necessary or proper.

We may now profitably turn to another subject having more important bearings on the future, and enquire whether a large and flourishing school of law can be hoped for in this city, and whether a connection with a seat of learning, where the whole circle of sciences is taught, is the best place for such an institution. In the past, especially in the most recent past, the discouragements have been very great. A gentleman was at the head of the department who, with all disposition to give his best services to it, was compelled to attend to the duties of his profession, if he would gain a support. Then he was called to the bench and left the school half-manned. The library was, so to speak, in rags. To raise the department seemed to need, not only zeal and ability, but the patience, the self-denying outlays, without immediate returns, to which no man connected with a public institution ought to be called. But even in its present revived condition, can the school be expected to increase to any very great extent. Or must it correspond in size with the demands of the State where it is situated? Here we must take into account the disposition of great numbers of young men to go for their initiation into practical life to some central spot, like New York, which, while it is not well fitted for the preparatory training, offers great advantages to those who wish to get themselves ready for the professions of law and medicine. There is no doubt that the present law school of Columbia College is mainly indebted for its very great success to one learned and most laborious instructor, Professor Theodore W. Dwight, who, it ought to be mentioned for the credit of the school here, was for a year one of its members; but if this distinguished teacher were here, and some man of much less ability and note *there*, the numbers in the two schools would not, for that single reason, be reversed. There would not be over four hundred scholars in law here instead of but a few over fifty. Still there is no question that, with present advantages, the ability and fidelity of the professors ought, ere long, to cause a large accession to the numbers. Another consideration deserves to be brought forward in this place. I refer to the attractions that a university town offers to many young men, to the opportunities for auxiliary studies, the comparative quiet and other charms which a large city given to commerce does not possess. Though we cannot expect that the law school of Yale College, in the best circumstances, would rival, in mere numbers, one equally well situated in the centre of business, we may expect to see its prosperity very greatly enlarged with its means of instruction and its growing reputation.

At this point, when I am about to close my address, I cannot help offering to my hearers a view of a law school which, although only ideal and possible at present, deserves to be looked at with attention. It is, moreover, one which harmonizes well with the whole circle of study pursued at Yale College, and could be realized in such a place as this, where some of the chairs already founded could be made to contribute to the carrying out of the ideal plan more easily than almost anywhere else in this country. I am the more willing to present the idea to my hearers, because I conceive it to be eminently needed as a reality in the United States. Let the school, then, be regarded no longer as simply the place for training men to plead causes, to give advice to clients, to defend criminals; but let it be regarded as the place of instruction in all sound learning relating to the foundations of justice, the history of law, the doctrine of government, to all those branches of knowledge which the most finished statesman and legislator ought to know. First of all I would have the training essential to the lawyer by profession as complete and thorough as possible. Let that be still the main thing, and let the examinations together with appropriate theses be a proof that every graduate has fairly earned his degree. But with this let there be ample opportunity for those who wish the aid of teachers in studying the constitution and political history of our country to pursue their studies in a special course by the side of or after the preparation for the bar. Let the law of nations, the doctrine of finance and taxation, the general doctrine of rights and the State, the relation of politics and morals, be within the reach of such as wish to prepare themselves for public life, and of those young men of wealth, of whom there is an increasing number, who wish to cultivate themselves and take their appropriate place of influence in society. Let there be the amplest opportunity for the study of English institutions, even far back into the middle ages, for that of Roman history and Roman law, for that of comparative legislation, and even for less immediately practical subjects, such as feudal and canon law. Let the plan of the library be expanded, so that it shall furnish the best books on all branches and topics connected with law, legislation and government. Can it be doubted that such an institution, of which I have sketched a faint outline, would be of vast service ; that its influence would reach into the halls of Congress, into the departments of government, that it might become a fountain of light through the whole land. Such an institution on so large a scale could not be self-supporting, and certainly men from every class of society ought to share its advantages, so that the best talents of the poor as well as the rich might be cultivated for the benefit of the country ; no small amount of funds, therefore, would be needed; but I present the idea in the hope that some man who can estimate the value of great and useful plans, and has the means to effect them, may be disposed by what I have said, or others hereafter may say better, to turn the idea into a reality.

And, now may I ask for the patience of my hearers, while I suggest one more thought touching the importance of law studies in connection with Yale College. The sciences of nature have grown immensely in theoretical and practical importance during the last century, and for a long time to come, it is probable, this growth will be unobstructed. Our system here is such that all new discoveries, all new sciences, with their practical applications, must form a part of it, and an increasingly important part. Now, these sciences have to do with natural law only, and their applications affect the development of the material side of civilization. There is danger, therefore, that the balance between body and spirit, the natural and the moral world, will be disturbed, which would be a state of things fraught with danger to the best interests of man. For this reason I desire to see all the sciences flourish side by side; the moral in their full power by the side of the natural in theirs. Only so can the best interests of society and of the individual man be promoted and a harmony be maintained in human culture. That a school of law, teaching a science whose foundation is right and justice, would contribute to this end, cannot be doubted.

ORATION

BY

EDWARDS PIERREPONT.

———o———

It is a singular fact in history, that the Normans, the most daring, brilliant and adventurous race that has ever yet appeared, by force of arms, established themselves in absolute and enduring power both in England and Southern Italy at the same period: and it is even more remarkable that what seemed a mere accident in the Italian Conquest should have produced such an immense influence upon England, in her Government, Laws, Commerce and Ecclesiastical policy, lasting and active even unto this day.

Along the lofty rocks which guard the shores on the Gulph of Salerno, you yet shall see remnants of the embattled walls and ruined towers which tell alike of the grandeur and decay of the once proud city of Amalfi. Here it is claimed that the mariners' compass was invented, and it is conceded that here it was perfected :—Here was founded the order of St. John of Jerusalem, made famous by the Knights of Malta ;—and here the Pandects of Justinian were found.

Six hundred years after the Pandects were published, and centuries after the Temples and palaces of Rome were in ruins and her laws almost forgotten,—Roger, a Norman king, descendant of the famed Count Tancred de Hauteville, took the City of Amalfi.—

In the Pillage of the Town a copy of the renowned Digest of the Roman Laws was discovered ;—a discovery whose effect upon the civilized world was greater in its consequences than that caused by the discovery of the Magnetic Needle.

Upon the discovery of the Pandects the study of the Roman civil law revived all over the Continent of Europe, and forthwith the Normans introduced it into England, and nearly every vestige of the common Law was for centuries almost destroyed.

Chancellor Kent remarks that: "The Pandects are the "greatest repository of sound legal principles applied to the "private rights and business of mankind that has ever "appeared in any age or nation."

Sir Mathew Hale said that: "The true grounds and rea- "sons of law were so well delivered in the Pandects, that a "man could never well understand law as a science without "first resorting to the Roman law for information":—And Lord Holt declares that: "The laws of all nations were raised out of the ruins of the civil law and that the principles of the English law were borrowed from that system." When we consider, that this Code embraced the wisdom of the Sages of the Law and the experience in jurisprudence of all nations for more than twelve hundred years, we need not be surprised to know that the general principles of the Roman Code rule the World to-day.

But it should never be forgotten by the American Lawyer that the Digests were compiled under a *Roman Emperor*, long after her legal sages were dead, after the last embers of civil and political liberty were cold, and when even the greatest Lawyers of Rome were abject at the Emperor's feet. Hence the "*Lex Regia*" expressly inculcates the foul doctrine of absolute power in the Sovereign, and that every right and all the authority of the people were transferred to him.

Perhaps it was well,—perhaps it was necessary, that a great Empire which by law had destroyed every trace of freedom

---

NOTE.—I prefer to adhere to the traditions so long accepted in relation to the revival of the Roman Law, notwithstanding the conclusions of the German Historical School.

should pass under the iron heel of the fierce Barbarian, who silenced even the wise teachings of the Roman Law while he destroyed the false doctrine of despotic sovereignty, but cherished in his rude way the dying spirit of political liberty ;—a spirit born in the half savage North,—cradled through the feudal ages,—scarce heard by the wild Soldiers who rocked it, became as the voice of an Earthquake, shook the Roman Hierarchy to its foundations, liberated the consciences of enslaved men, sent heads of tyrant kings to the bloody block, filled this vast continent with toiling freemen, and gave us the power to stand fearless on this platform and discuss the rights of the Government and the Governed, as I propose to do to-day.

In the City of Amalfi, of which we have spoken, a Council of the Roman Catholic Church decreed that no one who was engaged in the practice of the Law could enter the kingdom of Heaven.—

In the city of New Haven, Noah Webster taught the children of America, by picture before they could read, and by fable at their first lisping, that the farmer was honest and that the lawyer was a rogue :—But in spite of decretals of the Pope through his Council and of the teachings of the Puritan through his spelling-book,—Lawyers have continued to be an honored and a trusted class, the friends of liberty and the foes of oppression.

Not now stopping to debate which kingdom in the other World the Lawyer may enter, we can safely assert that in *this*, he will enter legislative assemblies, the Halls of Congress, the Senate and the Cabinets of the United States,—and hence it behooves us to know what kind of training, moral and intellectual, this great and ancient seat of learning is about to give to the young lawyers of its charge.

The founders of this Republic were wise in their generation, but of the great future not much was revealed.—In their day, no Steamer had ever ploughed the Ocean; no Locomotive had ever drawn a thousand men over the Earth at the rate of sixty miles an hour. Buffalo was then practically further from New York than San Francisco is to-day; then, communication between America and England was had after a long and weary voyage; while now, a letter written in London at the rising sun, is read in New York, *five hours* before his inspiring beams can gild the morn upon the topmost boughs of your Forest-City.

On the West, Asia with her strange civilization and her dateless history looks over into our face;—on the East, we can talk with Christendom as we will.—Mexico, fast dissolving, will soon, very soon, melt into our embrace, and then the Commerce of the World is at our feet! With every climate, with every soil, with every mineral and every tree which the needs of man can wish; with colleges, newspapers, free schools, free suffrage, free speech;—with slavery abolished, energy, enterprise, activity unparalleled, and intellect sharpened beyond any experience of the past, can we fail to become the greatest nation upon which the sun ever shone?

Yes; and fail we shall, unless a change comes over the spirit of this people, and sturdy honesty drives out imbecility and corruption! Moral forces as well as physical advantages must be considered in calculating the future of a nation. No Government can prosperously endure, which in the main, is not administered by the higher intellect and the higher moral sentiments of the people. It requires ability as well as honesty to govern a great nation wisely; and yet, our people make frequent protest against this simple truth;—they never employ a stupid Lawyer, to try an important cause, nor an ignorant Mariner to sail a valuable Ship, but they often elect Legislators to make laws, who know scarce anything, and about Laws and their operation,—nothing.

As the Country advances, new and complex relations make

Government the more difficult, and a higher order of Statesmanship is required.

Our fathers declared that all men were born free and equal, and to-day we have in several States Legislators who were born negro slaves, some of whom have no education whatever.

Our theory is, that the most ignorant must govern if they are the most numerous; and Arkansas, Louisiana and the other reconstructed States are giving our theory a rude test.

But we are told that the trouble in those States comes of the fault of the South:—But when your kitchen is on fire it does not help the matter to exclaim that it is the Servant's fault;—what you want is, to save your house.

When the War was ended a Statesman could see that tho' Slavery was dead its corpse was unburied and chained fast to the foot of the Republic, and would breed disease if not wisely disposed of:—But it was not thought desirable that Statesmen should meddle in this matter, and politicians hastened to re-construct the South, upon theories crude, ill-conconsidered and impossible of success.

The seeds of this folly are producing fruits after their kind, and bitter fruits they are,—more dangerous to liberty than any that ever ripened on our soil.

The States along the Mississippi voted large sums to repair the Levee and restrain the natural overflow of the Great River. The river would have respected a solid *dike*, but he disregarded the *votes*, and washing away his neglected banks, he overwhelmed in one disastrous flood the fields of rice, of corn, of cotton and of sugar,—destroying alike the dwelling of the rich and the cabin of the poor, and bringing ruin to the innocent for the crimes of dishonest rulers who had stolen the taxes and neglected their work.

What the flood left the pestilence will destroy, and the despairing people have cried to the Federal Government to protect them from starving.—How long do you think that Liberty can survive in States where such ignorance and iniquity prevail, tho' every living thing should vote every Sunday in the year?—Only virtue and intelligence can preserve a Republic.

Whether the Government of the States shall become absorbed by the central power will depend entirely upon the virtue and intelligence of the States. A people advanced in civilization and loving property as we do, will have a Government which can protect them in the enjoyment of their property; and if the people of the States show sufficient virtue and ability to maintain good government, then the States will retain their power; but if through ignorance or corruption their Governments fail to protect the Citizen in his rights, State Governments will perish and surrender to the Central Power.—It is all idle to talk of *Cæsarism* in this Country, and the cry awakens no alarm:—CÆSARISM is only possible when the people *seek* it as their last desperate defense against corrupt and despoiling rulers! A usurper of the Supreme Authority against the omnipotent power of public opinion would perish in a night.

We are a practical race, loving real material things—we live in the present and the future; we care nothing for the past; we have but little sentiment and no reverence for that which is merely "grey with age."

I can recall the name of but a single man in all antiquity whose advent here would awaken any great enthusiasm.

If Cicero, the most accomplished Orator and *litterateur* of Rome should come over, with his studied speeches, arranged with exordium, argument, and peroration, made up of sentences polished, formal, and wordy in the extreme, and should undertake to address the American People, they might gather once to see him and enquire whether this was the same man who in the Roman time coined so many new words to express a few old ideas; who was peevishly ambitious, timid and vacillating; whose insatiate vanity made him talk incessantly about himself, and induced him never to spare the feelings of his best friend if by the sacrifice he could gain the reputation of a wit at his friend's expense ; who was generally circumspect, well behaved, and in morals among the better Romans of his time, but too cowardly to be a faithful friend, and who in his old age divorced without just cause Terentia, the Wife of his Youth and the mother of his children, in order to marry his rich young Ward that he might get her money to pay the debts which his vanity and ambition had created :—The first curiosity being satisfied our people would tell him, that " he might have been a very respectable old fogy in a by-gone age, but that we had no use for that sort of Orator in our rapid Country and that he had better go back."

But if JULIUS CÆSAR, who lived at the same time, should arrive in the next steamer we should hail him as a native, or at least as a naturalized American, about 40 years old, who had landed in the very nick of time when the Republic wanted just that kind of man ;—we should send him immediately to Congress, and I dare say, talk of him for President before long notwithstanding the Constitution.

What was there about this Roman which should enable him to step down Nineteen hundred years and find himself at home in our midst?—He had some *flagrant* vices : but meanness and vacillation, treachery and cowardice had no dwelling in his soul.—

In the field,—with perceptions intuitive and quick as the electric flash, followed by celerity in movement never before conceived ;—unselfish in danger, sharing the humblest meal with the humblest soldier, and shunning no hardship and no peril which he asked other men to brave ;—fearless in battle as a man of fate, and generous in the hour of victory as no Conqueror had ever been before him.

In the forum,—eloquent and condensed, going right to the marrow of the thing, using words only to enforce ideas. Always forgiving, and liberal to excess; and when he came to the helm of State showing a grasp of mind, a grandeur of ideas and a greatness of soul which won the hearts of the people and awakened a jealously in mean rivals which only his blood could appease; And when they had murdered "this foremost man of all the world," under the false pretense of liberty for Rome, what did the Roman people gain? Freedom for Rome? Not at all;—The bloody deed but sealed her doom and hastened her destruction!

He comes through the centuries to our times like one born in our Generation because, while gifted with other transcendant faculties he was so richly endowed with the faculty of imagination;—a faculty which inspires the others.—This is the vestal fire which never grows cold, the flame of immortal youth;— it illumines the mind in every age to detect the truth;—to see things in their complex relations just as they are, and to behold in their train the events which are coming in the unerring sequence of causes which are passed.

It is this which makes Homer and Shakespeare poets of all time—which revealed to Plato and Lord Bacon their amazing wisdom:—which made Hannibal, Cromwell and Napoleon the wonder of their age,—which gave to the logic of Chatham, of Burke and of Webster its vital force, and lifted them intellectually above their compeers.

President Porter, in his work on the "Human Intellect," says: "In the communication of scientific truth there can be no question that a large measure of imagination is of essential service. * * * Indeed, we may safely say that in the history of speculation and science not a man can be found who was distinguished for philosophic genius who did not possess an active and a glowing imagination, and whose imagination did not render essential service in the operations of thought."—And further,—" that its workings are more fitly compared to inspiration than those of any other endowment of the soul."

Tyndall, in his "Fragments of Science,"—treating upon the scientific use of the imagination, says:

"We are gifted with the power of imagination, and by this power we can lighten the darkness which surrounds the world of the senses. * * Bounded and conditioned by co-operative Reason, imagination becomes the mightiest instrument of the physical discoverer. Newton's passage from a fallen apple to a fallen moon was at the outset, a leap of the imagination. * * In fact, without this power, our knowledge of nature would be a mere tabulation of co-existences and sequences. We should still believe in the succession of day and night, of summer and winter; but the soul of Force would be dislodged from our Universe; causal relations would disappear, and with them, that science which is now binding the parts of nature to an organic whole."

And Agassiz, in his geological treatise, says:

"Imagination, chastened by correct observation, is our best guide in the study of Nature. We are too apt to associate the exercise of this faculty with works of fiction, while it is in fact the keenest detective of truth."

I think we may assert that without a liberal endowment of this faculty no one in science, letters, art, statesmanship or war has ever gained an imperishable name.

I have said that we are not a sentimental race.—Look at the Washington Monument, on the Banks of the Potomac!—The association to rear it was started 41 years ago, with Chief Justice Marshall at its head and an Ex-President as his second:—According to the plan it was to rise high above the Pyramids.—It rose about 170 feet, and 20 years ago it stopped, and *looks* very determined never to rise any more! Intelligent Foreigners, now here, express amazement that we show no sentiment about the Centennial of our Nation's birth, and in contrast point to the celebration last month, of the raising of the Siege of Orleans, which has been continued through centuries with increasing enthusiasm.—Perhaps sentiment of this kind does not flourish in a Country whose history is so new, and certain it is that we have nothing like the raising of the Siege of Orleans where we can mingle fable and religious awe with the historic event, and enkindle anew at each returning May the sentiment of reverence for the simple shepherd-maid by whose almost miraculous power the siege of the City was raised.—But it is not surprising that the name of Jeanne D'Arc should be held is such reverence in France. No one can read her brief but beautiful life, her marvellous deeds, her wonderful trial, her cruel death, and fail to feel that no holier soul has ever lived on earth or ascended to the Savior through the flames!

Read over again the History of the Roman Republic to the death of Julius Cæsar, and the History of England from the reign of Elizabeth, and you will be startled by the parallels in our own time, and possibly you may fear lest we suffer some of the like punishments.

One and the same unvarying lesson is there taught,—that when the Government is conducted by able and upright men, the nation advances in civilization, riches and power; but when the nation is ruled by the dishonest, and spends lavishly through its debts,—luxury, corruption, injustice, fraud and their inevitable consequences are sure to follow, and like war, demoralize and destroy the innocent with the guilty.

Elaborate investigations have been made to find out the causes of longevity in men, but statistics have revealed only the single uniform fact, of early rising and early retiring.

When Statesmen shall have investigated the causes of longevity in States, I imagine they will find that moral causes alone and very simple ones, will give the solution.

China, whose history through the elaborate works of the Commission established by the French Government in 1851, we are just beginning to read, stands forth as the most illustrious example. As the increasing fleet of steamers on our Pacific Coast are bringing us every day in closer relations with that vast Empire, and as her laborers are pouring over to our Shores, it becomes the American Statesman to give heed to the great fact, and consider what effect this is to have upon the future of our country.

Her civilization, her polity, her religion differ widely from ours, and when at the Cannon's mouth we shall have forced commercial relations, steam-machinery, electricity, Hoe's printing press, and paper money upon the Chinese, we had better not forget that in exchange they will force upon us, an interminable throng of Emigrants, who will bring their peculiar morals, habits and religion, and their peculiar vices ; and that soon they will acquire the right to vote. Remember that China can send fifty million of voters to our shores and have more left than she knows what to do with. *This voting question* is a difficult one which the American people will reconsider some day, and perhaps we may then hear the honest inquiry, who will make the best rulers, as well as who can get the most votes ?

We just begin to hear a little murmur on the breeze coming up from the South,—but few note effects from silent causes which are stealing along like the unobserved rising of the tide.

When Governor Seward lately visited China he was surprised to find that the greatest work of human hands begun 240 years before Christ, was so well constructed that "but very slight repairs would restore it to its original state." A solid fortification some fourteen hundred miles long, built over mountains, rivers and ravines ;—A work which the Pyramids will not outlast, and which was all done in less time than it takes to build a Court house in New York, and—possibly at less expense. The great river, Yang-tse-Kiang runs three thousand miles through Central China and empties into the Pacific directly opposite San Diego in California;—it greatly surpasses in depth, breadth and volume of water our great Mississippi River, while the Imperial Canal, (twice as long as the Erie Canal) with its branches, makes a system of *artificial* navigation of Four thousand miles.

It is her relation to this Country which warns the American Statesman that he cannot neglect the present condition and past history of China. Her history is unique as her people. She was a populous kingdom three thousand years before the Christian Era. She saw the beginning and the end of the Assyrian, the Persian and of every Ancient Empire. She was powerful when the Pyramids were built, when Joseph was a slave, before Sesostris was King or Osiris was worshipped;— She was a mighty Empire when the first stone of the Temple of Solomon was laid and still greater when the Mosque of Omar was built upon its ruins. She was rich immensely, when Rome was conquering the World, yet no Roman Legion ever trod upon her soil; and to-day she is richer and more populous than at any period of her existence, and at her last census, as we learn through the French Government, she numbered over 530 Million of Souls. (530,595,887.)

There must be some great *moral* reason for this unparalleled longevity. The mandate, " Honor thy father and thy mother that thy days may be long," has been religiously obeyed in China, while her social and political organizations, however defective, have been governed by her wisest and best.

With the solution of the many grave questions in the near future, the educated Lawyer will have much to do, and the enquiry arises whether a great University is the best place in which to educate a Lawyer? A great University is the best place in which to educate anybody who is to take part in affairs; and this should be kindly told to the noble men who are giving their substance to endow small Colleges all over the country.

The influence of congregated numbers is not sufficiently considered, either in the intellectual, moral or physical development of men. The boy who comes in daily contact with crowds of other boys will be widely different in robust vigor from the one who is educated alone by a tutor at home.

That subtle influence, that magnetic force equally necessary for the development of a healthy body and a healthy mind, is lost in seclusion, and can only come of the congregation of numbers. Not only contact of mind with mind, but contact with many minds, is absolutely essential to a perfect growth.

The American artist finds his genius flag in his solitary home, and he goes to Florence or to Rome, where, in the spirit of the place, among an artistic crowd, he has new inspirations and capabilities which alone he could never attain.

Place even an educated man upon a fertile plain, with no companions but laborers, whose daily bread depends upon their daily toil, and though he may have the ASTOR LIBRARY in his house, at the end of a few years he will have rusted out. Association tends to culture and advancement; dispersion and isolation tend to barbarism;—and this is true the world over.

Equality is the central idea with our people, and I dare say that in this large audience there are many benevolent persons who would make all equally rich; but it would come to about the same to make all equally poor. The rich man would not do the menial work of another rich man, and the rich woman would not wash and cook for the rich man's wife;—the poor man will not brush the shoes of another poor man who can give him no pay, and all the social wheels would be ablock.—

Equality before the laws we can have; equality of condition is impossible.

A striking feature in our late development is an intense individualism, not favorable to the best interests of the State. The reason is obvious;—for civil services, however great, the State confers no permanent honors or lasting rewards, and in ordinary times, the working of our system does not admit those, who would serve for honor and patriotism, to serve at all.

We drift away from the economy of former days. During the early years of Washington's administration the entire ordinary expenses of the Federal Government were but $1,877,000 a year; while the taxes of the single city of New York this year are $39,218,945.79 ; and the cost of the Federal Government for the fiscal year, this month ending, as estimated by the secretary of the treasury. is $319,198,736.82.

A little arithmetic will show that our expenses have increased in far greater ratio than our population and resources ; —an ugly fact,—so ugly that no one seems willing to look it in the face.

The city of New York will best illustrate how easily great natural advantages may be destroyed by moral causes.

Better placed for commerce than any other great city on the globe, New York is losing her trade. A corrupt and imbecile government, neglecting the piers, docks, storehouses, elevators and other facilities for business, has through fraudulent practices so increased the taxes and other exactions upon the merchant, and thus made his expenses so enormous that other places can undersell him, and trade, never sentimental or æsthetic, goes where it can buy cheapest.

Money has a closer relation to morals than is generally admitted. In all history, whether of individuals or communities, I find that laxity in money matters is followed by looseness in morals ; and among other evidences I note a favorite theory, quite prevalent just now, that there ought to be increased facilities in obtaining divorces, on the ground that facility of divorce will diminish the temptations to vice,—That is,—*legalize Robbery to prevent Burglary ?*

However great our boasted independence may be, we are nevertheless, in some respects, facile imitators of older nations.

We are hardly conscious of the increasing influence of England upon this country;—an influence somewhat reciprocal. She has a glorious history, and you cannot breathe her air and see the evidences of her perfect order, her progress and her collossal power without a thrill of reverence for the old fountain of our blood :—But to reach her present greatness England struggled for several centuries through ignorance, tyranny, wars and corruption of which we have no parallel, and out of which we draw much consolation for our future.

The reign of Queen Elizabeth is regarded as one of the most glorious in English history.—It was the time of Walsingham and Burleigh ; of Shakespear, Bacon and Raleigh.

About the court of Elizabeth was a young courtier named Christopher Hatton; he had never been admitted to the Bar, and his only qualification for the highest Judicial Office in the Realm was comeliness of person, skill in dancing and foppery in dress; and yet, to the amazement and chagrin of all the great Lawyers of the time, this handsome dandy was made Lord High Chancellor of England, and held the Office until he died.

Under all our Presidents the highest judicial places have been given to able men, and when the great office of Chief Justice fell vacant by the death of Chief Justice Chase, the President selected no personal favorite, but bestowed the high honor upon an eminent lawyer of tried integrity, a native of your State, a son of old Yale, and I may add with pardonable pride,—a member of the class of '37.

When James, the successor of Elizabeth, tried to extend his Royal prerogative against the liberties of England, he found Coke and other great Lawyers stoutly to resist. When Wentworth, by far the most able, the most eloquent, the most resolute Commoner who had ever appeared in England, entered Parliament, he took the side of the people against the encroachments of Charles; but after seven years he became an apostate, and turned all his vast abilities, his experience, sagacity, determined purpose and his inflexible will, to the establishment of that thorough system of kingly power which should forever crush the liberties of the people; But he found a legal lion in his way, and when ruling Ireland with iron hand and adamantine heart, striving with all his might to subject every private suit in the Courts of Justice to the Royal prerogative, he writes to Laud: "I know very well that the Common Lawyers will be passionately against it, who are wont to put such a prejudice upon all other professions, as if none were to be trusted, or capable to administer justice but themselves; yet how well this suits with *Monarchy*, when they monopolize all to be governed by their year books, you in England have a costly example."

At times, England has had her prostrate judges and a slavish Bar, but in the main, her Lawyers have fought valiantly for liberty, and to-day we can point to every Christian Government on earth and be certain that its liberties can be measured by the influence of its Lawyers.

As the price of his apostacy Wentworth was made the Earl of Stafford, but under the lead of Pym and the resolute Lawyers of the time, the Earl was arraigned for attempting to subvert the Laws and the liberties of England. Even his bold spirit grew alarmed at the tone of the Commons, and he sought the King.—

Charles gave him the most solemn assurances that "not a hair of his head should be hurt," and a few days after gave his royal assent to the Bill of Attainder which brought this ablest minister, whom the king had used to make himself absolute, to a bloody and an ignominious death! Few years passed by,—uneasy years for this perfidious king;—and Charles walked up the scaffold to die, as he had let his faithful Stafford die;—and when the beheading axe was seen, we may well believe that the shade of the Earl appeared to the faithless king, who mournfully exclaimed,

> ——— " When we shall meet at compt,
> This look of thine will hurl my soul from heaven.
> And fiends will snatch at it."

Now calmly standing near the vacant throne we see by far the greatest sovereign that England has ever had.

Literary sycophants have been accustomed to revile the character of Cromwell and to represent him as a low born vulgar hypocrite or bigot. He had not the parlor graces of Lord Chancellor Hatton, but he would have walked alone, thro' an army of Hattons as an ox walks through a field of grasshoppers.

Born of an ancient family, descended from some of the high nobility, he was related to Thomas Cromwell the Earl of Essex and sometime minister to Henry VIII. His grandfather was Sir Henry Cromwell the Lord of Hinchinbrook, known as the "Golden Knight," on account of his great riches; and his mother was of the best of English blood, and her relationship to James I induced that Monarch on his way to take possession of the English Crown to become a guest at the Cromwell Mansion, where Oliver, then but four years old, saw the King at the family table;—James little dreaming that the head of his own son would be cut off by this kindred boy, who should reign in his stead.

He was educated at the University of Cambridge, and when but 18 years old he was called home by the death of his father to be the sole protector of his mother and sisters.

While reading law in London at the age of twenty, he fell in love with Elizabeth, the beautiful and accomplished daughter of Sir James Bourchier, a wealthy knight.

At the age of 21 he married, and under the same roof with his mother took his young bride, who afterwards coming to her exalted station showed a purity and nobleness of character more beautiful than her personal loveliness. She was the first and *only* love of Cromwell, and in the height of his greatness and near the end of his reign, when necessity had separated them for a short time, she, like a true and loving woman, chided him for not writing oftener ; and to her chidings he replied :—" My beloved Wife,—You scold me in your letters because by my silence I appear to forget you ; truly it is I who ought to complain, for I love you *too much :*—Thou art dearer to me than *all the world.*"

He was in Parliament at the age of 29 and again at the age of 40, and when the Civil War broke out he raised two companies of soldiers at his own expense and devoted his entire estate to the public service :—

And, when he came to power, the haughtiest kings and nobles of Europe sought political and matrimonial alliance. At his death the court of France went into mourning, tho' he had required Louis XIV to banish the sons of Charles, whose widow was Henrietta of France, the daughter of Henry the Great :—He was buried in Westminister Abbey as a legal monarch beside the annointed kings.

There was a time when all seemed lost of the liberties of England, and Cromwell thought of leaving his country. But in those trying times, when all good men began to despair,— Cromwell and the just men who sympathized with him " sought the Lord in prayer ;" and it was " His guidance," as they believed, to gird on their swords for war and rescue England from her slavery :—and from that hour they never faltered and they never feared. Prince Rupert, the nephew of Charles, was accustomed with his gay troopers to carry all before him by his dashing onsets. At the battle of Marston Moor he led 20,000 eager Royalists, and for the first time, he dashed against the " Ironsides " of Cromwell. It was like the dash of sea-foam against a granite mountain ! After the battle, Cromwell wrote to his wife:—" God made them as stubble to our swords."

When in the plenitude of his power, young Lely, afterwards the Court painter of the frail beauties of the Second Charles, wanted to paint him.—"Paint me as I am" said Cromwell; "If you leave out the scars and wrinkles I will not pay you a shilling." Go to the Pitti Palace,—the picture with the scars and the wrinkles you shall see, but a kinglier head reposed on kinglier shoulders you shall never see!

Voltaire, in his history of Louis XIV, says :

" He increased his power by knowing when it was proper to restrain it: he made no attempt on those privileges of which the people were jealous : Soldiers were never quartered in the city of London : he imposed no taxes that might occasion murmurs : he did not offend the eyes of the public by appearing with too great pomp and grandeur : he did not indulge himself in any pleasures : he accumulated no treasures : and he took care to have justice administered with that strict impartiality, which makes no distinction between the high and the low, the rich and the poor * * Commerce had never been so flourishing or so free before : and England had never been so rich. Her victorious fleets made her name respected throughout the world."

But England had grown tired of being virtuous and honest, and thought that she could prosper without these inconvenient restraints, and with intoxicated joy she hailed home that "merry monarch" the second Charles ;—and a merry time they had ;— The dead body of the Great Ruler who had brought such riches and power to England, was dragged from its coffin in Westminster Abbey, hanged and mutilated at Tyburn and thrown into a ditch.

The Court was crowded with men, rival scoffers at every sacred thing ; and with women rivals in the open shamelessness of their vices. Wanton luxury and extravagance appeared in every form; But retribution came swifter and more terrible than the people had anticipated.—From the demoralized condition of the kingdom, commerce fell off, trade languished,— the spirit of the nation was gone :—England, so powerful under Cromwell, became the scorn of the Nations; her King the Vassal of France, and her Navy but lately the terror of the world became too feeble to protect her coast.—The Dutch sailed up the Thames, and English Merchants saw the flames of their burning ships from London Bridge. The Goldsmiths and Bankers of London were accustomed to borrow money of their dealers at a low rate of interest and lend it to the Government at a higher rate, to be repaid out of the taxes of the year.—Millions of coin had thus been deposited by the Bankers in the Royal Exchequer : the King wanted money for his dissolute Court, and he did not like to face the Commons. —Clifford suggested that an easy way to raise the means would be to close the Treasury and rob the Bankers and their clients of these millions of Coin :—This suited Charles exactly, and he made Clifford a Peer, gave him part of the stolen money and squandered the rest. The effect of this perfidious robbery can well be imagined :—Consternation followed; thousands of Widows and Orphans, poor Clergymen and men of humble means, together with the Goldsmiths and Bankers were brought to poverty in a day, and every honest cheek in England was blanched or blushed with shame, and every honest soul prayed for an hour of stern old Cromwell's rule.

But England remained in vassalage suffering the punishment of her "*merry making*" for many long years, nor did she even *begin* to recover the prosperity or the rank which Cromwell had given her until after the peace of Ryswick, and not even until the early years of the 18th century.

Economy is a sterling virtue in the administration of the

State, and without it neither justice or honesty is possible in Government.

Extravagance is one of the most corrupting vices and leads by easy grades to numberless crimes. It is the curse of our day ; it came of the issue of irredeemable paper money to carry on the war ; and when the war was ended luxury had produced an intoxication too dreamy to be voluntarily abandoned.

Our duty was plain ; and to any one worthy to be called a Statesman our interest was as plain as our duty.—We should have turned all our energies to keep our faith, to redeem our promises, to stop our luxuries and end the sham which has corrupted the nation.

Like cowards we have shut our eyes to the truth and reveled in delusions until we can deceive ourselves no longer. The reconstructed States, eager to prosper with the rest, issued Bonds which they never hoped to pay, ruined their credit and their thrift and tumbled into anarchy,—while we of the North have piled up our debts until our taxes are a burden too grievous to be born.—We wake from the deceiving dream to learn that the American people are subject to the same laws of Nature and of Finance as other mortals ; that a promise to pay a dollar is not a dollar ;—any more than a promise to deliver a horse, for a load of wheat received, is a horse ; that our industries are paralyzed because confidence has ceased, and that the issue of a thousand millions of new greenbacks would not restore the lost confidence for an hour, or revive trade in the least.

It will dawn upon the popular mind before long, that during the war the Government printed "*legal tender*" and paid it out for everything which the country produced, and thus gave a temporary prosperity, but that now the Government do not pay out a dollar for anything until it has first collected the money from the people,—when the changed condition is understood it will be seen that a new issue would be a delusion and a fraud. The farce of attempting to create property by legislative enactment was long since played out by older nations, and always with the same disastrous results.

It is now thirteen years since specie has been our currency: —For more than twenty years England, through the influence of the Napoleon wars was in the same condition, and she listened to the same shallow arguments which we now hear; but her prosperity never returned until under the manly lead of Sir Robert Peel, she faced the situation, accepted reality and rejected sham : from that hour her onward progress begun.

We have been as extravagant as England after the restoration and we are in debt for the revelry :—But some well-to-do Citizen looks up with innocent surprise and says, "I am not in debt."—But you *are*, my deluded friend, and your house and your store and all that you have is heavily mortgaged, and so are the wages of the humblest laborer, and none can escape.

That our prosperity will revive again I make no question; it is the tribulation preceding the revival which we ought to avoid. A country with a people so active and resources so boundless will get along; but wise statesmanship might save us many setbacks and heavy troubles into which the lack of statesmanship may plunge us.

A Government which gets money from its Citizens on a promise which it never tries to keep does not differ in the least from the King who took his subjects' money without the pretense that he ever meant to pay. When a Government cheats its Citizens, its Citizens will cheat each other. The hardest strain which free government has ever had is close at hand: the next Presidental election is the turning point; it begins a new century in our history—the public mind will be awake, and that will be an eventful day. It will settle the question whether our Government will keep its faith, and turn its determined face towards justice, economy and truth, and thus begin with the new century a new career of prosperity and grandeur and riches such as the world has not seen, or whether it will imitate England in her corruptest times and take the curse which afflicted her so long.

When the conflict comes may every lawyer and every man whom this great college educates stand for the public faith, for the honor and the glory of his country, with his face to the enemy and his trust in Heaven.

SPEECH

OF THE

HON. EDWARDS PIERREPONT,

DELIVERED BEFORE

The Republican Mass Meeting, in the Hall of Cooper Institute,

NEW YORK,

October 31st, 1878.

NEW YORK:
PUBLISHED BY THE STATE CENTRAL COMMITTEE.
1878.

Fellow Citizens :

We have come to talk about money. The subject is not new, but the substance is always attractive.

If, I could show each one of you how to make a million of dollars within two years, I suspect that no one would grow impatient or drowsy; or if with Aladdin's Lamp I could reveal to you a vault in the earth piled with heaps of gold, and should warn you that in five minutes the door would be shut forever, but that during those minutes you might all enter and carry away as much treasure as you could, the strife would be immense, and I fear that the magic door would close over many, who in their eagerness, had forgot the limit of time, and must starve to death with plenty of gold in their hands.

I have not the lamp of Aladdin, nor can I tell you how to make a great fortune in a little time; but, I may, perhaps, say something which shall tend to lighten the laborer of his toil, through a better understanding of the principles upon which prosperity rests.

Quite early in the history of civilization, it was found that men were endowed with very different faculties. Some had skill in the working of metals; some in rude tools and machinery; some could make a boat, and others could sail it; and some understood the tillage of the soil.

Finally, it became apparent that if each would use the peculiar talent which he possessed, the products of the same hours of labor would be largely increased and the community proportionately enriched. The stone-cutter could not cut a coat, nor could the farmer made a scythe; but each could supply his wants by exchanging the results of his especial work, and thus by dividing labor according to the faculties and facilities of different individuals the aggregate product would be multiplied many fold. But the difficulties in making exchanges were great. The butcher had a slaughtered ox which he wanted to sell, and fifty people wanted to buy a small portion of the beef. The wheelwright had a cart which the butcher wished to buy, but the owner of the cart wanted no beef, and least of all enough to pay for the cart. Such, and other inconveniencies in making exchanges led to the invention of MONEY. But money would not answer the purpose of exchanging products of value, unless the money had also value; could be easily divided without loss; would not perish with the use and could be carried from place to place.

The beef could be divided; but it would soon decay, and was not convenient to carry in the pocket. Many other things could be divided and not perish, but the division would destroy the use, and the bulk or weight would prevent them from being carried about.

In the ruder ages and in the newer colonies,—beads, shells, bright plumage and skins were used as money; and to-day, sheep are the currency among the great tribes of Central Asia; and a human life is valued at more than a hundred head of sheep. By the Statutes of New York its extreme limit of value is five thousand dollars.

Beads, made of polished shells, with much skill and labor by the Indians, were a legal tender in the colony of Massachusetts, and the red men received them as money in exchange for furs; but the white man soon showed his superiority in finance by inflating the currency with counterfeit beads made of colored wood, and caused a collapse. If the *first settlers* of Massachusetts had been as advanced in political science as one of her descendants, they might have turned the counterfeit beads into " fiat money " and got along for awhile.

A Dutchman who had imigrated to Manhattan Island about this time, hearing of the wooden beads, and learning that the English colonists of Massachusetts were very intelligent, refused to let his son go to school at all lest he should become a counterfeiter.

Homer speaks of oxen as the greenbacks of his time, and gives the number of oxen which the armor of Diomede and the more splendid trappings of Glaucus cost.

But quite early, gold and silver were regarded as precious metals; and long before kings or emperors were ever invented, " Abraham, weighed to Ephron for the cave of Machpelah four " hundred shekels of silver current money with the merchant."

The love of gold seems implanted in the nature of man, and it will not be eradicated by Legislative enactment. The civilized man who does not love gold, is extremely rare; I have not seen one.

A substance of universal desire has, of course, great commercial value, and when you add uniformity everywhere, divisibility without loss, incorruptibility, density, portability, and quantity sufficient, you have the best substance out of which to make money wherewith to facilitate the exchange of products, save labor and waste, and advance the civilization of man, which has ever been discovered.

The desire for gold and its value as money, does not depend alone upon its scarcity.

Its endless uses and its alluring beauty, make it more desired than other metals of greater costliness. There are twenty known metals, a pound of which will buy more silver dollars than a pound of gold will buy, but these metals have no beauty and their uses are few.

I hold in my hand some paper money, issued by a once powerful government. I know it to be genuine; while General Dix and I were trying the Prisoners of State, we took it from a Rebel Spy.

I will read the stamped inscription:

```
OOOOOOOOOOOOOOOOOO OOOOOOOOOOOOOOOO
O                                                      O
O      Six months after the ratification of a Treaty of O
O   Peace between the Confederate States and the United O
O   States                                              O
O  oooooooooo      THE CONFEDERATE STATES               O
O  o Receivable o                              50       O
O  o    in     o        OF AMERICA    A                 O
O  o Payment   o
O  o of all dues o                 No. ——— oooooooooo   O
O  o  except   o
O  oExport Dues o                            OFundable inO  O
O  oooooooooo    Will pay Fifty Dollars to bearer. oConfederate o  O
O                                                oState Stock  O
O                                              o bearing 8 o  O
O                       RICHMOND VA.              per cent.
O                                              o interest, o  O
O                                                oooooooooo O
O                                                      L     O
OOOOOOOOOOOOOOOOOOOO OOOOOOOOOOOOOOOO
```

You cannot buy an apple with it.

It is just as worthless as the paper without the stamp.

I hold another piece of stamped paper which reads thus:

"THE UNITED STATES. $50.
Will pay to bearer
FIFTY DOLLARS.
Washington, D. C.

This note is a legal tender for fifty dollars."

With this you can buy anything you need. Why? Is it on account of the paper? Not at all. As paper it is scarce better than the Confederate rag. But the faith in the stamped promise to redeem the paper in coin gives the purchasing power.

I present you here a piece of fine gold, upon which there is no stamp whatever. Its weight is equal to $552\frac{1}{2}$ dollars of coined gold.

Any banker in Wall street will gladly give me six hundred and sixty coined silver dollars for it. Its value then does not depend upon the stamp, while the value of the paper depends entirely upon the faith reposed in the promise of the stamp to redeem the paper.

If an insane delusion shall seize this people, and they shall decree that the Government must issue ten thousand millions of paper money, and distrust, confusion and anarchy follow, the stamped paper will not buy bread to feed a starving child, while this unstamped gold will be eagerly received in exchange for any of the needs of man.

It has a value then, quite outside of any stamp of the Government, or of any Legislative enactment.

FELLOWS CITIZENS :—You may be deluded by ignorant or misguided men about the Legislative powers of the Nation; you may be impiously told that Congress by its fiat can make money, as the Omnipotent God, by his fiat, made the light ; but all such attempts will perish in confusion.

The Congress can no more make fiat money, than they can make fiat potatoes.

But the greenback orators point you to the time when paper money was issued by the Government; when laborers were employed at high wages and when all seemed prosperous; and they tell you, that the same prosperity would return if the Government would again issue new Greenbacks. This is a plausible suggestion; it is rather taking ; and if it cannot be fully met and clearly refuted, then the inflationists have the argument.

FACTS, dependent upon truthful figures will be useful in this discussion ; and they will prove that when confidence vanished, the crash came, and labor ceased to be in demand, a greater amount of paper currency was afloat—far greater than in the seeming prosperous days of 1869.

Surely then, it was not the lack of paper currency which caused the collapse and deprived the laborer of his hire.

But let us go back to what are called the prosperous days of the war, and see how it was.

The Government, then less than a hundred years old, sent more than a million of able-bodied men to the field. These were all diverted from productive industry and actively engaged in waste. The rebel States had vast armies also employed in destruction. It was not the property of a foreign foe that these armies were eating up and destroying, but the property of our own people. The Government needed food and clothes, arms and ammunition, horses and harness, ships and wagons, and blankets and saddles, and all the thousand nameless things needed in the movement of great armies; labor was in demand, and made scarcer by calling so many soldiers to the field. To pay for all these things the Government issued Greenbacks, made them a legal tender, and promised to redeem them in coin. This was simply a forced loan, tolerated by the exigences and perils of the War, AND IT WAS RIGHT.

After four years, war was conquered by the valor of our troops, and the soldier who had not gone down to death to save his country, returned to peaceful life and increased the supply, while the demand for labor was diminished.

Now commenced the change; scarce perceptible at first, but soon too palpable to be unheeded. The Government, no longer a buyer, cancelled vast contracts for arms and other supplies, and ceased to pay out any money except that which it had first collected from the people in some kind of tax.

Three thousand million of national debt had been created, much of it bearing a high rate of interest, and enormous State and County debts had been created in addition. Sagacious men saw that unless the public could be brought to face the real situation a crash must come.

It grew evident that the seeming prosperity was purely delusive, the Government had been living upon its debts, not upon its income. As the young heir to a great estate may, through his credit, spend ten times his income for years, and fancy that all is prosperous; so we, when the nation was lavishly spending its borrowed money called this prosperity, and shut our ears to the warnings of those who said that the day of reckoning must come.

Statesmen saw that we must gradually contract the paper currency, in order to return to a healthy condition; and between the close of the war and 1868, laws were passed to that end; but so many preferred false appearances to honest truth, that contraction was stopped by law, and the paper currency was expanded until in 1873, it reached the enormus sum of 750 million of dollars; thus the currency in 1873, was fifty-six millions more than in 1869.

But did this vast volume of currency, afloat in 1873, bring prosperity? You all know that then came the collapse, from which we are suffering at this hour. But what did we do to lift the country from its prostration, when its paper currency was so immense? Will it be believed fifty years hence, that we added over thirty one million to the inflated volume? We did; and thereby added largely to our distress. The severity of the distress brought the dawn of reason to a deluded people, and we began to see that we must return to the currency, which the experience of ages has proved to be the only one under which a commercial nation can long prosper.

The Resumption Act has not hastened that return one hour; it would have come before this from a higher law, and without the Act, if the President's veto of the Silver Bill had not been trampled under.

I labor so long upon this question of an inflated, irredeemable currency, because I regard it as the turning point in the great issue. If our people become satisfied that more Greenbacks will not bring even the apparent prosperity which we had before, but increased disaster instead, then the Greenback delusion will vanish as did the dream of our paper riches.

But suppose the Congress should pass a law directing the Secretary of the Treasury to print two thousand millions of greenbacks, and the President should sign the bill;—tell me, how would that help you;—how would you get the greenbacks? The Secretary would not present them to you;—have you anything to sell which the Government wants to buy; does the Government owe you anything? If no, then you cannot get the Greenbacks from the Secretary, and if you have anything to sell you can get a full price for it now without any new issue. But would you part with houses, or lands, or goods for part of these two thousand millions of new Greenbacks? *Not if you reflected over night.* But no such law can ever go into operation.

Let us see how the new project is to be worked. First, the bill must pass Congress, and then the President, who shows great judgment, patriotism and firmness upon this question will veto it; and it cannot pass over the veto. There is many an honest, intelligent patriot in the Democratic party who will never let such wrong be done to his country, even if the Republicans are not strong enough to arrest it. But even if such a law passed the veto, then the Supreme Court would stand as a granite mountain to resist the enormity.

You will ask then what is the harm of the agitation? The harm is great. It breeds distrust; it leaves men of business uncertain about the future; it prevents any new enterprise; paralyzes industries, and destroys much of the demand for labor.

Capital is always timid, and when it distrusts the honesty or intelligence of the Government, it conceals its means and remains inactive. Capital and labor must always prosper or suffer together. Capital which is inactive brings no income, and when the action of the Government is such that capital feels insecure, it will not embark in any industry.

In a country like ours every class of the community is dependent for his income upon some other class. The owner of houses cannot get rent unless the tenant can get money; the merchant cannot get pay for his goods unless his customer can get something with which to pay. The owner of money, even, can get only a very low rate of interest when distrust prevents enterprise, and he must then, as a rule, spend upon his capital to live.

If favored by Divine Providence in abundant crops and other products, as we have been, we shall very early start upon a career of prosperity surpassing anything which the world has ever seen, unless it is destroyed by the unwise action of the Government.

If the specie basis is our settled policy, and a real, honest resumption takes place in January, we shall have restored confidence, and in due time a healthy expansion from liberated coin and convertible paper, leaving the gold of the commercial world to flow in as it may be needed.

This will, before long, bring similar, if not greater, stimulus than that which occurred in England on her return to specie payments after a suspension of more than twenty years.

I speak of an honest resumption, such as the Act contemplated.

But I understand that some of our advanced statesmen propose to have paper money which does not purport to be redeemable in anything. "Fiat money;" that is money made out of nothing, and to be redeemed in nothing. It is a good name, "Fiat money;" we can understand that. Pieces of paper are to be stamped $5, $10, $20 and $100; and by the fiat of Congress they are to be as many dollars as the stamp indicates.

The Almighty alone can make something out of nothing; the Congress can make nothing out of nothing, and nothing will buy nothing.

The stamp of a horse upon a piece of paper is not a horse, and no government can make it one; and the farmer who found himself compelled by the law to take the pictured animal instead of the live one which he had paid for in labor or in wheat, would rightly conclude that his government was a fraud.

You will ask if I would banish paper money from use? By no means; any more than I would banish bank checks. Paper money is convenient, and saves much labor and risk. I would allow anybody to bank and pay out any amount of paper money, the convertibility of which he had secured under the law. No government can determine in advance the limit of needed currrency, that can only be settled by the laws of trade. You cannot have too much paper money which is convertible into the standard coin of the commercial world. The moment it becomes redundant the surplusage will return for redemption. That will be regulated by a law unerring as the motion of the spheres. We have had for many years a striking illustration of this principle. The law authorized the issue of $50,000,000 of fractional currency, convertible into legal tender on demand. It was found that only about $40,000,000 of this paper could be kept in circulation, it being all that the country needed. To the paper issues of the Bank of England there is no legal restriction whatever, except that which springs from certain conditions. It may issue £15,000.000 of paper money without having any coin behind it; and upon coin or uncoined gold in any form of bullion it may issue notes without limit; not only that, but it is compelled by law to buy any amount of uncoined gold of 22 carats fine which may be presented, and to pay for it in paper at the rate of £3, 17s. 9d per Troy ounce, and the seller of the bullion who has received the notes can forthwith convert the paper into sovereigns without leaving the Bank. If the holder of the bullion chooses to wait to have it coined, the Mint will do it without charge and give him at the rate of £3, 17s. 10½d. per ounce, but as a penny-hapenny would only be saved upon some $19 the interest and inconvenience of delay is of course much greater than the small difference, and Bank notes are invariably received. For the privilege of issuing this £15,000,000 of paper without gold behind it, the Bank pay the Government about £200,000 per annum; but the redemption in coin of this fifteen million of paper issue is secured in this way —eleven millions of it is actually owed to the Bank by the Government, and the other four millions is secured by investment in Exchequer Bills, bearing three per cent. interest or other safe interest-bearing securities, saleable at all times. In case of a run upon the Bank, long before the gold lying behind its notes could be exhausted, the four million of the securities above-named could be converted into cash and the eleven million which the Government owe the Bank could be converted into three per cent. Government Stock by the Chancellor of the Exchequer, with which the Bank could buy up its outstanding notes or redeem them with the proceeds of the National stock.

Thus the £15,000,000 of paper issued by the Bank with no gold behind it is invested in safe securities bearing 3 per cent. interest which the Bank gets and these are a security for the redemption of the paper, much as our Government Bonds are a security for the currency issued to the National Banks. Hence there is absolutely no limit imposed by parliamentary law, to the amount of coin and Bank of England notes which may be put in circulation, except as before mentioned—but it is all regulated by the higher law of trade.

On the first of next January, the Secretary of the Treasury will have abundance of gold with which to resume and maintain specie payments, unless prevented by the Silver Bill. Very little gold would have been needed for actual use, and no more would have been drawn. Now, the danger is imminent, that the alarm caused by making a depreciated Silver dollar a legal tender, will make a run upon the Treasury and clear it of gold.

There is no question, that the Secretary desires faithfully to execute the law as expressed in the Resumption Act and in the Silver Bill, and to have gold and silver dollars circulate on a par, but of course, he sees that no such equal circulation is possible.

Avowed enemies of resumption with consummate tact, helped the Silver Bill through, forseeing, as they did, what a powerful hindrance it would be to any real resumption.

The principles of that Bill will slowly mature their fruits. For a while, the mischievous influences may not be very apparent, but as the silver coin accumulates, and long before it reaches two hundred million of dollars, as it may do in less than four years, disturbances must arise in our currency which will be serious.

The present value of pure silver to pure gold is about as 1 to 18. Silver has fallen largely since the beginning of the year, and promises a further decline. The present silver dollar is 15 to 18 cents less in value than the gold dollar, and the difference may increase. Gold being the standard currency of all the great commercial nations with whom we most deal, we cannot ignore the general standard of commerce.

It may have escaped your notice that great changes have occurred in the monetary standard of Europe.

It is now some sixty years since England commenced to coin the gold sovereign and abandoned the coinage of silver except for subsidiary use. By the Act of 1816, passed in the reign of George III., gold was made the sole legal-tender for sums above 40 shillings. The States comprising the Great German Empire demonetized silver in 1873.

The Latin Union, composed of the two great States of France and Italy, adding the three smaller States of Belgium, Switzerland and Greece, by treaty of January 1874, limited their silver coinage in effect to subsidiary coins.

In Holland, silver coinage for general circulation ceased in 1875, and by law, it ceased in Spain, except on Government account, in 1876.

In Denmark, Sweden and Norway silver ceased to be the standard in 1873, and gold is the standard in Portugal, Turkey, Brazil and the Argentine Republic.

Thus silver, ceasing to be coined as a monetary standard in all the great commercial nations of Europe, and the annual product being large, we can see why it has diminished in value, and why it will decline still more.

The Silver Conference invited by the United States for the purpose of trying to establish some fixed ratio value between gold and silver, met in Paris last August, but the object was soon found to be utterly impracticable.

If you get a dollar of gold and find that you can sell it to a broker for a dollar and twenty cents in silver, knowing that under our law you can discharge any debt by silver, you will of course sell the gold, and everybody will do the same, and gold will disappear from circulation.

From the beginning of our coinage in 1793 up to 1878, a period of 85 years, we had coined of legal tender silver only eight millions of dollars, while during the same period we coined above nine hundred and eighty-three millions of gold. In practical fact, gold has always been our standard, and silver, which had already demonetised itself by fluctuations in value and inconvenient bulk, was after an exhaustive discussion, running through three years, demonetised by the law of 1873, and so remained until the present year.

Down to 1853 the total amount of coined silver dollars which remained as a legal tender for amounts not exceeding five dollars, was only two and a half million. Between 1806 and 1836, a period of thirty years, not a legal tender silver dollar was coined. It was never used as the standard of value; no appreciable amount of it ever remained in circulation; and after 1834 up to this year the money of commerce as well as the standard of value was gold. Indeed, the standard silver dollar has not been found a necessity, or even a convenience, in our currency, during a single year of the present century. A silver dollar occupies twenty-seven times the space of a gold dollar. A purse which twenty silver dollars will fill can carry five hundred and forty gold dollars, and if you pack two hundred millions of silver in the usual boxes, it will take eight hundred railroad cars to take them from Philadelphia to New York.

It has been supposed by some men that we must have silver currency over and above the subsidiary coin, " because there is not gold enough in the world to do the business." If that is true, then surely we ought to have a double standard, or a quadruple, if need be. But if I show that for more than twenty years last past, gold has in fact been quite the chief coin used in the great business of the Christian world, we must conclude that with the large annual product of that metal we can get along in the future.

On the 12th of September, 1877, before the convention of bankers, held in the City of New York, the Hon. Wm. S. Groesbeck, of Cincinnati, read an able and elaborate argument strongly condeming an inconvertible paper currency. He expressed himself in favor of having gold and silver coins to circulate on a par, and mutually aid each other. He said : " The production of gold throughout the world is greater than that of silver; so also, is its production in the United States ; and the stock of gold in Europe and the West, is more than twice as large as their stock of silver ;" and he cites reliable tables to prove, that the product of gold for the twenty-four years next preceeding 1876, was far more than twice the product of silver.

During the period above named the production of gold, in round numbers, was three thousand millions of dollars, and the product of silver, was twelve hundred and nine millions. Of this silver, one thousand million was shipped to India and China, and once divided amongst that innumerable throng of the populous

East, into currency, personal ornaments and other artistic work, very little ever returned. This left of the entire production of twenty-four years, only two hundred and nine million for subsidiary coins, plate, ornament and use in the various arts, hence we have conclusive proof that there has been gold enough to do all the business of Christendom.

But England, the great commercial nation of the world, and who for the last sixty years has done more business with the silver standard countries, India and China, than all the European nations beside, has during these sixty years, coined no standard silver whatever; and England after long experience shows not the smallest disposition to return to the double standard.

But let us see whether the United States does not produce more gold from her own mines than she needs for her currency.

Since the discoveries in California, we have produced in round numbers, fourteen hundred millions of dollars in gold, and the rest of the world has produced more than we. Thus vanishes the fallacy that there is not gold enough with which to make the only commercial standard of value.

There is no greater misapprehension, than that which leads men to suppose a necessity for a large amount of coin or other legal currency in order to conduct, even the most varied and collossal transactions.

I am favored, by a most reliable banker, long experienced in finance, with a table showing how fallacious is the idea.

The daily transactions in the City of New York, alone, amount to more than sixty million of dollars, while the actual cash which is used in all these transaction is less than three million.

You sell a house in New York, or a shipment of flour in Liverpool, for $20,000, and as a rule, no coin or currency is used in the transaction. It is extremely rare that any considerable sum of money passes from hand to hand.

The great merchant in New York may buy and sell in the the course of six months goods valued at fifty million of dollars, and close the business without having received or paid in actual cash a single dollar. Very little currency is needed in the great transactions of commerce.

We need no silver coins except for fractional use, *any more than we needed them in the years gone by*, and if the silver dollar coinage continues, and its weight is not increased, before the amount of two hundred millions is reached, it is likely that a million of gold dollars will buy at least one million two hundred thousand of silver dollars. Such difference in the value of the two standards must finally bring confusion and drive all the gold from the country, or lock it, as a useless hoard, in the Treasury.

To the laborer, to those who have a little in the savings bank, and to those men and women who have small incomes from mortgages or cheap houses, and to all who, live on salaries or other fixed incomes, and to every employé of the Government, or of any public or private establishment whatever, I have a word to say touching the future action of the Silver Bill, so far as you are personally concerned. The rich can far better protect themselves against bad legislation than you possibly can. You agree to work for $40 a month; at the end of the quarter you call for your wages, and you are paid in silver, no matter that it is 20 per cent. below par, and will only buy you 80 cents worth of food; it is a legal tender, and you cannot refuse it— the same will be true of every person who lives upon a salary or other fixed income, and it will work a greivous wrong, and oppress those whom the Government should most carefully protect.

It is amazing to see with what romantic honor our Government has protected every Foreigner who has sought to make money by investment in our bonds, and with what scorn of justice it proposes to trample upon the plainest rights of our own citizens.

The earlier bonds were issued at the highest interest and at the lowest cost to the purchaser, and all have been paid in gold, and gold at enormous premium—even though the bonds did not purport to be payable in any coin.

The Texas Indemnity Bonds matured in 1865, the six per cent. bonds in 1868, the five per cent. bonds in 1871, and others in 1874; all were paid in gold coin; the coin ranging from 234 to 110; and yet there was no obligation expressed upon one of these Bonds or in the Acts under which they were created to pay them in coin, and when they were paid in gold, at this ruinous premium, Greenbacks were a legal tender for all debts public and private, except customs, duties, and mere *interest* on the public debt. The world can but admire the sacrifices which we made to preserve our faith by paying *in gold* every one of our obligations as they matured, no matter at what cost of premium, and no matter what nation held them, or at what low price they were obtained. But this year, when it was discovered that nearly all of the Government Bonds had returned from Europe and were held by our own citizens and the premium on gold had substantially disappeared, and when it was known that every one of these Bonds had been paid for in gold at par or above, the Congress passed a law over the President's veto, which compels American citizens to accept depreciated silver both for the principal and interest of the Bonds, even though the silver may fall 20 per cent. below the gold which they paid for the Bonds. It will be an interesting page in history for our children to read, that after the Amer ican Government had paid off (mostly to Foreigners) one-third of its war debt in gold, at enormous premium, and the greater part of the remainder of the Bonds having been paid for by the people of the United States *in gold*, the Government turned upon its trusting citizens and compelled them to take silver for their Bonds, worth less by many cents on the dollar than the gold which the Government had actually received from its own people for the self-same Bonds!

Two years from this, there will be a Presidential election, and before that time our people will discover whether they have been treated with justice.

We are slow to perceive the results of causes which are silent and gradual in their action; we did not realize that the gradual inflation of the currency between 1869 and '73 must surely bring disaster; and we did not see that the still further inflation of 1874 would only intensify the suffering; and I question whether we are now awake to the fact that we have turned the tide and are on the rising wave of prosperity, likely to increase and continue if we will resolutely insist that the Silver Bill shall be amended and that no new issue of paper money shall be made by the Government.

I cannot think that we are blind to our glorious heritage, or forgetful of what we have achieved, or ignorant of the boundless resources which we possess! Can we forget, that, after the great war, when the Government, in funded and unfunded debt, owed 3,000 million of dollars, we went bravely to work, and within this short time have paid off one thousand million of the debt, and that we have so reduced the interest as to make it fifty-six million a year less than it was?

There is no parallel in the history of nations! Well may *The London Times* say, as it lately did in commencing a leading article. "The United States are the richest nation on the face of the earth." And with a little patience and wise statemanship, every citizen of THE GREAT REPUBLIC can feel as proudly as did the subject of old Rome, when in any part of the world he deemed it protection to say: " I AM A ROMAN CITIZEN."

No class of the community suffer half so much by an inflated, irredeemable, and hence fluctuating currency as the laboring class.

The broker, the banker, the man of watchful skill in finance —the rich men can take care of themselves; yea,—and *make money by the fluctuations*; the laborer has no chance under such a system but to be kept in grinding poverty.

Tell me, laborer;—during these years of paper expansion and high wages, did you save anything for the days of darkness which began in 1873? Of course you did not, you could not, and I will presently show you why.

By an inexorable rule, as paper money increases, its purchasing power grows less, and as the inflation steadily advanced, the wages for which you contracted at the beginning of the year would buy not near so much at the end, and you were the loser, which you could not afford.

Your wife and children needed the same food and clothing as they did when the same wages would purchase twice as much.

By the courtesy of the President of the Produce Exchange, and by the kindness of a great merchant of New York—one of the greatest in the world—I have obtained tables showing the prices of food and clothing through all the so called prosperous years up to this date. These voiceless figures tell a tale with more eloquence than any words of mine, and they tell what you may have forgotten.

In 1864 when the Government was issuing Greenbacks, and wages were high, the average price of mess pork for the entire year was $33.19 a barrel, and of flour, $8.63 a barrel. Such has been the action of the Republican Party upon the finances that we are at specie payments, and the dollar which you get for your wages *is* a dollar, and the pork which would then have cost you $33.19, you can now buy for $10½; and the flour which would then cost you $8.63, you can now get for $4.63.

Brown sheetings which sold at 77½ cents a yard, now sell at 7¼. Bleached sheetings which sold at 77 to to 80 cents per yard, can now be had for 10½ cents.

The best calicoes, which sold at 50 to 51 cents a yard, now sell at 5½ to 6 cents.

From these tables I might multiply examples, but I will not detain you. You see why you could not support your families and save a dollar from your wages in the flush times of paper expansion. Irredeemable paper money long forced upon a nation will reduce the free laborer to a serf.

No truer remark of a great Statesman was ever made than that of Daniel Webster, who said; "Of all contrivances for *cheating* the laboring classes, none has been more effectual than that which deludes them with paper money." Be not deceived; the laws of nature, the laws of justice and the laws of God will not be violated without retribution.

It would seem strange that in this year of the world it is necessary to argue that the passage of laws could be other than a crime, which compels the citizen to receive instead of food, which was agreed to be delivered for work done, the promise of food which was not to be kept, or that money, any more than a ship, can never be made by a fiat of Congress.

This idea about irredeemable paper money is not new. It prevailed in China seven hundred years ago; it has at some time appeared in nearly every commercial country of Europe; it existed in the continental days of our history; it has brought every nation to the verge of ruin who adopted it, and they only have been saved who abandoned the pernicious fallacy.

This great people, intelligent and enterprising, favored with blessings never before vouchsafed to any nation has set its face in the right direction, and after all the depression and suffering through which it has passed, and now on the very edge of the rising wave which will lift it upon the rock of safety, surely will not sink back into the returning tide of ruin and distress.

The " Ohio–idea--irredeemable–greenback–fiat–money-Party," will soon disappear, leaving only the embodiment of its *principles* well expressed in the negro refrain:

" Beefsteaks when I'ze hungry,
Whisky when I'ze dry ;
Greenbacks when I'ze hard up,
Yes—allerz 'till I die."

SPEECH

OF THE

HON. EDWARDS PIERREPONT,

DELIVERED BEFORE

The Republican Mass Meeting, at the Hall of Cooper Institute,

NEW YORK,

October 15th, 1879.

L. W. LAWRENCE,
89 Liberty Street.

SPEECH
OF THE
HON. EDWARDS PIERREPONT.

Fellow Citizens:

I propose, to night, to take a brief survey of the situation,—to see what are the perils of the hour,—by what stealthy steps they have approached, and how they may be averted. The causes which lead to convulsions in Nations, however slow in development, are more uniform than is generally supposed.

The Presidential contest opens with this canvass; and when the vote of New York is counted on the 4th of November, we can pretty surely know whether a Republican or a Confederate will be the next President of the United States.

Momentous issues hang on this result,—perhaps the issues of peace or war!

To judge wisely of the future we must know the past; and with our intense and busy people the past is soon forgotten.

Read the future in the record of the past.

Remember, that the love of power, of riches, of dominion;—human passions, and human nature are enduring forces, upon which we can depend.

What has been,—may be again.

Thomas Hart Benton was born in a Slave State. He was for thirty years a Senator of the United States from another Slave State;—he, like all the able men of the Democratic party in the days of its purity, was earnest in favor of hard money. He was called "Old Bullion."

In the winter of 1857–8, I met in the City of Washington, the Hon. Benjamin F. Butler, an eminent citizen of New York, once a member of President Van Buren's Cabinet, a true patriot and a charming man. He proposed to take me to see his friend Benton, then an old man, that I might listen to his forecast of our political future. I met the venerable Senator by appointment the next morning. He immediately launched into politics. As I wrote to a class-mate and friend on the same day the substance of his conversation, I am able to reproduce it. "The South, sir," said he, "means to break up the Union: it has been the plan of their leading men for years. For a long time I was in their confidence, and I know their purpose: they do not confide in me now; they know, sir, that I denounce their treason. No matter what you of the North concede, the more you yield the more they will exact; they are determined to have a separate government in which laborers shall be slaves, where an oligarchy may rule and a middle class form an army. They know that the increasing population of the free States will so outnumber them before long that their rule over the Union must cease. They will dissolve the Union, sir, and you will live to see it. I shall not. Nothing will satisfy them which the free States can do. Concessions will make no difference."

Mr. Benton died in the following April. His prophecies, though true, like those of Cassandra, were disbelieved at the time.

On the 18th of May, 1860, Mr. Lincoln was nominated for President by the Republican Party.

The South saw their opportunity. They broke up their Democratic Convention at Charleston, divided the Party into factions, had two candidates in the field, and thus, purposely aided in the election of Lincoln, whose success, by Northern votes alone, they desired, in order to make the South solid for Secession. They thought that Lincoln was ignorant and vulgar, without prestige or power; and that his election by the North would unite the South in the formation of a new government, "whose corner stone," as their Vice-President said in a public speech, was "The stone of slavery!"

For fifty years before the war the slaveholders had ruled the Union. Neither their wealth nor their intelligence, nor their numbers entitled them to this rule.

In Congress, their strongest arguments were the pistol, the Bowie knife and the bludgeon, aided by frequent threats that they would dissolve the Union. They knew that the North hated duelling, violence and blood :—they thought that no outrage would provoke the North to fight. But their wiser men saw that there was a deep religious sentiment at the North hostile to slavery :—they called this "*Fanaticism.*" They saw that it was increasing, that it was earnest, and that scoffs and persecutions only multiplied its votaries. They saw also, that Northern thrift, intelligence and skill were increasing the riches and the population of the Free States, and that the day was near, when the ideas engendered by freedom and education would uproot their accursed system of human bondage. They saw that the oligarchy was doomed, and that their barbarous institution itself must fall, unless they could establish the doctrine of the supremecy of the States, that slavery was the normal condition of all in whom there was negro blood, and that it should be extended over newly acquired territory upon which no slave had ever trod!

So soon as Southern leaders perceived that the Northern conscience would revolt at such monstrous propositions, they set about the destruction of the Union, and planned the formation of a Confederate Government.

No concessions, no Union-saving conventions, no sermons from whey-faced preachers of the North, " Clothing their naked villany with old odd ends, stol'n forth of Holy Writ " could satisfy the South ; they made war ; and on the 12th of April, 1861, they commenced the bombardment of Ft. Sumpter!

You know the rest! We pass over the horrors of that war ; four years of carnage, and of bloody death! Five hundred million of treasure was wasted. Five hundred thousand American citizens were hastened to their graves!

Who broke up this peaceful, happy, benign government and draped the land in mourning?

Not the North, surely.

Well ; Lee surrendered at Appomattox in April, 1865 ; the rebel armies were dispersed ; Jefferson Davis was a fugitive, and then a prisoner about to be tried for his life, and President Lincoln was murdered.

The nation had had enough of war, and all re-echoed the phrase, " *Let us have peace.*"

The South was vanquished, prostrate, and exhausted; ready to accept any terms which the victorious North might impose.

Suppose that some prophetic Benton, had then said to the North,—" On the 4th of March 1879, these whom you now call " prostrate rebels" will dominate both houses of Congress in your Capitol at Washington; The Eleven Confederate States will have on that day, in the Senate and House, *ninety three* Representatives! Of these, *eighty five* will be of those who were soldiers in the rebel armies, and three more who held high office in the rebel States.—On that day, twenty Rebels will sit in your Senate, who fought to destroy the Union; with three more who held high office in the Confederacy: In the House, Sixty-Five Confederate Soldiers will proudly take their places to legislate for their conquerors, and block the wheels of government by withholding supplies, unless at their bidding, the wholesome laws are repealed which loyal men passed to preserve the purity of Elections"!

Would you not have laughed to scorn, such a prophet? Would you not have read to him the XIV amendment to the Constitution, showing how impossible was the fulfillment of such prophecy? Would you not also have shown the madness of the prediction by reading the XV amendment in these words:

Amendment XV.

1. The right of citizens of the United States *to vote* shall not be denied or *abridged* by the United States or by any State, on account of race, color or previous condition of servitude.

2. The Congress shall have power to " enforce this article by appropriate legislation."

And if he had answered you, that terror, torture, the shot-gun and the halter would drive every loyal voter from the polls, in the entire Confederacy, and that the disabilities imposed by the third division of the XIV amendment would all be removed, would you not have thought such prophecies the ravings of a lunatic?—!

And yet the number of Confederates which I have named, rule both houses of Congress to-day; and of the two hundred thousand colored soldiers who, in the crisis of our fate, and at the Presidents' call, bravely fought to save the Nation, none dare vote in all the Confederacy!

The Vice President of the Rebels is in the House, Wade Hampton is in the Senate, and Jeff. Davis is likely to be there soon!

Both legislative branches of the government are ruled by the Confederates, and they boast that next year they will have the Executive also.

This is no idle boast.

It seems idle, to those who contemplate only the superior intelligence, wealth, and the vastly preponderating numbers of the North, and who do not understand how a President is elected.

I dare say that some of you fancy that you have voted directly for a particular man to be President of the United States. You have done nothing of the kind. You have only voted for *Electors* to choose a President for you.

The framers of our Constitution did not think that the people could be trusted to express their direct will, and they contrived that the people might select a few men called "Electors" to choose a President for them.

The system is most vicious. Under it Presidents have been, and will be chosen in opposition to the direct vote of the people.

Let me show you how it works. You vote once in four years for Presidential Electors. Each State has just as many Electors as it has Senators and Representatives together. Each State prescribes its own mode of choosing its Electors.

In this State you vote for thirty-five Presidential Electors, and every other State chooses Electors in the same proportion. These electors meet in what is called "Electoral College," and choose the President. They may choose a man whom not a voter ever thought of, and he would be the President. In the practice of later years the electors have chosen the one whom their party nominated in convention, but that is not necessary, and in an emergency it may not be done. But a *covert* and grosser fraud upon the people grows out of the system in another way.

Take the State of New York, which is called a "doubtful

State;" and Wisconsin, Maine, Massachusetts and Vermont which are considered Republican States.

A fair estimate of the vote for next year is, 1,100,000 for New York, and for Wisconsin, Maine, Massachusetts and Vermont ogether, 800,000.

New York has the same electoral vote and counts exactly the same in electoral college as the four States last named. Now, if New York goes Democratic by 1,000 majority, she leaves 549,000 votes of the State unrepresented in choosing a President; and if in the four Republican States mentioned, the Democratic vote should be only 4,000, then you would have one million three hundred and forty-five (1,345,000) thousand Republican votes exactly balanced in a Presidential election by 551,000 Democratic votes!

But let us go South and see how elections go there.

South Carolina has the same electoral vote as Maine; her citizens are largely Republican. In the late contest Gen. Hayes received 91,786 votes and carried the State. Last fall the vote for Governor Wade Hampton was counted, one hundred and nineteen thousand five hundred and forty-five (119,545)! And how many Republican votes were cast? Not one!!

In Alabama Gen. Hayes received for President 66,230 votes; but at the election for Governor last fall not a Republican vote was reported!

In Mississippi Gen. Hayes received 52,605 votes. But in one year after, Governor Stone was counted in by 96,382 votes! The Republican vote had disappeared, and under the head of "scattering" was returned 1,168! And yet, in Electoral College, meeting to choose a President, Mississippi exactly equals New Hampshire and Nebraska combined.

Louisiana, in the year of Gen. Hayes' election, had a *registered* colored vote of 115,268, and a registered white vote of but 88,179. Mr. Hayes received a vote of 77,154; and yet Louisiana has but a single white Republican in Congress and not a colored member.

What means this sudden disappearance of 317,346 Republican votes from these four States!

We are told that the Southern climate is unhealthy for Republican voters, and that they have all died out!

Before the war five slaves added three votes to the whiteman's count: Now, five negroes add five votes to the whiteman's count in the election of President. Emancipation increased the Southern Electoral vote by 35, but the whiteman allows no negro to vote a Republican ticket; the white electors cast the entire electoral vote *which is not diminished by the exclusion of the colored voters.*

Remember that if two States have each 400,000 voters, and each is entitled to 14 electors; the electors chosen in one State by two hundred thousand and one votes, will have the same voice in choosing a President as the 14 Electors in the other State chosen by 400,000 voters. You see that the South have gained 35 electoral votes by Emancipation, and that under our unequal system, if the South drive every freedman from the polls, the South will have precisely the same Electoral vote as tho' every colored man voted the Confederate ticket. Hence you see, why, by violence, by terror, and by atrocities unnumbered the freedmen are disfranchised.

Turn to the Census of 1870; make any reasonable calculation for the changes since, and you shall see, that the population of New York is just about the same as the white population of the eleven Confederate States, and that her wealth is just about three times the wealth of all these eleven States together.

Against the 35 electoral votes of the State of New York, with her intelligence and her wealth so many times larger, and with a population nearly equal to the white population, (*which alone casts the Electoral vote*) of these States, how many Electoral votes do you think these same States cast?

NINETY-FIVE (95)!

FELLOW CITIZENS; how do you like the working of this electoral system, since the slaves are freed and our Southern brethren have come back into the Union?

You perceive there is some danger. By large majority the popular will may express itself in favor of your candidate, and yet, the Electoral vote may give the Presidency to another; and this mockery, we call, "*free election by all the votes of a free people.*"

How then can we escape the danger? Not by sentimental emotion, not by throwing up our hands and exclaiming what tremendous majorities Massachusetts or Vermont, Pennsylvania or Iowa will give. In a Presidential contest it matters not whether their majorities are five or five hundred thousand; it is all the same. Our only way is to secure the electors; and to do that we must face the situation.

The South is solid; made so by fraud and violence. She has 138 electoral votes. It requires only 47 from all the North to give the Government to the Confederates!

New York has 35, and Indiana has 15; both given for the South, transfers the power, with three votes to spare. Morton is dead; and Indiana is fairly claimed by the South; that leaves New York alone for the great battle; and here the last battle against the enemies of the Union will be fought. Next year we take the census; after that, there will be a readjustment of the electoral vote. The increased population of the North will then settle the future: the South know this, and hence their last mad struggle to seize the Government at the next election.

Without New York the Confederates have no chance of victory: without New York the Republicans have no better chance.

Elect your ticket this fall and the Presidential contest will be easy. The prestige of success, and the possession of the government of this great State steadies the wavering and assures the rest.

A BETTER TICKET was never presented for your votes. I have but time to speak of him who is nominated for Governor. I dare say that some of you may have preferred another. It is always so. But no fair-minded man will say that Mr. Cornell will not make an excellent Governor; and when we go to war, we ask who can lead us to victory, not whom do we like best?

No man has a more honorable record than Mr. Cornell. He has been long before the public. He has been a member of the Assembly and one year he was the Speaker. He served as one of the Commissioners for the erection of the Capitol at

Albany. He was Surveyor of the Port of New York, during a period of four years, and Naval Officer for a year and a half.

He has discharged the duties of all these great trusts with eminent good judgment, ability and success, and upon his fidelity, honor or integrity there is not a stain. He is the son of a sire who earned a fortune, of which he largely gave to endow a great Institution of Learning to benefit the people. He will be an honor to the name he bears, and to the State of which he will be Governor.

Let us explore the consequences of neglecting to carry the State this Autumn. If we do not carry it this year, it is pretty certain that we cannot carry it next; and if the enemy carry it, we can safely predict some things that will happen. If our 35 Electoral votes are given to the Southern candidate,—by every reasonable calculation, the executive government of the Nation will be transferred to the rule of the Confederates.

Swiftly following the transfer of power, you will find, that distrust about the financial question returns, that Northern capital timidly retires, that labor ceases to be in demand, that new enterprises are abandoned, and that the bright confidence and auspicious dawn of prosperity, but lately begun, will grow dark with gloomy apprehension.

A demand will be made that the freed slaves shall be paid for, that Southern damage-claims shall be settled, that the Emancipation Proclamation, the new amendments to the Constitution and the Re-construction Acts shall be declared void; that the Union and Confederate soldiers shall be alike pensioned; and that each State shall be declared sovereign, with full power to create Banks of issue without let or hindrance from the Federal government!

Do you doubt this? of course many of you do. You would not believe that the sacred pledge of freedom, called "the Missouri Compromise," could be shamelessly violated until the infamous deed was done. You would not believe that the South meant war until Ft. Sumpter fell.

Now, the South boldly tell you what they are going to do; and again you will not believe them. They do not propose to *secede* and leave you in possession of the Army, the Navy, the

Treasury, the Federal Courts, the Capital, the Archives, and all the machinery of an established government, in full and friendly recognition by all the powers of the earth!

They propose to leave you no such advantage: They propose to take your government into their own hands. They have grown wiser.

If they can once get control of the Government they will rule with relentless hand, and make you pay back, *with interest*, all that they lost by the war.

How are you to help it? Do you point to the constitutional amendments? They proclaim them "void."

It is well known that each man has kept a list of the number and value of his slaves.

With President and Congress in their interest, they can pass a law for the payment of their claims. The Secretary of the Treasury pays it in obedience to law (I do not mean Secretary Sherman).

What could you do about it? Bring it before the Supreme Court? But where would the money go meanwhile?

And who would enforce the mandate of the Court, if you get one? Armed governments never trouble themselves about mandates of a Court, if they don't like the mandate. A pair of Confederate soldiers would take care of the Court if it stood in the way. But perhaps you say that you would resist such wrong by force. Would you? We should find ourselves at a disadvantage in such a contest with the organized power of this great government, and many a pillaged city would smoke, and many a brave soldier bite the dust before we could gain the victory.

The South has commendable traits; it rattles before it strikes. It has told you from the beginning that it repudiated the Emancipation Proclamation; that the new amendments to the constitution and the Re-construction Acts were "null and void," and that they meant to elect a President who would "*trample them into dust.*"

When the Constitutional Amendment abolishing slavery, came before the House of Representatives in 1864. Mr. Pendleton in his place said: "But neither three-fourths of the

States, nor all the States, save one, can abolish slavery in that dissenting State, because it lies within the domain reserved to each State for itself, and upon it the other States cannot enter."
More than three years after the war, Gen. Wade Hampton, now a Senator of the United States, in the National Convention of his party held in New York, inserted in the platform this : " And we declare that the Re-construction Acts are revolutionary, unconstitutional and void," which was unanimously adopted.
At the same Convention, Gen. Blair was nominated for Vice-President, he having but a short time before published his declaration of principles, in which he said, " We must have a President who will execute the will of the people, *by trampling into dust* the usurpations of Congress known as the Reconstruction Acts." And Col. Herndon, complimenting Blair in a speech at Mobile, exclaimed, " Who but a brave, true, generous heart could utter such a sentiment as this?" And Senator Pugh, in a public speech, said, "I would not give a three-cent postage stamp for their Fourteenth Amendment. It is no part of the Constitution, and it never will be. It is a base fraud."
All the leading men of the South, from Blair to Blackburn, and their Northern allies, have uttered similar sentiments.
But the sagacious and philosophic statesman, Alex. H. Stephens, the ex-Vice-President of the Confederacy, in a speech before the Georgia Legislature, after the war had failed, proposed a plan to got possession of the government, which the South have persistently followed. He said, " We are not without an encouraging example on this line, in the history of the mother country. * * * The truest friends of liberty in England, once in 1642, abandoned the forum of reason, and appealed, *as we did*, to the sword as the surest means of advancing their cause. * * * But they retraced their steps. * * * *The House of Lords and the House of Commons* were henceforth *the theaters of their operations.* * * * The result was, that in less than thirty years *all their ancient rights and privileges,* which had been lost in the civil wars, *with new securities,* were re-established."
The South have accordingly transferred " *the theater of their operations,*" from their lost battle-fields to the Senate and the

House, hoping in this way to "*re-establish all their ancient rights and privileges, with new securities.*" And we must concede, that so far, their success has been encouraging.

The audacity of the Confederates may well excite our wonder! Civilized paople have supposed that intelligence, the payment of honest debts, the possession of property, and numbers of population, with the raising of taxes to support the government, gave such people the right to govern.

The states so clamorous for power have repudiated their debts, they pay but little tax, they have but little property, their numbers are comparatively few, and the masses of their people are very ignorant.

The Confederacy was formed of eleven states. In several of these States there are more colored people than whites. The entire white population is scarce five million and a half, and terror now keeps the colored men from the polls. Since the war, and from 1866 to 1878, there has been raised *from internal revenue* to support the government and pay its obligations, $2,055,397,846.18! Of this sum the eleven Confederate States have paid only $201,906,096.15!

The single State of Ohio alone paid $13,104,524.39 more than all the Conferete States combined; and New York alone has paid very nearly twice as much as all the Confederate States together.

From official reports it appears that of the taxes to support this government about 89 per ct. are paid at the North, and but 11 per ct. by the entire South; and that of imports 96 per cent. come to Northern Ports; and that of our vast internal commerce only 8 per ct. is in the South.

President Hayes received in the Eleven Confederate States 785,000 Republican votes. He was not suspected of being over harsh towards that rebellious people. On the contrary, his great desire for brotherhood and peace led him to many acts of generous conciliation which elicited sharp criticism from his party. Before two years of his gentle administration were passed, those who voted for him in the South, were by intimidation or violence driven from the polls.

Mr. Hays has learned what every Northern President and

every Northern Statesman, who went before him learned, that no conciliation, no soft words, no generous deeds will ever pacify the South. Mr. Hays has evidently had enough of the experiment; his robust, patriotic speech at Youngstown shows that he understands the situation, and that the same good sense which prompted his admirable vetoes will wisely guide him through his administration.

There are many able, patriotic Statesmen of the Democratic Party in the North, any one of whom would make an admirable President; *if elected by Northern votes;* but such an one, has no chance of nomination by the dominant South. They will take no man from the North unpledged to do their bidding:

And if to their 138 Electoral votes, they add 47 or 50 gleaned from the North, and thus elect their President, may they not with reason demand that the thing created shall be subject to its Creator?

I am glad that Mr. Hayes adopted the policy of conciliation towards the South. I think it was greatly wise. It was a necessity; considering the state of the public mind. Had it not been done, the Northern sentimentality would never have been satisfied.

Had the plan succeeded, it would have been well; having failed utterly, it proves that endless conciliation is not the remedy for Southern troubles. It proves what had been proved before, that Northern magnanimity, Northern sentiment, and Northern character are wholly unappreciated by the South. They stand upon a lower plain. They breathe an atmosphere of demi-barbarism; they cannot understand the larger humanity and the more enlightened conscience of the North. Slavery blunts the moral sense and brutalizes the passions. It stamps its curse too deep to be wiped out in a single generation.

Before Rebellion it met every concession with new and more arrogant demands. It met unanswerable arguments in Congress with threats and violence and challenge to mortal combat. A Northern Senator was stricken down and nearly murdered in the Senate House for words spoken in debate! Then they made war. Having had their fill of that, they were met by a magnanimity unparalleled in the annals of time; since the war not a rebel estate has been confiscated; not a rebel has been punished. Not a Confederate in all the Confederate States is now deprived of the rights of suffrage, and Jefferson Davis is as free to vote as President Hayes. None but Union men are deprived of this sacred privilege in all the Confederacy!

When late,—DEATH spread his dusky wing over a portion of the South, and there was scarce a house in which there was not one dead, the North hastened to their relief with a liberality unknown. True charity asks no gratitude. But even charity demands that her innocent friends shall not be treated with outrage.

They seem to regard every act of concession or kindness from the North as born of cowardice or as a just tribute to their personal superiority.

It were better for all, that we administer temperate justice instead of maudlin generosity.

We have a clear forecast of what the enemy will do, by looking at what they have done.

So soon as was possible, the new Congress forced an extra session, and organized their committees through which all business is done.

In the Senate, the Democratic party count forty-two; only twelve of these are from the North. The Confederates have the Chairmanship of seventeen of the most important committees of the Senate; and in constituting all the committees they have so contrived that every committee is controlled by the Confederates. In each case the majority of the Committee is Democratic; and in every case a majority of that majority is Confederate.

All important measures are determined in caucus, and the Confederates are a majority in every caucus.

Virginia has the Committee on Pensions; Georgia the Committee on Commerce; little Delaware, so little, that she has but one lone Representative, takes the important Committee on Finance. And what do you think the great commercial State of New York, with a population more than 35 times larger than Delaware, and with wealth five hundred times greater, gets in the Senate Committee? The Committee on PATENTS.

Gentlemen of the South; you over-play this little game; you show an unfair adroitness for which we were not prepared. You have so contrived every committee as to give the control to the Confederates—and the legislation in Congress is all shaped by the committees. We concede that you are solid, and that we of the North are slow to wake up. But do you mean to wake us again to to the *drum call?*

The South have always had some pretended *grievance*, with which to reproach the North. In 1824 it was because trade was pretty free and the North grew rich on commerce. Under the lead of Clay they forced a high protective tariff, against the protest of Webster. The North diverted much of its capital and prospered on manufactures. Then the South clamored for "*free trade*," and threatened nullification.

In 1850 they made vague charges of " Aggressions " by the North ; and when Mr. Webster demanded of Senator Berrien, and other Southern statesmen, to know what these "aggressions" were—they proved to be: " that the growing religious sentiment of the North disapproved of the right of one man *to sell another's children into slavery!"*

The resistance of the North to the destruction of the Union was another grievance. And after the war they were aggrieved at the re-construction of the rebel States.

Re-construction was a difficult problem with which our statesmen had to deal, and the North differed widely as to the best mode. I never believed that " universal amnesty, and universal suffrage " was the specific solvent for this difficult question. I did not believe that the African race, just passing from generations of slavery, could legislate wisely. But Southern leaders would not come forward to aid in re-construction, resume their loyalty, and honestly try to help an indulgent government to restore the impoverished States to harmonious prosperity. They stood aloof; and in sullen conceit refused to assist. Had they returned to a sincere allegiance they would have had every possible aid from the over-generous North.

They have only themselves to blame. They are not prosperous, they are not happy; they do not march abreast with the advancing civilization of the age. They mire in a dismal swamp and refuse to be lifted out. They neglect education and the teachings of Christian humanities; and they trample down justice, and thus banish their most useful population. They must face about or they are doomed.

Their present grievance is that the North will still remember some of the atrocities of the war. In derision, they call this "The Bloody Shirt," with small piping voice the doughfaced, knock-kneed idiots of the North, cry feebly, "Bloody Shirt."

But while massacres like that of the Chislome family, murders like that of Dixon and of Bryce, horrors like those on the Southern Mississippi, recently made public by the Memorial of Judge Dillon, the Mayor of St. Louis, Senator Henderson and others; atrocities which have lately driven thousands from their homes, to brave cold and hunger, nakedness and death, rather than remain in that abode of cruelty continue, you will not bury in oblivion the memories of the past through fear of mockery from your foes.

When William, the great Conqueror, the Bastard son of the Duke of Normandy by Arletta, the handsome daughter of a tanner, (whom, from a window of his Castle, the Duke first saw washing clothes in the brook,) held his army before the revolted town of Alençon, the besieged hung raw hides along the walls of the town with the jeering cry, "WORK FOR THE TANNER." The young hero remembered his mother with love; He was not ashamed of a hide for his banner, and the revilers of his mother perished before his fiery onset as stubble before the flames?

WOE, BE THE DAY! when for battle-banner, the "Bloody Shroud" shall be unfurled, and earnest men tread onward to the fray! The bloody corpse of Lucretia drove the last Tarquin from Rome, and the "*crimsoned garment*" now mocked at by fools, may yet rouse a people more wildly than did the beat upon the human skin, which formed the head of Ziska's drum.

The son of a tanner has just landed on our shores; I hope that he will not be called to do the kind of work which the Norman Tanner did. But if he is so called, he will do it, *thoroughly*.

I have seen him where Sovereign, and Princes, Ambassadors and Nobles rose up to do him reverence,—calm,—self-poised,—unruffled as a sphinx.

He is wiser than when he went away ; of broader intelligence; loftier in tone ; more exalted in his moral nature. But he will retire to his home in Galena, the same single-minded, unpretending, brave and honest man; a fitting product of our noble institutions.

Pardon me for detaining you so long. But a word more and I have done.

I have spoken of the future as it unrolls to the eye of the mind ; of the present and of the past, as truthful history will record them.

I have not spoken with the least feeling of personal hostility towards any individual in all the Confederacy. I, like all the North, would gladly treat them with generosity, if they would manifest any sign of loyalty, justice or duty. But I abhor their preposterous assumption, their cruelty to the freedmen and to all who differ with them in opinion ; and I will resist to the uttermost their audacious and insatiate desire to gain by violence and fraud the control of this government, which Northern valor preserved, and which Southern treason aimed to destroy. We endured four years of terrible war. We have passed through five years of heavy depression and much suffering, consequent upon that war. By patience, by self-denial, by persistent effort, against foes, even of our own household, we have restored the credit and financial stability of our country. Confidence has returned, labor is in demand, wages are advancing. The tide of emigration again sets in. We have sold within a year $500,000,000 of our products abroad, and every week brings heavy shipments of gold to our ports. The most auspicious dawn of a prosperous future opens before us ! Shall it be turned to sudden night? I call upon the people of this great State to come up once more to the battle for freedom and human rights. Carry the State this fall, and the strife is nearly over. Then the prosperity which has so happily begun may continue, and we may fairly count upon long years of peace, and brotherhood with our recent foes, and see the South, " *sitting,* clothed, and in her right mind," devoutly thanking God that he did not " leave her to eat of the fruit of her own ways, and to be filled with her own devices! "

SPEECH

OF THE

Hon. Edwards Pierrepont,

DELIVERED BEFORE

The Republican Meeting,

AT THE

Hall of Cooper Institute,

October 6th, 1880.

New York:
CORNWELL PRESS, BOOK AND JOB PRINTERS, AND LITHOGRAPHERS,
243, 245 & 247 Pearl and 18 & 20 Cliff Streets.

1880.

SPEECH

OF THE

Hon. Edwards Pierrepont,

DELIVERED BEFORE

THE REPUBLICAN MEETING,

AT THE

HALL OF COOPER INSTITUTE,

OCTOBER 6TH, 1880.

NEW YORK:
CORNWELL PRESS, BOOK AND JOB PRINTERS, AND LITHOGRAPHERS,
243, 245 & 247 Pearl and 18 & 20 Cliff Streets.

1880.

My Fellow-Citizens:—

The Democratic orators and the Democratic press boastfully tell you that the South is solid for Hancock. Well——

It was solid for secession;—solid for Jeff. Davis!

There is not a *loyal State* solid for Hancock. Every Northern State is either very doubtful, or else certain for Garfield.

If there is a free vote and a fair count every Northern State will declare for Garfield. What does it mean, that the South are solid for Hancock, and that not many at the North are for him; except those who sympathized with secession? It bodes evil to the Republic if you let him be elected.

Believing, as I do, that General Hancock is a loyal man, I was puzzled to know why the South nominated him for President.

General Toombs excuses it, by saying:

"We *cannot* put one of our own men in *this time* and *have to take* a Yank."

But J. B. McClures life of Hancock, containing the speeches of the Southern gentlemen who nominated him throw calcium light upon the motive.

Governor Hubbard of Texas said:

"I rise by request, a request which meets the impulses of my own bosom, to second the nomination of the soldier satesman Winfield S. Hancock.

"Sir, he is not only a soldier—that is something in the contest that is to be waged, as the gallant Hampton has told you. The South will be united, whoever you may nominate. But failing in principle, failing upon every issue upon finance or of reform or of good government, to attack the record of the Democratic party, mark it, the slogan will be 'The bloody South; the old haven of rebellion still lives.'

"If you nominate Hancock, where is the argument? We can say everywhere. Here is a man whom one hundred thousand Northern soldiers, if they are like Southern soldiers, will rally around his standard. Gentlemen, I believe him to be to-day the most available candidate of all the great names that have been presented. And, as I said awhile ago, what we want is votes, more of them, in God's name, whether they come from Republican soldiers or otherwise!!"

Judge Daniel of Virginia, arose and said among other things; "The nomination of General Hancock means *instantaneous* and *continuous* aggression." And General Wade Hampton said; "Mr. President and Gentlemen of the Convention. On behalf of the "Solid South," that South which once was arrayed against the great soldier of Pennsylvania, I stand here to pledge you its *solid vote*."

On page 91 we read that "Hancock was superb," and on page 92 that "General Hancock was grand and magnificent, and the very incarnation of war!" That is good:—

MARS himself, the GOD of War, couldn't beat that in his best days. In these prosperous times of peace, we do not want the "very incarnation of War" for President. We would rather have a Statesman.

When the General telegraphed to the Greenback-Republican fusion candidate for Governor of Maine, "Accept my congratulations on the *glorious result of your campaign;*" he evidently felt with Gov. Hubbard, ready to exclaim what we want is votes, in God's name give us votes, even tho' they come from Greenback-Republicans or otherwise.

Up to the time of that dispatch, as General Hancock had no experience whatever in civil affairs, the public did not know whether he was for Greenbacks or Gold, or how sound his mind or steady his judgment. They now have an inkling of both.

A revolution in the eminently successful policy of our Government is attempted, and the question is whether you will allow it. A great war was fought out, costing much treasure, blood and sorrow, to save the Union, and, it is now proposed that those who conspired to destroy it, SHALL RULE. This is a fair statement of the case, and no false pretences about "running a Union Soldier" will change it. If the South get New York and Indiana they take the Government with three electoral votes to spare. It is conceded on all hands that the country was never so prosperous. Shall we take the insane risk of a change in the Governmental policy under which we are doing so well?

To-night I propose to speak of General Garfield and General Hancock and of the parties which they represent. On another occasion I shall say something of our fellow citizen General Arthur, whose life and well earned reputation is known to you all, and whose letter of acceptance, in style, in strength of view, in clear and masterly handling of the questions upon which he touches, is one of the best State Papers which we have ever read. In every walk of private life and in every public trust his honor and integrity are without reproach.

We take exception to the intense sectionalism of the South; to their perpetual boasting that they are "Solid;" to their incessant efforts to keep alive and inflame sectional hate; to their constant avowal that their cause was just, and hence that the North was wrong in suppressing rebellion. They say:

"We believe as firmly as in the eternal word of God, that we were in the right."

A stranger reading Southern journals and Southern speeches would suppose that the North were rebels, and that the South had not forgiven them. The speeches of public men and the utterances of public journals are an index of the sentiment in their locality.

(From the Memphis Avalanche.)

"White men who dare to avow themselves here as Republicans should be promptly branded as the bitter and malignant enemies of the South. The name of every Northern man who presumes in this community to aspire to office through Republican votes should be saturated with stench. As for the negroes, let them amuse themselves; if they will, by voting the Radical ticket. *We have the count.* We have a thousand good and true men whose brave ballots will be found equal to those of *five thousand vile Radicals.*"

This threat about the count was lately carried out in Alabama, a State which gave 66,230 votes for Hayes, now counts no Republicans, and a Democratic majority larger, I believe, than the lawful vote of the entire State.

Mr. Field, Attorney-General of Virginia, Sept. 15th, 1880.

"We killed a great many Yankees during the war, and I wish we had killed twice as many more, enough to have given us the victory and our cause success."

General Fitzhugh Lee, at Portsmouth, Va., Sept. 2d, 1880.

"If you desire that those heroes buried yonder (pointing to the Confederate monument) shall not have died in vain, vote the Democratic ticket and vindicate the principles for which they sacrificed their lives."

Batavia, O., Sept. 23d.—Congressman Blackburn, of Kentucky, said in his speech here, on the evening of the 20th inst.:

"Let the Radicals cease their brawl about a "Solid South." She is solid, thank God! She was solid for Jeff. Davis in 1860, and we will be solid for Hancock in 1880."

When General Grant arrived in Chicago last November, it was deemed a fit time to send friendly messages to the prominent men of the South. *Governor Wade Hampton* declined to reply: *General Toombs* sent this;

"Your telegram received. I decline to answer, except to present my personal congratulations to General Grant on his safe arrival to his country. He fought for his country honorably, and won; I fought for mine, and lost. I am ready to try it over again. DEATH TO THE UNION. R. TOOMBS."

In January following, the Southern journals said;

"General Toombs has been selected to deliver the annual oration before the literary societies of the University of Mississippi in June next, by the *unanimous* vote of the students."

These fairly express the prevailing sentiments of the South. The only Union which they wish, is annexation of the North under such conditions that they can rule the whole. Toombs, always outspoken, says;

"We cannot put in one of our own men this time, and have to take a 'Yank.' That being the case, let us take one who is less 'blue bellied' than the most of them. You may depend upon it, sir, that 'Yank' or no 'Yank,' if elected, the old boys of the South will see that Hancock does the fair thing by them; in other words, he will run the machine to suit them or they will run the thing themselves."

This effort to create sectional bitterness is an old trick and ante-dates the war. It was the prelude to secession, and the same precise game was played, as now, charging the North with "*aggressions*," and with "*irritating*" the South.

Stephen A. Douglas who knew their plans ; in his dying speech to his countrymen thus exposes them :

"The election of Mr. Lincoln is a mere pretext. The present secession movement is the result of an enormous conspiracy formed more than a year since." "They desired a Northern Republican to be elected by a purely Northern vote, and then assign this fact as a reason why the sections cannot live together. Every man must be for the United States or against it. There can be no neutrals in this war; *only patriots or traitors* !"

When Abraham Lincoln died, the work of destroying slavery was finished:—a martyr's blood sealed the doom of that abomination forever !

We take a new departure.

Great issues of vital moment will be pressing for solution.

Whether having two legal standards of coin, we shall clip 12 to 15 per cent. from one, and declare by law that its value in payment of debts, shall be equal to the other :

Whether we shall place resumption upon a solid basis, which can stand the shock of commercial crises, and make the two standards so nearly equal that the bill-holder may take his choice."

Whether every good citizen, who pays taxes, without regard to race or color, shall have the same right to vote, and whether every citizen who has a right to vote shall be protected in that right:

How shall the laborer be protected in his wages, how shall we deal with Chinese immigration and how shall we restore our ruined commerce ?

How shall the sectional prejudices and hostilities, the growth of years and remaining from the war, be uprooted and absolute harmony be restored between the States ?

These and other issues will soon demand attention.

We stand in the very presence of the question, which party is the fittest to lead in the settlement of these grave issues, and which of the two Presidential Candidates is the more likely to guide us to a happy result ?

We shall not advance one step in this discussion until we have settled the Supreme question whether secession was *right;* whether the war to coerce the seceding States was an act of patriotic duty, or whether the Northern idea about the preservation of the Union was born of cant,—a wicked and insane delusion,—creating a Moloch.—an infernal Deity,—before whose altars we burned millions of our property, and in whose bloody sacrifices we offered more than three hundred thousand of our sons!

First settle this question in your minds;—was the Rebellion a terrible crime, for which its authors deserved condign punishment, and was the war for the Union a deed of lofty virtue? As you decide, you will have answered the question, "which party can be most safely trusted for the next four years?"

The chief concernment of Government is to protect life, liberty, and property.

Property is the base of modern society. Its accumulation is the primal stimulus to every industrial enterprise :—Its influence has increased with Christian civilization, which protects the possession and regulates the pursuit by just laws.

He who has not studied the science of National Wealth and long habituated his mind to the consideration of the questions involved in it, is not fitted to be President of the United States or to be a cabinet adviser of the President, however eminent he may be as an Astronomer, Engineer or Sculptor, or however "superb" he may have shown himself on the battle field.

Forty Eight years ago last November, in a log-cabin, some fifteen miles from Cleveland Ohio, James Abraham Garfield was born. When less than two years old his father died, leaving a widow with four little children, and naught else but a small, uncleared farm.

As the youngest boy grew up he showed a love of reading which he seems to have inherited from his mother; But from very early years he was obliged to work all day upon the farm in Summer and at carpenter-work in Winter.

When sixteen years old he became a driver on the tow-path of the Canal which ran near his home; but the frequent wettings in the canal, the exposure to the sun and the chill malarious air of night gave him a terrible fever of which he lay ill in his mother's house five months. When he recovered, his desire for learning was so great that his mother, with her scanty savings determined to send him to the Geanga Academy. He hired a little room and with the simple utensils which his mother gave him he cooked his own food, which cost him less than fifty cents a week. By laboring at carpenter-work morning and evening and in the vacation, and at haying and harvesting in summer, and by teaching school in winter, he was able to study at the Academy during the Spring and Autumn terms and to save a little every year with which in time he hoped to be able to go through College, if he could so prepare as to enter the junior year.

At the end of his first twelve weeks he went home to Orange, helped his brother build a barn for their mother, and then worked at day wages in haying and harvesting:—With the money thus earned he paid off the arrears of his Doctor's bills left from his long illness.

When he returned to the Academy he had but a single sixpence:—Going to church the next day he dropped it into the contribution box!

Think you that the casting of the poor boy's mite was not recorded above,—or that all the vile slanders which envy can invent will keep him from that place for which the Lord has raised him up?

Having spent his last penny in charity on Sunday, he went with a brave and trusting heart, to study and to work on Monday. Thus he toiled on, until he was twenty-three years old, when with all his self-denial he had only half enough saved for two years of the most frugal College life. His prospects were gloomy enough, but his heart never failed and hope did not forsake him. He found a man who was willing to advance the needed balance, provided he would get his life insured and assign the policy, which to the great joy of the young man was done, and in the fall of 1854 at the age of twenty-three he entered the junior class of Williams College, where he graduated in 1856 with honors. Soon after he was made professor of Greek and Latin, and two years later President of Hiram College.

In 1859 he was elected to the Ohio Senate. Early in 1861 he was made Colonel of the 42d Ohio Regiment, and soon he had command of a Brigade. By forced marches he surprised and routed the rebel forces under Humphrey Marshall in Kentucky, and continued in active service until after the battle of Chickamauga; for gallant conduct in that battle he was made a Major General. While in the field he was elected to Congress but remained in the service some fifteen months after. He has been returned to Congress from his District at every subsequent election. In January last he was elected to the Senate of the United States, receiving every vote of his party, a compliment never before paid to any Senator from the State.

After such a life,—after such a record of twenty years in the public service,—after such long continued and never faltering confidence, on the part of his especially intelligent District and the people of his state, it would seem superfluous to notice the attacks made by hostile partisans upon his integrity.

To the honest, to the just, to all the fair-minded no vindication of General Garfield is needed; his manly life; the testimony of all who have known him from his youth up; the frank statement of every eminent Democrat of his acquaintance vouching for his incorruptable integrity. The public speech of Governor Fish in which he says;

"Of General Garfield I can speak with the confidence which an intimate acquaintance of very many years, and close official relations during eight years, of that time, have given to me. No purer, no nobler man ever left the council chamber of the Nation. In private life an affectionate son, a kind father, a careful parent, good neighbor and honest citizen; in public life able, far-seeing, truthful. None doubt his ability, none doubt his integrity, although the necessities of parties and of politics have led to the circulation of several petty slanders against him. No better and purer man ever lived."

The published letter of that distinguished Democrat, Judge Black, written on the nomination of General Garfield saying; "I have been General Garfield's devoted friend for many years. If he would carry the principles which regulate his private life into his public conduct he would make the best Chief Magistrate we have ever had," should be enough. But nothing is enough for those in whose malignant breasts are hidden caves, where loathsome envy, (like the fabled Ghoul feasting on corpses of the dead) gloats over the defamed and mangled reputations of good men! But General Garfield is a candidate for the Presidency. Go to the great Library in Philadelphia and among the pamphlets and journals of the time you shall find viler calumnies upon Washington, than upon any Presidential candidate of our day; and John Quincey Adams during his canvass, wrote;

"The bitterness and violence of Presidential Electioneering increases as the time advances. It seems as if every liar in the country was at work day and night to destroy my character. It does not surprise me, because I have seen the same species of ribaldry year after year heaped upon my father, and for a long time upon Washington."

It is a strange fact that in a free Republic, the man who rises to greatness by his own unaided merits is more envied and reviled than he who is lifted by family influence and hereditary wealth.

The life of General Garfield is known from boy to eminent manhood; it is the earnest, honest, religious life of a good and able man. Have no fear that calumny will obscure his fame or embitter his temper, tho' it may sadden his heart.

His rival for the Presidency is General Winfield Scott Hancock;—born in easier life, who never soiled his hand with toil and never paid a doctors' or a tailors' bill, except with money furnished by the Government, since he entered West Point at the age of sixteen; precisely the age at which Garfield, barefooted and half-clad commenced driving on the tow-path of the canal.

The handsome, unsunned Hancock in his comely uniform and spotless gloves on the campus at West Point, and the shoeless Garfield along the muddy canal, do not look much alike,—and, their future hopes would be equally unlike in any other country than this, where alone, liberty and fair chance have ever been permitted. But in the race of life, the tow-path boy,— younger by many years, has overtaken the fortunate cadet, though poverty and illness, with none to help, retarded the one and powerful friends and the Government of the United States paid every debt and supplied every want of the other.

They are both men of stainless life. But the one is a noble representative of the principle of equal rights and the Christian civilization of the North;—the other fairly represents the privileged class of the old slave-holding South, to which is added a small exclusive element of secession sympathizers in the Northern States.

General Garfield is a statesman of enlarged views and varied experience. He has risen from the people; he feels their sympathies and knows their wants; unless they are cheated, they will lift him to the Chief Magistracy of the Nation.

If we were at war, there is not a Military man or a civilian in the country who would not think it preposterous to place Senator Thurman in command of a great army, tho' no unprejudiced man doubts that he is one of the ablest statesmen of his party, and no Democrat would make a better President.

The accomplished soldier Hancock would be as unsuited to the Presidency, as the accomplished statesman Thurman would be unsuited to the command of an army.

The American people have a keen sense of the fitness of things.

There is no more exalted station than that of President of the United States!

What has General Hancock done to merit this high place? What civil experience has he had, what studies has he pursued to fit him for the great office?

The sole thing which entitles him to public favor is, that he fought well for the Union against the Rebels.

Do the Solid South wish to make him President *for that?* Have they suddenly turned loyal to the Union and repented of secession? Not even a maudlin doughface of the North believes it, and there is not a Southern Rebel who would not scorn to pretend it. The South have never concealed their purposes and they have never mistaken their man. They take General Hancock because they know that the party is stronger than he, and they know that they can force him to their use. They hope that the Union soldier may win a few votes from the credulous North,—enough to transfer the Government.

If the South had 185 Electoral votes instead of 138, do you for one moment suppose that they would have nominated Hancock?

The Solid South makes chiefly the Hancock party; they call it the Democratic Party. Without the South the Democratic Party would be nowhere. At the Extra Session last year, commenced the "aggressions" which Judge Daniels told us should be "continuous" if Hancock was nominated. They took possession of both Houses of Congress. In the Senate were 42 Democrats: Twelve only from the populous North, and seventeen Confederates were made chairmen of the seventeen most important committees.

To this party General Hancock addressed his long-delayed and carefully prepared letter of acceptance. He announces that the war was over long ago, and that "the time has come to *enjoy the substantial* benefits of reconciliation!" The white Republican and the freedmen of the South have been "*enjoying*" these substantial benefits for some time,—and the North will begin to taste of that *enjoyment* soon after they surrender the government! He says, that the "bayonet is not a fit instrument for collecting the votes of freemen:" but he does not say, whether he thinks the shot-gun, the halter, tissue ballots and torture, fit instruments with which to disperse and destroy the votes of freemen!

In that letter he is silent about the millions of Southern damage claims against the payment of which the Constitution makes no provision; but he now frankly says that he would veto them. It is amazing to hear men, supposed to be intelligent tell you that the 4th Section of the XIV Amendment forbids the payment of these claims: The words are

"But neither the United States nor any State shall assume or pay any debt or obligation incurred in aid of insurrection or rebellion against the United States, or any claim for the loss or emancipation of any slave; but *such* debts, obligations and claims shall be null, illegal and void."

You would suppose that the wayfaring man, however great a fool could understand this. There is no Constitutional provision against the payment of damage done or against giving a pension to every Confederate Soldier; and General Hancock is too manly to make any such false statement.

I read from the journals of the day that when he was nominated at Cincinnati, "The band was playing DIXIE!" "The nomination was then made unanimous, amid great cheering, and the band played DIXIE *first*."

This was all consistent, and if Hancock is elected, "Dixie" will be "played first" again.

The Union soldier crippled in the war, will be turned out of his little place to make way for the Confederate who helped to cripple him; and when the limping one-armed "boy in blue" is begging for employment to give his children bread, point him to your sons, and tell them, "this is the outcome for ruined health and maimed limbs sacrificed in battles for the Union! Let "Dixie" be played again, and become the National air!"

General Hancock is the selection of the South, and a sectional candidate. I know him to be a courtley gentleman; if President, I believe that he would feel in honor bound to do all that he could for—his party,—and that he would insist that no President could resist the will of that party whose principles he had espoused, and by whose power he had been exalted.

Whoever gains the Presidency will find himself powerless unless supported by his Party. The President cannot make a village Post Master without the consent of the Senate, or get his own salary without the consent of the house. He is powerful while backed by his party—powerless when he breaks with it. Even the Queen of England is subject to the party in power.

On the recent change the Queen did not wish Mr. Gladstone for her Prime Minister, but the party *forced* her to send for him.

Few consider how absolutely the value of our property depends upon an able and just Government. You may own a richer mine than ever tempted the cruelties of Cortez in Mexico, but if the Government does not protect you in its development a thousand million of the unmined gold is not worth a two dollar greenback.

The action of the Government may decrease or destroy the value of your property in many ways. We are apt to forget that when the Government issues bonds or incurs debts for any purpose these obligations must be paid by those who have property, and who earn property, by the laborer and the man of substance. If by sectional legislation extravagant expenditures are made by the Government in the South, Northern capital and Northern labor have to pay the chief part.

Let those who tell you that State Sovereignty and the right of secession was given up with the surrender at Appomattox, read the following :

OFFICE OF STATE SUP'T PUBLIC EDUCATION,
STATE OF LOUISIANA,
NEW-ORLEANS, Aug. 21, 1880.

Messrs. CLARK & MAYNARD.—GENTLEMEN : Please accept many thanks for the "Government Class Book" sent this office. I have examined it with much care, and while there is much to admire in its beautiful and attractive dress, and typographical neatness and accuracy, in its clear and perspicuous as well as condensed statements, yet it contains many statements which are not borne out by a strict construction of the Constitution of the United States; and the heresy now so popular in some sections that this is a Nation, is one that I, at least, am unwilling to be taught the children of Louisiana, for it is not true, if the early Fathers of the Constitution knew whereof they affirmed. I regret that any such sectional idea (perhaps I should say "National" idea) should pervade the book. I regret I cannot introduce it into the schools of Louisiana, for with this exception I like it. Very respectfully,

EDWIN H. FAY, A. M.,
State Superintendent of Public Education.

Do you think that Superintendent Fay will lose his place ?

Tell me candidly, *Fellow Citizens,* which of the two parties can you most safely trust for the next four years ?

The party which saved to the Nation the only hope of Union, and freed a fettered race ; under whose lead peace and confidence and unexampled prosperity have come ; the party of the enlightened, progressive civilization of the free North, or the party trained in the sentiments, traditions and tardy civilization of the slave power?—which when the war was near success, declared in National Convention, that it was a failure and ought to be abandoned; which pronounced the emancipation Proclamation, the re-construction acts and the Constitutional amendments "revolutionary and void;" which committed the enormous election frauds of 1868, and the tissue ballot crimes of a more recent date; which when resumption of specie payment was near, proclaimed it impossible and wanted to repeal the resumption law; which, last year threatened to put out your light houses, stop your commerce and block the wheels of Government by withholding supplies unless the wholesome laws were repealed which loyal men had passed to preserve the purity of elections; which opposed every plan to restore the National Credit, and which coming into the Legislative power this Government at the Extra-Session, commenced these "aggressions" which justly alarmed the North.

General Hancock says that he will veto the rebel claims; But Wade Hampton speaking for the "Solid South" says;

"We believe as firmly as in the eternal Word of God, that we were in the right; and we have a settled faith, which no trials can shake, that in his own good time the right will be made manifest."

What is the inevitable logic of this "settled faith?" "Faith without *works* is dead!" To what works will not this *settled faith* lead?

Governor Vance, now Senator from North Carolina tells in his recent speech to what it leads;

"The South asks no bold and unfair thing when she demands her rightful compensation for homes destroyed, farms laid waste and pillaged, property stolen, and slaves released by the Yankee plunderers who lived upon us and then refused us bounty. And it is time that the whole North should understand this. It is time that the North should understand that it must atone, as far as it can, for all the South has suffered in body, pocket and soul. Our time is coming, boys, and the long purgatory that we have gone through will only make our paradise the brighter when we get there."

They honestly believe that they had a right to secede; that the war to keep them in the Union was a wrong; and that the damage to their property caused by armed forces coercing the States back ought to be paid by those who caused the damage:—they have proclaimed the doctrine from the first. They insisted that under the Constitution the States were Sovereign; that Slavery was a State institution inviolable by the Federal Power.

By arms the South was vanquished, but not a man, woman or child in the Slave-States was convinced by this rude argument. They believed then, and they believe now, that might prevailed over right; that depriving them of their property in Slaves, and damaging their estates by an invading army was a grievous wrong for which the Northern Government ought to make reparation!

As I have shown, that Wade Hampton speaking for the South says:

"We believe as firmly as in the Eternal Word of God, that we were right."

General Garfield, speaking for the North on the 3d of October last said;

"It was part of the policy of the Confederate authorities from Jefferson Davis down to make Union prisoners idiots and skeletons, and to exchange broken and shattered bodies and dethroned minds for strong, robust well-fed rebel prisoners. * * * Finally, and in conclusion, I am willing, and I think that I speak for thousands of others—I am willing to see all the bitterness of the late war buried in the grave of our dead. I would be willing that we should imitate the condescending, loving kindness of Him who planted the green grass on the battle-fields, and let the fresh flowers bloom on all the graves alike. I would clasp hands with those who fought against us, make them my brethren and forgive all the past, only on one supreme condition : that it be admitted in practice, acknowledged in theory, that the cause for which we fought and you suffered, was and is and forever more will be right, eternally right. That the cause for which they fought was and forever will be the cause of treason and wrong. Until that is acknowledged, my hand shall never grasp any rebel's hand across any chasm, however small."

I have asked many of my Democratic friends, whether in case of the accession of the South to power they did not apprehend such action as would impair public confidence?

And the answer has been uniform; "Oh-No;-the North would never stand that : why,—it would destroy the Democratic Party forthwith, and not a Northern Democrat would be left in Congress two years."

My friends,—are you quite sure that the enforcement of Southern doctrines would destroy what you call the "Democratic Party ?" It would not destroy the Southern *wing* of that party, the *only wing* with which it can soar to power.

Give the South the control of the vast power of the Federal Government, with a hundred thousand official places, the annual disbursement of untold millions, the handling of Government loans, with the authority over Banks, and do you think that they cannot continue to get the 47 votes needed from the North? It is childish folly to imagine otherwise. If you cannot keep the power which you have, you cannot get it back when it is lost.

It was said of old; "The warrior's strong bow to him who can bend it, and the heavy sword to him who can wield it." If we have not the manhood and the will to maintain our sovereignty, be quite sure that the mass of the people will turn to those who have. Lose the control of the Government now and you lose it for a generation.

We may boast of our education, our culture and our wealth, but if we are subtle Greeks instead of valiant Romans, if we lack the persistent courage which makes great rulers of a Nation, we heap up riches for the bolder Spoiler and Empire passes to those who can handle it. The Nations of the world look on, and they will rightly judge by the result, whether we of the North were born to command, or whether we are of meaner race, fit only for industries, trade and inventions; destined by the laws of Nature and of God to take inferior place among the great powers of the earth. May it be possible that our valor and our virtues are spasmodic and wilt away before the sterner will of more heroic souls!

Wade Hampton the leader of Democratic leaders has lately in a public speech proclaimed the Democratic doctrine thus;

"With a united South casting one hundred and thirty-eight electoral votes, we need only New York and Indiana, and I believe we shall have them. If we elect the Democratic nominee the Republican party will go to pieces like a rope of sand."

"Consider what Lee and Jackson would do were they alive. These are the same principles for which they fought for four years. Remember the men who poured forth their life blood on Virginia's soil, and do not abandon them now. Remember that upon your votes depend the success of the Democratic ticket"

MEN AND WOMEN OF THE NORTH:—So nobly brave and self-sacrificing in the war, so broad and generous in your charities, who pay most of the taxes, produce most of the wealth, have nearly all the commerce and manufactures of the United States, do we lack some of the loftier aspirations which make an exalted people? When we reach the highest field of the human intellect and character,—the wise Government of a great Nation,—shall we show indifference to honor, and infirmity of will, by which we throw away an Empire and submit to the aggressive rule of bolder men, who never "let I dare not wait upon I would?"

A strange fatuity blinds the Northern mind to public dangers which are at all distant, and no experience seems to awaken our apprehension. We would not believe that the sacred pledge to freedom, known as the "Missouri Compromise" could be trampled with infamy! When on the election of Lincoln the long-threatened secession began, I heard our most eminent statesman tell the believing merchants of New York that in sixty days it would all be over. When the South made war and General Sherman said it would require 250 thousand men to put down the rebellion, the Northern press and the Northern people declared that he was insane:

After the ballot was given to the freedmen none of us would believe that the large Electoral vote thus added to the South would all be counted for the Confederates, precisely the same as tho' every freed negro had voted for the Southern white man; nor would we believe that in the spring of 1879, that twenty-three would sit in the Senate who conspired to destroy the Union; or that Wade Hampton would proclaim in public speech on the 26th of July in this year, that the principles for which Lee and Jackson fought were the same as those which the Democratic Party, with Hancock at its head, now advocates.

We have cherished pleasant delusions about the Census, which prove to be as false as our dreams about the increased power which negro suffrage was to give us:—It turns out that the South is reported to have increased much faster than the North, and that Southern representation will be relatively larger, intead of greatly less, as we boastfully predicted! We look bewildered,—and wonder how it can be! Will we never have done wondering? Is it a marvel that the Party which made the false count in 1868 and committed the tissue ballot crimes quite lately, should return a fraudulent Census?

The Enemy have us at disadvantage in this Contest. They have no scruples:—They can stuff the ballot, falsify the count, and fire the shot-gun; while we hesitate to use even the lawful means of victory.

The Presidential Canvass opened last autumn—the issues were presented—we knew then, as well as now, that all would depend upon New York. We won Governor and both branches of the Legislature, and thus obtained the certainty of gaining the Electoral vote of the State if we chose. *Not by fraud but by law.* Until the time of Van Buren we always chose Electors by the Legislature. He opposed the change, but it finally came. All we had to do last winter was to put the law back and thus secure the State. Do you suppose that any Southern State would have thrown away the certainty and taken the chance of a Presidential defeat? We did clearly right, if we think it of no importance which party wins. It is not so clear, if we believe what we profess. Chinese gongs are poor weapons of war against shot-guns and Winchester Rifles. If we are counted out next November we shall realize our danger, and find, perhaps, too late, that what the people demand is good Government, and that canting flattery of the people, which they see through and despise, is not Government. Millionaires, rich men, respectable conservatives of New York, you will get waked up some day! It only wants a resolute leader of the populace with courage in his heart, and brains under his hat, to make you very uncomfortable. We are prosperous just now, and all is quiet—it will not be so always—and then you will want a Government, such as you will not find, if you shirk political duties. We would most gladly see complete harmony restored between the two sections of our country, but upon terms which are not humiliating; and when I daily read the boastful speeches about the "Solid South," and recall the wrongs by which it has been made solid, I know full well that some day, somehow, there will be a Solid North. There can be no lasting peace which is not founded on justice. When Wade Hampton told the Virginians the other day, that they only needed 47 votes and that New York and Indiana would give them, he expressed no union sentiment, but the purest Sectionalism; and when he added, "If we elect the Democratic nominees the Republican Party will go to pieces like a rope of sand," he made no idle boast. Power attracts votaries, and especially a new and resolute power. I have no hatred towards the South; I respect their courage, their frank avowal of their principles, their persistent and unfaltering purpose to rule within or without the Union; but I do not wish them to reign over the North—it would be a grievous rule—humiliating, degrading, and for us, shameful in the extreme. It would prove that every word of scorn which they formerly heaped upon us was deserved.

The party of Hancock is the party of State rights—the party of secession—it has never recanted its heresy or repented of the Rebellion. It caused the war from which came the burden of our National debt. It has opposed every measure for the restoration of the Public Credit, or for the return to specie payments. Senator Blaine, than whom, no man is better informed, has shown in a recent speech that, "Against every one of these measures the Democratic Party offered a stern resistance.

Mr. Thurman and Mr. Bayard, as usual, in the lead. Mr. Bayard further advocated the substitution of the old State bank system for the National bank system—a measure fraught with merciless disaster to the whole financial and commercial community."

I ask the merchants, manufacturers, operatives and laborers of the North, are you willing to see your reviving trade diminished, your busy wheels stand still, your furnaces go out, foreign iron and foreign goods flooding the market, wages fall and crowds of willing men seeking in vain for work? So sure as night follows day, this you will see if you turn over the Government to those who hate the Union and tried to destroy it!

Tell me; are you ready to admit that we made a wicked blunder when we went to war for the Union, and to confess with shame that secession was right and that coercion was a crime!

If the Democratic South elect their Candidate, no sudden convulsion will follow, and scoffers will say, "where is the promise of its coming?" They will slowly consolidate their plans;—they will know that the same defects of character which made the North surrender, may be relied upon to keep the North in subjection. They will give us no excuse for war; they will not secede and leave us in possession of the vast power of this great Government; they will keep it in their own hands: With its places, the collossal disbursements of the public funds, and the favors they can grant, this will be an easy work for courageous men who make politics the business of life, and whose pride would make them "rather reign in Hell than serve in Heaven."

We shall never change their determined purpose by yielding or soft words: They are bold and persistent in the game for Power: But I pray that we may never see Union Soldiers begging their bread, and Rebel Soldiers in revelry on the spoils of the out-witted, befooled, emasculated North.

In the words of that true patriot General Grant, in his letter to Senator Logan, "IT WILL NOT DO TO BE BEATEN NOW."

REMARKS

OF

THE HON. EDWARDS PIERREPONT;

At a meeting of the New York Bar, held on the 13th of January, 1882, to take notice of the decease of the late

EDWIN W. STOUGHTON.

Mr. Chairman, and Gentlemen of the Bar :—We are told, that "it is better to go to the house of mourning than to the house of feasting."—

The funeral brings out the nobler generosities of our nature, and lifts the soul far higher than the feast.

In the heated race of life the better impulses are often suppressed;—but when a fellow laborer falls by the way, we pause, and would gladly lift him up.

In the sepulchre, we bury every unkind thought or feeling which strife or rivalry may have engendered, and sorrowing, we plant flowers upon the grave and water them with our tears.

"It is apointed unto men once to die."—"If it be now, 'tis not to come; if it be not to come, it will be now; if it be not now, yet it will come: the readiness is all."

At the age of sixty-three years and nine months, Mr. Stoughton died.

There still-lingers in the world a belief that when a man has completed the multiple of years which the mystic numbers 7 into 9 make, the chances are, that his constitution will break up before the year is over, and 63 is called the "GRAND CLIMACTERIC" of man's life.—Burk mentions this with respect, and even Sir James Clarke, the late eminent physician to the Queen, in his very interesting book upon the preservation of health, speaks of what he calls, " CLIMACTERIC Disease," and shows how all important it is to guard against the dangers of the "*climacteric age.*"

Our brother of the Bar;—at whose grave we mourn, and to whose memory we would do honor, made his reputation as a LAWYER;—

The full merit of what he accomplished in a difficult and learned profession will not be justly estimated without reference to the obstacles which he had to overcome.

To his youth, fortune did not come smiling, and she gave him no golden key to the chambers of success;—At each door his right to enter was challenged, and he had to make good that right,—and he did it, VALIANTLY.

He came down to New York from his native Vermont, at the age of 18:—he had no advantages of collegiate or university education, and commenced the weary drudgery of a lawyer's boy in a lawyer's office: By industry he earned his frugal support, and by diligent reading in spare hours, he was able, at the end of five years, to be admitted to the Bar.

The protracted time of toil which he spent before any commanding position was reached, but tells the story of every man who has attained eminence at this Bar:--whoever imagines that such eminence can be reached without great labor, diligence and native ability combined, does not reason wisely. Within its inner temple, the LAW tolerates no idler, or man of ordinary faculties,—and the lawyer who reaches it, enters by right of his own good brain and force of character.

When he opened an office in this great city,—without means, without any powerful friends,—with no family connections to aid him,—his prospects, to the ordinary mind, were gloomy enough;—but then, as now,—the young man who has that "audacity of faith," which comes of youth, and the conscious possession of great native gifts, and determined purpose, casts out fear;—

"And with ambitious feet, secure and proud,
Ascends the ladder leaning on the cloud."

As his income increased he lived with profuse hospitality, and at his luxurious table he was fond of quoting the saying of a great barrister, that "Lawyers worked hard, lived well, and died poor." He certainly "worked hard and lived well," but the latter part of the quotation, I think, will not apply. He was always liberal with his household and equally liberal with all who were dependent upon him. He was successful in life, regretted and honored at its timely close. He had reached the full measure of professional eminence, and after the mid-autumn of life no lawyer can reasonably hope to add fresh laurels to his fame. He was able in the general practice, but especially distinguished in the department of Patent Law. I believe that he left no one to suffer who had any just claim to his aid, except to suffer that deep sorrow which many in no wise related sincerely feel. "His dust shall return to the earth as it was, and his spirit has returned to God who gave it."

Modern science, nothwithstanding its manifold benefits, has, in its narrow bigotry, cast some shadow over a happy faith in the immortality of the soul and the consolations of religious belief. But this will not last very long; it will by and bye dawn upon the minds of intelligent men that the scientists study only the *material* part of man, and finding no evidence of soul in the dead man's brain which they dissect; they rashly conclude that St. Paul was mistaken when he said "There is a natural body and there is a spiritual body."

This one-sided view will pass away when the soul of man is studied with the same earnest fidelity as material substance is investigated. During the temporary obscuration of faith it may be that chastisement and perplexity of nations will arise. Past history shows that when a people forget God and disbelieve in the immortal soul it is near the time when the right of government is disputed and anarchy ensues. There is no record of a people with any degree of civilization which has not a religion, and which does not pray to a Supreme Being in the day of trouble, and no revelations of science will ever eradicate this deep religious conviction from the human heart. We shall miss our departed brother from the daily walks of life and after a little while we shall follow him.

In an honored grave, "after life's fitful fever, he sleeps well." Peace, to his ashes,—and to his undying soul a GLORIOUS IMMORTALITY.

LETTER OF JUDGE PIERREPONT

ON THE

CREDIT MOBILIER CHARGES.

To the Editor of the New York Sun:

The New York *Sun* of the 15th instant has an editorial headed " LET US REASON TOGETHER," and calls upon me to meet the *Credit Mobilier* charges against General Garfield with a " lawyer's calm logic," and offers the columns of the *Sun*, and through it " an audience of half a million."

I like the proposition, " *Let us reason together ;*" if the South would but make the same to the North, the over-generous North would hasten to yield the most liberal concessions for peace and brotherhood.

The reason given by the *Sun* for its call upon me is in these words:

"Mr. EDWARDS PIERREPONT, Republican, Grant's Attorney-General and Minister to England, made a speech the other evening at the Cooper Institute, and in that speech he gave utterance to the following language : ' Although the necessities of parties and politics have lead to the circulation of several petty slanders against him (Garfield), no better nor purer man ever lived.' "

The words quoted are not mine; they were credited by me to Gov. Fish, but I may be fairly held responsible as indorser. I am sincerely obliged to the *Sun* for its vast audience,

2

On the 14th of January, 1873, Gen. Garfield, before a committee of Congress, swore :

"I never owned, received, or agreed to receive, any stock of the Credit Mobilier or of the Union Pacific Railroad, nor any dividends or profits arising from either of them."

It is charged that "this was a perjured statement." It was deliberately made, and in the course of the testimony it was reiterated, with emphasis. If it was false, no honest man ought to vote for Gen. Garfield.

At the outset, it must strike every thoughtful man with amazement that one "convicted of legislative bribery and perjury" seven years ago should have retained the unfaltering confidence of his district, should have been continued in Congress, should have been chosen to the Senate of the United States last winter by every vote of his party, should have been nominated at Chicago last June for the most exalted place on earth, and should have received on the 12th of this month such overwhelming evidence of the love and confidence of his great State.

All this is quite contrary to human experience, if the charges are true.

But let us look at the evidence. It is all printed in Congressional documents and lies before me. I shall cite from its pages verbatim.

So early as 1859, the "Credit Mobilier" Company was chartered under the Laws of Pennsylvania.

In the winter of 1867–8, Mr. George Francis Train told Mr. Garfield that the company proposed to buy lands along the line of the Pacific Road where towns and cities were likely to spring up, and asked him to take $1,000 of the stock. Gen. Garfield had no money, and declined the proposition. Some time later Mr. Oakes Ames made a similar proposition, and Mr. Garfield told him that, however tempting the enterprise, he had not a thousand dollars to invest, but that, on the contrary, he was in pressing need of even $300, which he owed; that he had been to Europe the past summer, and had to pledge his salary in advance. Mr. Ames said that he would loan him $300, remarking that if Mr. Garfield finally concluded to take the stock, this loan could be adjusted in that way.

Several months later the loan was repaid, and that is the only business transaction ever had between the two men.

As Gen. Garfield swears, and as Mr. Ames' testimony hereinafter cited proves, not a share of stock was ever transferred to Mr. Garfield or ever stood in his name, and not a dividend was ever received by him on any share or stock whatever, and not a dollar from the sale of any interest therein. In the Presidential contest of 1872, it was charged that sixteen members of Congress had received shares in the "Credit Mobilier," and Mr. Garfield's name was mentioned as one. He was then away in the Rocky Mountains.

On the 15th of September he reached Washington, long before Congress met, and forthwith he caused to be published in the Cincinnati *Gazette* a statement denying that he had ever held, subscribed for, owned or seen a bond or share of the stock. When Congress met in the following December, Mr. Speaker Blaine, whose name was also mentioned, moved a committee of investigation, of which Mr. Poland, of Vermont, was chairman.

Investigation revealed that Mr. Oakes Ames held one hundred and eighty shares of this stock as trustee for the purpose, as the phrase was, "*of placing it where it would do the most good.*" On the 13th of July, 1867, Gen. Garfield sailed for Europe, and on the 9th of November following returned to New York. In the winter of 1867-8 the conversation between Garfield and Ames and the loan of the $300 is said by General Garfield to have occurred. Whatever sum was loaned or paid to Garfield, whether it was $300 or $329, it was loaned or paid *before* June 22, 1868, or on that day, as all admit, and that not a dollar passed after that date. On the 17th of December, 1872, Mr. Ames gave his testimony (pp. 15-58), and said:

"Q. In reference to Mr. Garfield, you say that you agreed to get ten shares for him, and to hold them till he could pay for them, and that he never did pay for them nor receive them? A. Yes, sir.

Q. He never paid any money on that stock, nor received any money from it? A. Not on account of it.

Q. He received no dividends? A. No, sir; I think not; he says he did not; my own recollection is not very clear.

Q. So that, as you understand, Mr. Garfield never parted with any money, nor received any money on that transaction? A. No, sir; he had some money from me once, *some three or four hundred dollars*, and called it a loan; he says that is all he ever received from me, and that he considered it a loan; *he never took his stock and never paid for it.*

Q. Did you understand it so? A. Yes; I am willing to so understand it; *I do not recollect paying him any dividend,* and have forgotten that I paid him any money (p. 28).

Q. Who received the dividends? A. Mr. Patterson, Mr. Bingham, James F. Wilson did, and I think Mr. Colfax received a part of them; I do not know whether he received them all or not; I think Mr. Scofield received a part of them; Messrs. Kelley and Garfield never paid for their stock, *and never received their dividends*" (p. 40).

On pp. 19-21 he mentions by name eleven who bought stock, but (p. 21) he says: "He (Garfield) did not pay for it or receive it."

On pp. 23-41 he mentions having paid dividends to eight members of Congress, and he says that to several of them he paid all the dividends that accrued. He says, p. 28: "I do not recollect paying him (Garfield) *any dividend* and have forgotten that I paid him any money." Page 40: "Messrs. Kelley and Garfield never paid for their stock, *and never received any dividends.*"

This completely sustains Gen. Garfield.

This testimony of Mr. Ames was given (be it remembered) December 17, 1872. It was published January 6, 1873.

On the 15th of January, Mr. T. C. Durant, a heavy stockholder, and long president of the company, was examined (p. 173) and said :

"The stock that stands in the name of Mr. Ames, as Trustee, I claim belongs to the company yet, and I have a summons in a suit in my pocket waiting to catch him in New York to serve the papers."

After this testimony of Mr. Durant, and on the 22d of January, 1873, Mr. Ames took the stand again, and testified (pp. 267-290) that he gave certificates of stock to others, but that he never gave any to Mr. Garfield, and that none were ever spoken of (pp. 295-6). In the case of others he took regular receipts, but none were ever pretended to have been taken by or given to Mr. Garfield (pp. 21, 113, 191, 204, 337, 456, 458). To five members he gave checks payable to them by name on the Sergeant-at-Arms, which were produced (pp. 333, 334, 449), also three others bearing the initials of the parties ; but no check with name or mark or letter relating to Gen. Garfield, or writing or receipt with his name, initials or mark, was it pretended ever had existed.

Mr. Ames swears that he paid to various persons the dividends which accrued, and that one purchaser sold his ten shares at a profit of $3,000, and that dividends went on for some *four years* after the time when he says he gave $329 to Mr. Garfield, in June, 1868 (pp. 191, 337, 217, 461, 454), but that he never paid Mr. Garfield a dollar *after that date*, and never spoke to him about it (pp. 40, 296, 356).

At p. 296 he says:

" Q. Was this the only dealing you had with him in reference to any stock? A. I think so.
Q. Was it the only transaction of any kind? A. The only transaction.

Q. Has that $329 ever been paid to you? A. I have no recollection of it.

Q. Have you any belief that it ever has? A. No, sir.

Q. Did you ever loan Gen. Garfield $300? A. Not to my knowledge; except that he calls this a loan.

Q. There were dividends of Union Pacific Railroad stock on these ten shares? A. Yes, sir.

Q. Did Gen. Garfield ever receive these? A. *No, sir ; he never received but* $329.

Q. Has there been any conversation between you and him in reference to the Pacific stock he was entitled to? A. No, sir.

Q. Has he ever called for it? A. *No, sir.*

Q. Have you ever offered it to him? A. *No, sir.*

Q. Has there been any conversation in relation to it? A. *No, sir."*

It is simply preposterous to suppose that during these *four years*, from 1868 to 1872, Mr. Garfield owned stock paying large dividends and never received a dollar, and never sold the stock, while he was in debt, building a house, in urgent want of money, giving mortgages to raise it, and has never received anything, either by way of dividend or sale, to this hour.

There is not a pretence that he ever received but $329, which sole sum it is admitted was paid, if at all, so early as *June* 22, 1868. In discussing this question, we are to presume that a sane man will act with ordinary common sense.

Mr. Ames admitted that after December, 1867, the various dividends amounted to more than 800 per cent., but reiterated that Mr. Garfield never had a dollar of stock or bonds, and never any dividend save the $329.

Mr. Ames produced his diary of 1868 containing a statement of an account with twelve Members of Congress relating to these shares (pp. 450–461). All but three are crossed off (pp. 451, 458, 459). At pp. 459, 460, Mr. Ames admitted that the account with Garfield's name had *never been adjusted.*

"GARFIELD.

"10 shares Credit M............................	$1,000	00
7 mos. 10 days..................................	43	36
	$1,043	36
80 per ct. bd. div., at 97........................	776	00
	267	36
Int'st to June 20th...............................	3	64
	$271	00

1,000 C. M.
1,000 U. P.

Q. This statement of Mr. Garfield's account is not crossed off, *which indicates, does it, that the matter has never been settled or adjusted?* A. No, sir; *it never has.*

"Q. Can you state whether you have any other entry in relation to Mr. Garfield? A. NO, SIR."

Here note that Mr. Ames swears that he has *no other entry in relation to Mr. Garfield.* But subsequently, on the 22d of January, 1873, he presented the following (p. 297):

	"J. A. G.		Dr.	
1868.	To ten shares stock Credit Mobilier of A..	$1,000	00
	Interest...............................	47	00
June 19.	To Cash	329	00
		$1,376	00
1868.	By dividend, bonds Union Pacific Railroad, $1,000, at 80 per cent., less 3 per cent	$776	00
June 17.	By dividend, collected for your account.....	600	00
		$1,376	00 "

It will be seen that these accounts do not agree; and it was found that this last account was *not in his memorandum-book at all.* The celebrated $329 is here added, *for the first time.*

Every lawyer of much experience knows that accounts made

up to suit a purpose are apt to carry within themselves some evidence by which their falsity can be detected.

This one is no exception. It says:

"June 19, to cash..........................$329
June 17, by dividend, collected for you. 600"

Ames admits that the dividends continued, and that he never paid Garfield another dollar. But he is asked how he paid the $329, June 19, 1868; and (at p. 295) we have it:

"Q. How was that paid? A. Paid in money, I believe."

But he could show no voucher, or even a memorandum of his own; and he swears (p. 297):

"Q. You say that $329 was paid him; how was that paid? A. I presume, *by a check on the Sergeant-at-Arms*; I find there are checks filed, without indicating who they were for."

Now we are coming to something not dependent on memory. The check was found, and, one week after, it was produced (p. 353):

"JUNE 22, 1868.

Pay O. A., or bearer, three hundred and twenty-nine dollars, and charge to my account.

OAKES AMES."

The other checks showed, by name or initials, to whom they were given; but "O. A." did not look much like *Garfield*, but more like *Oakes Ames*. The truth was, that Oakes Ames kept the stock himself and drew the dividends, and he never attempted to show that he had transferred them to anyone, and it was natural that he should fear the law-suits which were to make him account; but hear his testimony (p. 353):

"Q. This check seems to have been paid to somebody, and taken up by the Sergeant-at-Arms; those initials are your own? A. Yes, sir. Q. Do you know who had the benefit of this check? A. I cannot tell you. Q. Do you think you received the money on it yourself? A. *I have no idea;* I may have drawn the money and handed it to another person; it was paid in that transaction. It may have been paid to Mr.

Garfield. There were several sums of that amount. Q. Have you any memory in reference to this check? A. I have *no memory* as to that particular check."

But there is another little trouble about this $329. He says: "It may have been paid to Mr. Garfield." But the check was not made until the 22d of June, and was paid the same day, as the teller proves; whereas Ames brings a written account to prove that he paid Garfield on the 19th, three days before the check existed. But he was still further examined (p. 354.):

"Q. In regard to Mr. Garfield, do you know whether you gave him a check, or paid him the money? A. I think I did not pay him the money; *he got it from the Sergeant-at-Arms, upon a check.*"

Still later, in the same examination, occurs the following (p. 355):

"Q. You think the check on which you wrote nothing to indicate the payee must have been Mr. Garfield's? A. Yes, sir; that is my judgment."

On the 11th of February, twelve days later still, the subject came up again, and Mr. Ames said (p. 460):

"A. I am not sure how I paid Mr. Garfield."

Still later (p. 471):

"Q. In testifying in Mr. Garfield's case, you say you may have drawn the money on the check and paid him; is not your answer equally applicable to the case of Mr. Colfax? A. No, sir. Q. Why not? A. I put Mr. Colfax's initials on the check, while I put no initials on Mr. Garfield's, and I may have drawn the money myself. Q. Did not Mr. Garfield's check belong to him? A. Mr. Garfield had not paid for his stock; he was entitled to $329 balance; but Mr. Colfax paid for his, and I had no business with his $1,200."

"Q. Is your recollection in regard to this payment to Mr. Colfax any more clear than your recollection as to the payment to Mr. Garfield? A. Yes, sir; I think it is.

"Q. Is it your habit, as a matter of business, in conducting various transactions with different persons, to do it without making any memoranda? A. This was my habit; until within a year or two I have had no bookkeeper, and I used to keep all my own matters in my own way, *and very carelessly, I admit.*"

Mr. Ames says in his testimony (p. 281):

" Q. What was the character of the book in which the memoranda were made? A. It was made in a small pocket memorandum, *and some of it on slips of paper.*"

In the examination of Mr. Dillion, cashier of the Sergeant-at-Arms (p. 479):

" Q. There is a check payable to Oakes Ames or bearer; have you any recollection of that? A. That was paid *to himself; I have no doubt* myself that I paid that to Mr. Ames (p. 53.)

Mr. Ames continued:

Q. You may state whether in conversation with you Mr Garfield claims, as he claims before us, that the only transaction between you was borrowing $300? A. No, sir; he did not claim that with me.

Q. State how he did claim it with you; what was said? A. I cannot remember half of it; he (Mr. Garfield) stated that when he came back from Europe, being in want of funds, he called on me to loan him a sum of money; he thought he had repaid it; *I do not know; I do not remember.*

Q. How long after that transaction (the offer to sell Credit Mobilier stock) did he go to Europe? A. I believe it was a year or two.

Q. Do you know that he did not go to Europe for nearly two years afterward? A. No, I do not; it is my impression it was two years afterward, but I cannot remember dates."

Such is Mr. Ames' defect of memory. He complains of it in his testimony, and says:

" People ask me about things that happened a year ago, and I cannot tell whether it was ten years ago or one."

The proof is clear that Gen. Garfield sailed July 13, 1867, the *year before* June, 1868, instead of *two years after.*

It is worthy of note that Mr. Ames testified five years after the transaction.

On page 356, he said he " considered Mr. Garfield the purchaser of the stock, unless it was borrowed money," and on page 461, at the conclusion of his testimony, he said:

" Mr. Garfield understands this matter as a loan ; he says he did not explain it to him.
Q. You need not say what Mr. Garfield says ; tell us what you think ? A. Mr. Garfield might have misunderstood me ; I supposed it was like all the rest, but when Mr. Garfield says he mistook it for a loan ; that he always understood it to be a loan ; that I did not make any explanation to him, and did not make any statement to him ; I may be mistaken ; I am a man of few words, and I may not have made myself understood to him."

If Mr. Ames had not been sued by Mr. McComb and been threatened by Mr. Durant with another suit to make him account for the stock, no such charges would have been made againt Gen. Garfield. Gen. Garfield's testimony is positive and explicit.

Every circumstance confirms its truth and there is nothing in the evidence which shakes it. The report is not evidence, nor is there evidence to sustain the report.

The report says :

" He (Garfield) agreed with Mr. Ames to take ten shares of Credit Mobilier stock, but did not pay for the same. Mr. Ames received the 80 per cent. dividend in bonds, and sold them for 97 per cent., and also received the 60 per cent. cash dividend, which, together with the price of the stock and interest, left a balance of $329. This sum was paid over to Mr. Garfield *by a check on the Sargeant-at-Arms.*"

This is in direct conflict with Gen. Garfield's sworn statement, and it is fairly argued that if the report is accurate, Gen. Garfield's testimony is false. The report was signed by Judge Poland, Chairman, by Judge McCrary and by Gen. Banks, all of them Republicans and men of character and honor, and each of them has since publicly announced his fullest confidence in the integrity, truth, purity and honor of Gen. Garfield, thereby admitting the inaccuracy of this part of the report. Judge Poland says:

"I only desire to have an opportunity to express to the Convention and to Republicans everywhere my entire approval of the nomination made at Chicago. Probably no man in Vermont knows General Garfield more intimately than myself. He was in Congress during the whole of my ten years' service, and for eight years we stood together in the House, and ever on terms of friendship and intimacy. But our political opponents affect to question his personal integrity and purity of character, and to base their accusations upon the evidence taken before, and the report of a committee of Congress, of which I was chairman, known as the Credit Mobilier Committee. I believe him to be a thoroughly upright and honest man, and one who would be so under all circumstances and against any temptation. The use that is being made of my name and of the report of the committee which was drawn by me, in my opinion, makes it proper for me to express my personal judgment as to the character of the man."

Judge McCrary, one of the committee, in a public letter of July last, says:

"With respect, however, to this transaction, I must say *that subsequent developments and further consideration of the matter long ago led* me to the conclusion that the memorandum of Mr. Ames was very unreliable, and I have for years felt *assured of the correctness of General Garfield's recollection of the facts in dispute.*"

Senator Hoar says:

"I was one of the committee who investigated the Credit Mobilier, and wrote the greater part of the report of the committee known as the Wilson Committee. There was nothing in the transaction which in the least gave me reason to distrust General Garfield's *absolute integrity*. I expressed my opinion of the *absolute honor and integrity* of General Garfield in this matter *years ago*. No man, Democrat or Republican, who ever served with Garfield does, I think, doubt that he is *absolutely incorruptible*."

And Judge Black, who investigated the whole matter at the time of the report, wrote a letter to the Speaker of the House acquitting General Garfield of any wrong; and last June, when General Garfield was nominated, the judge again wrote, saying: "I have been General Garfield's devoted friend for many years. If he would carry the principles which regulate his private life into his public conduct, he would make the best Chief Magistrate we ever had." Such men do not publicly commend one "who has been convicted of taking bribes or swearing falsely." That part of the report reflecting upon General Garfield was wholly wrong, unsupported by the evidence, made in haste from a mass of testimony disjointed and running through a long period, and at a time when Congress was frantic at the revelations made, and too ready to find scapegoats for the multitude of sins.

Macaulay says:

"We know no spectacle so ridiculous as the British public in one of its periodical fits of morality * * * But once in six or seven years our virtue becomes outrageous. We must make a stand against vice.

Accordingly some unfortunate man, in no respect more depraved than hundreds whose offences have been treated with lenity, is singled out as an expiatory sacrifice. * * * He is, in truth, a sort of whipping-boy, by whose vicarious agonies all the other transgressors of the same class are, it is supposed, sufficiently chastised. We reflect very complacently on our own severity, and compare with great pride the high standard of morals established in England with the Parisian laxity. At length our anger is satiated. Our victim is ruined and heart-broken. And our virtue goes quietly to sleep for seven years more."

It is barely possible that some touch of these ancestral traits unconsciously hurried honorable Congressmen to inconsiderate and unjust conclusions.

EDWARDS PIERREPONT.

NEW YORK, October 19, 1880.

THE IMPENDING CRISIS IN OUR FINANCES.

A PLAN TO MAKE GOLD AND SILVER CIRCULATE EQUALLY.

—BY—

EDWARDS PIERREPONT.

THE IMPENDING CRISIS IN OUR FINANCES.

The Secretary of the Treasury in his able and very suggestive report shows that of gold, including coin and bullion, the Government owns but $134,670,790 ; that of this sum $95,500,000 was obtained by the sale of bonds under the Resumption act of 1875, to be applied to the redemption of the legal-tender notes ; that by the 12th section of the act of July 12th, 1882, the Congress implied that at least $100,000,000 of gold must be held in the Treasury for the redemption of these notes as presented, and that the late Secretary, Mr. Sherman, under whose administration of the Treasury specie payments were resumed, held that gold equal to forty per cent. of the outstanding legal-tender notes should be held in reserve for their protection ; and further, that of those notes there are now outstanding $346,681,016.

The Secretary says : " Many persons regard the legal-tender notes as money ; that this is a delusion will be proven whenever there is a large demand for gold for export. They are not money, but merely promises to pay it ; and the Government must be prepared to redeem all that may be presented *or forfeit its character for solvency.*" Referring to the table showing the small amount of gold in the Treasury, the Secretary says:

"From this statement it is seen that there is no surplus gold in the Treasury, and that the reserve has been trenched upon; that there is no plethora of any kind except of silver dollars, for which there is no demand.

"After giving the subject careful consideration, I have been forced to the conclusion that unless both the coinage of silver dollars and the issue of silver certificates are suspended, there is danger that silver, and not gold, may become our metalilc standard. This danger may not be imminent, but it is of so serious a character that there ought not to be delay in providing against it. Not only would the national credit be seriously impaired if the Government should be under the necessity of using silver dollars or certificates *in payment of gold obligations*, but business of all kinds would be greatly disturbed; not only so, but gold would at once cease to be a circulating medium, and severe contraction would be the result."

A simple computation shows that all the gold in the Treasury is less than the forty per cent. reserve to protect the legal-tender notes by over $4,000,000.

It is estimated that there is now in the country at least $610,000,000 of gold. Demonetize this large sum, and turn the gold into merchandise, then the "*severe contraction*" mentioned by the Secretary would be inevitable. He speaks, in the above extract, of the serious injury to the national credit which must follow from paying "*gold obligations in silver dollars,*" and he several times, in the course of his report, speaks of our "*gold obligations.*"

He evidently, and as we shall show, justly, considers the $346,681,016 of legal-tender notes and all the coin-bonds of the Government, with their coupons, "gold obligations."

Take a legal-tender one dollar note of March 3, 1863—it reads: "The United States will pay to bearer one dollar." At that time the silver dollar of 412½ grains was worth considerably more than the gold dollar.

By the act of March 18, 1869, "*The faith of the United States is solemnly pledged to the payment* IN COIN *or its equivalent of all the obligations of the United States not bearing interest, known as United States notes, and of all the interest-bearing obligations of the United States, except in cases where the law authorizing the issue of any such obligations has expressly provided that the same may be paid in lawful money or other currency than gold and silver.* * * * *The faith of the United States is also solemnly pledged to make provisions, at the earliest practicable period, for the redemption of the United States notes in coin.*"

At this time also the silver dollar of 412½ grains was worth two and a-half per cent. more than the gold dollar.

The act of July 14, 1870, authorized the issue of $200,000,000 of five per cent. bonds.

$300,000,000 four and a-half per cent.

$1,000,000,000 million at four per cent., "*principal and interest payable in coin of the present standard value.*"

This agreement as to payment was printed on all of these bonds. At this time also the standard silver dollar was worth considerably more than the gold dollar. Indeed, for 20 years next prior to 1873 the silver dollar bore a premium ranging from 2 to 5.22 per cent., in consequence of which, added to its inconvenient bulk, it had ceased to circulate as coin, and had become merchandise, and was by law demonetized in 1873. The "*coin of the* [then] *present standard value,*" in which the bonds and interest were made payable was evidently *gold coin*, and so understood by every one at the time. Such, clearly, was the Government contract. There was no other *standard coin* in circulation at that date ; the Government exacted, in gold, the duties on imports, which by the act of Feb. 25th, 1862, were set aside to pay interest on the coin bonds ; the Government uniformly paid interest on its bonds in gold, and in gold up to the present time it has always paid its coupons and called bonds ; and placing this question beyond debate the Congress by the act of Feb. 12th, 1873, demonetized the silver dollar and left no standard coin but gold in which the bonds, coupons and legal-tender notes could possibly be paid, and when the Resumption act of January 14th, 1875, was passed there was not such a coin of the United States as a standard silver dollar. The uniform custom of the Government was to exact all its duties in gold, and to make all its payments relating to the coin bonds in gold ; and upon every precedent in the fair interpretation of contracts and of good faith the Government were bound to pay these obligations in gold coin of the then "Standard value," and the bondholders were bound to receive the same for their bonds and coupons, and could not exact payment from the Government in standard silver dollars of $412\frac{1}{2}$ grains, whether the same dollar was at a premium of 5 per cent., or at a discount of 15. Suppose the silver dollar had not been demonetized, and to-day bore its former premium, will any one maintain that the bondholder could claim the right to be paid in the more valuable silver instead of the gold coin? Surely not, for the reason that every surrounding and attending circumstance proves that the "coin" mentioned was understood by all parties at the date of the contract to be *gold coin*, and no other.

From the foundation of this Government only eight million of standard silver dollars were coined until after the recent Silver bill of Feb. 28, 1878, went into operation, and the act of Feb. 12, 1873, declared that silver should be a legal-tender for only $5 in any one payment.

The Resumption act of 1875 contemplated the redemption of the legal-tender notes *in gold*, and in the 12th section of the act of July 12, 1882, the redemption of the United States notes *in gold* was recognized, and it was therein clearly implied that the *gold reserve* held for such redemption should at no time *fall below* $100,000,000.

On the 14th of January, 1875, the Resumption act was approved. In sec. 3, it provides that,

"On and after the first day of January, 1879, the Secretary of the Treasury shall redeem, *in coin*, the United States legal-tender notes [then outstanding, on their presentation for redemption, at the office of the assistant Treasurer of the United States, in the City of New York, in sums of not less than fifty dollars. And to enable the Secretary to prepare and provide for the redemption in this act required, he is authorized to use any surplus revenues from time to time in the Treasury not otherwise appropriated, and to issue, sell and dispose of, at not less than par, in coin, either of the descriptions of bonds of the United States described in the act of Congress approved July 14, 1870, entitled 'An act to authorize the refunding of the National debt,' with like qualities, privileges and exemptions, to the extent necessary to carry this act into full effect, and to use the proceeds thereof for the purposes aforesaid."

Under the authority of this act the Secretary issued and sold bonds, for which he received, in *gold coin*, $95,500,000 to be held for redemption of legal-tender notes.

Be it remembered, that when the Resumption act was passed, the silver dollar of $412\frac{1}{2}$ grains *was not a coin of the United States*, and that no silver was a legal-tender for more than $5, and that the $95,500,000 in gold which was obtained by the sale of bonds under this act, was always regarded as a part of a gold reserve to be sacredly held towards the redemption of the legal-tender notes.

On the 1st of November, 1884, the Treasury held of coin and bullion, all told, but $134,670,790, with which to redeem $346,681,016 of legal-tender notes, pay interest on a bond debt of $1,206,475,600, and principal of the called bonds.

From this it appears that the redemption reserve of gold has been trenched upon, and that upon gold obligations the Government must default when a panic or a large shipment of gold occurs.

On the 28th of February, 1878, an act was passed, entitled "An act to authorize the coinage of the Standard Silver dollar, and to retain its legal tender character." The President vetoed the bill, but it was passed over his veto. This act required the coinage of a silver dollar of 412½ grains of standard fineness, made it a legal-tender for all debts public and private (except where otherwise exprsssly stipulated in the contract), and compelled the Secretary of the Treasury to purchase silver, not less than two million dollars a month, and have it coined. Section 3 of the act reads: "That any holder of the coin authorized by this act may deposit the same with the Treasurer or any assistant Treasurer of the United States, in sums not less than ten dollars, and receive therefor certificates of not less than ten dollars each, corresponding with the denominations of the United States notes. The coin deposited for or representing the certificates shall be retained in the Treasury for the payment of the same on demand. *Said certificates shall be receivable for customs, taxes, and all public dues, and when so received may be reissued.*"

Up to this time nothing but gold had been received for customs, which under the act before cited, was set apart; first of all to pay interest on the public debt, and even legal-tender notes were not receivable for duties, but silver certificates, *not a legal tender*, are made receivable for duties by the act. At this date silver had fallen largely in value, and those interested in keeping up the price expected that this compulsory coinage of silver, would raise the value; but it has been falling ever since.

Section 2 of this act provides for an international conference to adopt a common ratio between gold and silver, and "internationally to establish the use of bimetallic money," &c. Three Commissioners were appointed by the President and proceeded to Europe on their mission. The writer of this article was in England at the time, and having every facility for the investigation took much pains to ascertain the views of the Ministry and of the more prominent financial men in London, and he became satisfied that so far as England was concerned, the mission of the Commissioners would be fruitless —that England having then had the gold standard ever since 1816, desired no change and would listen to none in the direction proposed. This Commission entirely failed. In 1881 another Commission was sent out and failed equally.

We can send out another Commission at equal cost, and be courteously snubbed for a third time if we will, but since it is conceded that we are by far the richest nation in the world and claim to be the most intelligent, and are large producers of gold and silver and of nearly everything else which minister to the wants of man, we shall consult our dignity and our interest better by attending to our own financial system and go a begging to Europe no more. So far as England is to be considered we might as well send out a commission to persuade her to dethrone the Queen and elect a President every four years. Suppose the chief nations of Europe should agree with the United States upon a ratio, say 15 to 1, and soon after new discovery of silver mines should reduce the price of silver in London to half its present cost, does any sane man think that silver coined on the international ratio could circulate at its face value for a single day?

As easy would it be to make, by international treaty a quartz crystal, equal in value to a Golconda diamond. Coin does not make the only use for gold and silver, nor does it chiefly determine their relative value.

In July, 1882, Congress passed a law forbidding any bank from being a member of any clearing-house in which silver certificates are not receivable for clearing-house balances; the Treasury is a member of the New York Clearing-house, where by far the greater part of its business is done, and yet not a single silver certificate or silver dollar has been received for clearing-house balances, and the Treasurer reports that, being obliged to use gold, his available gold ran down from $155,429,600 on the first of January, 1884, to $116,479,979 on the 12th of August following.

All this shows that the laws of trade, supply and demand, values established in the great marts of commerce, and the convenience and will of the people combined, can defeat any treaty or legislative enactment relating to trade.

Until the Silver bill of 1878, we could hardly have been considered in practice a bi-metallic nation. Up to that time we had coined of the standard silver dollars only eight million, while during the same period we had coined of gold close to a thousand million dollars—to be exact, $983,159,695. The silver dollar had not generally circulated as currency for many years prior to 1873, when it ceased to be a coin.

Fractional silver coin was in free circulation, and, long years before, foreign silver coins passed current.

By the act of Feb. 21, 1853, the fractional silver coin was so reduced that a dollar in fractional coin weighed but 384 grains. This was done to keep them in the country, because a silver dollar of $412\frac{1}{2}$ grains was then worth more than a gold dollar.

A dollar in fractional coin, since the Coinage act of Feb. 12, 1873, weighs only $385\frac{8}{10}$ grains.

By the Coinage act of 12th Feb., 1873, the silver dollar of $412\frac{1}{2}$ grains was demonetized and the gold dollar of $25\frac{8}{10}$ grains was made the standard of value.

In the words of the Act: "A one dollar piece which, at the standard weight of $25\frac{8}{10}$ grains, *shall be the unit of value.*"

The act further says: "The standard of both gold and silver coins of the United States shall be such that of one thousand parts by weight, nine hundred shall be of pure metal and 100 of alloy.

This is the standard of purity, not of value.

By the same act, the gold dollar of the standard fineness, and weighing $25\frac{8}{10}$ grains was made the unit OF VALUE.

The English sovereign has 917 parts of pure gold in a thousand.

In other civilized nations, as well as our own, gold is the standard by which all values are measured, and all exchanges between us and the European nations are settled on the gold basis. When we say that prior to 1872 the silver dollar was above *par*, we all understand the par of gold.

Thus it is seen that for 86 years we got along pretty well by coining about a thousand million dollars in gold, and but eight million of standard silver.

Many sensible men, familiar with affairs, think that "there is not gold and silver enough in the world with which to do the business."

Such are generally old men, who have but a drowsy idea of the changes in the modes of business which swift steamers, the cable, the telegraph, the telephone, bank checks and clearing-houses have wrought since fifty years ago.

The transactions of the London Clearing-house are over *thirty thousand million dollars a year;* the differences are all settled by checks on the Bank of England, so that not a coin or bank note passes from hand to hand in all these immense transactions.

The business of the New York Clearing-house is now about the same, but as the balances are not settled by checks on any one bank, a comparatively small amount of money passes in their settlements.

In a country like England, small in area, dense

in population, with unparalleled rapidity of communication, and having all the modern facilities for exchanges, a gold currency, with subsidiary silver and bank notes based on gold are all that is needed. But in a country like ours, vast in extent, thinly peopled, and in many parts, lacking the means of rapid transit, a much larger currency is required than gold can supply.

France, considerably smaller than the State of Texas, and thickly populated, has an active circulation of $43 per capita, while the United States has less than $24 per capita.

But it is useless just now to discuss the question whether a single gold currency or a bi-metallic currency is the better. The judgment of the country is decidedly in favor of a gold and silver currency, and considering what large producers we are of both metals, this settled judgment is probably right, and the real question is, how can the two metals be made to circulate so that one shall not demonetize and drive out the other?

The silver advocates in their inconsiderate eagerness to benefit their patrons have unwittingly reduced the value of silver, and if there is not a change in the coinage law it will be reduced still more.

Secretary McCulloch foreseeing the coming trouble, proposes, as some measure of relief, a withdrawal of one and two-dollar notes, and thus force silver dollars into circulation, which dollar he distinctly says is worth but 85 cents, and that a dollar in our fractional coin is worth but about 78 cents.

The Secretary further says:

"The amount of one-dollar notes in circulation is $26,763,097.80; the amount of two-dollar notes in circulation is $26,778,738.20. Congress, would, I think, act wisely in putting an end to their circulation. Nor do I hesitate to express the opinion that the country would be benefited if all five-dollar notes should be gradually retired and the coinage of half and quarter eagles should be increased. If this should be done, the circulating medium of the United States below ten dollars would be silver and gold, and we should be following the example of France, in which there is an immense circulation of silver coin, which in all domestic transactions maintains a parity with gold."

The example of France is not a happy illustration to apply to our country. It is true that in France there is a considerable circulation of silver coin, but France is a thickly populated and compact country. A single State of the 38 United States contains 26,324 square miles more than the whole of France, and one Territory of the United States is twice as large as France, with 157,757 square miles besides.

France has, of legal-tender silver coin, about $540,000,000, and she coins no more, but most of this lies dormant in vaults; she has, of gold coin, about $870,000,000, and notes of the Bank of France, in circulation, $568,727,469. By far the larger part of her actual circulation is gold and bills of the Bank of France. There is no very large amount of silver in active circulation. Everywhere in France, in settlement of the balance of your bill at the hotel, the railway, the restaurant, the factory, the shop or the market-place, you will receive in exchange for a Bank of France note, gold, or gold and bills with a dollar or two of silver—never as many as ten. No large amount of silver is carried about in France or kept in shops of trade.

The habits of a people come of their conditions, necessities and convenience. Our habits require paper money and small bills. We travel over vast distances, and in going from New York to New Mexico, and from thence to Alaska and back, a considerable amount of small money is required— exchange offices are not thick along the way. To carry sufficient silver is impossible and unsafe; the bearer would be relieved of his burden by "road-agents and missionaries," as they call them, before half over his journey.

Silver, in proportion to value, is about $28\frac{1}{2}$ times as bulky and $15\frac{1}{2}$ times as heavy as gold. Paper money is convenient and safe to carry, and we are not going to bear about us many silver dollars. We want a paper currency convertible into coin on demand. That suits our conditions and necessities.

The Secretary says: "It is estimated that there are in the country at this time some $75,000,000 of fractional silver coins, and that nearly $30,000,000 are in the Treasury unavailable as assets."

And he suggests a recoinage so as to bring them up to the standard of the silver dollar.

The suggestion is a good one, and the reason

given, namely, that this debased coin "is not an available asset," appeals equally for the recoinage of the silver dollar.

The Secretary shows that silver has been falling ever since the passage of the Silver bill, and "that it is now lower than at any time since the summer of 1879."

By Government estimate, there is now about $610,000,000 of gold in the country. Every one knows that a considerable demand for shipment and a distrust which would cause hoarding must turn this gold into merchandise, withdraw it from circulation and force the Government to default on its gold obligations, or pay them in silver worth not more than 85 cents to the dollar.

When that happens, the "*severe contraction*" which the Secretary foretells will be upon us.

Now, what is the remedy? To force out silver dollars by withdrawing the one and two-dollar bills would avail but little, and to stop all coinage of silver *surely* will not meet the difficulty.

The Bank of England is by law obliged to take *any amount* of standard gold offered at the rate of £3 17s. 9d. per ounce, and give for the same its notes at that rate, payable on demand in gold coin.

A Bank of England note is simply a gold certificate. The coinage is free, and if the holder of gold bullion wishes to have the coin instead of a Bank of England note, he can wait the coinage and have the advantage of receiving £3 17s. 10½d. coin for his ounce of standard bullion.

The Secretary of the Treasury has not been able to put in circulation but $41,000,000 of coin out of the $184,730,829 of silver dollars already coined, and it seems well settled that not more than $50,000,000 of silver dollar *coin* can be kept out.

Laws more powerful than legislative enactments have changed the relative value between silver and gold—a fact which those dealing with finance must recognize.

The Trade Dollar.

As the legislative department of the Government in the Silver bill seemed disposed to slight its gold obligations, so in its treatment of the trade dollar it seems inclined to ignore its obligations regarding that coin entirely.

THE TRADE DOLLAR holds an anomalous place among our coins. By the act of Feb. 12th, 1873, it was made a coin of the United States, and made a legal-tender for $5 in any one payment. By the same act the silver dollar of $412\frac{1}{2}$ grains was demonetized, as was the silver dollar of 416 grains. The trade dollar weighs 420 grains, and retained its limited legal-tender character until July 22, 1876, when by joint resolutions of Congress the legal-tender quality was taken away.

When this resolution was approved there had been coined of the trade dollar $9,256,400, and after the beginning of 1876 up to the end of 1878 there were coined $26,672,960 when the coinage ceased, but of this sum $11,378,010 were coined in the last year of the coinage.

The trade dollar is now, and always has been, by the Act of Congress, "*a coin of the United States.*" Its intrinsic value is greater than the standard dollar; its circulation has never been prohibited, nor is there a suggestion in the law authorizing the coinage against its general circulation; on the contrary, the people were led to believe, and they were right in believing, that when the law expressly says, "the silver coins of the United States shall be *a trade dollar*, a half dollar, a quarter dollar and a dime," it meant what it so plainly said, and meant that a trade dollar was just as much "a coin of the United States" and had the same right of circulation as any of the other coins issued. And Secretary Sherman, in his circular of Sept. 3, 1878, says: "There could be no objection for "the owner to put the coins into circulation."

Before the legal-tender quality was taken away, the Government had issued of these dollars between nine and ten millions, and an eminent banker in New York now has over eighty thousand of these dollars, every one of which were issued before they were deprived of their legal-tender character.

Secretary Folger, in his last report, dated Dec. 3, 1883, presents this subject in its true light, and reveals the discreditable reason for "the hue and cry" against the calling in of this coin. The Secretary says:

"The act of 1873 made the silver coins of the United States and hence the trade dollars, a legal tender at their nominal value for any amount not over five dollars. Thus the reading of the laws taught the people that the trade dollar was a coin of their Sovereignty, and for the redemption of which, *at an unabated value, their Government was bound.* * * * It is plain that a busy people, finding this coin afloat in the channels of business, syled a coin of the United States, would readily believe that it was an authentic issue of the Government, and to be redeemed by the Government, the same as other money put out by it. From time to time, however, as it suits *scheming men and the occasion fits, a hue and cry is raised against it,* it is discredited in the marts, and unwary holders suffer loss or inconvenience.

As it is a coin of the United States, having the image and superscription thereof, sanctioned as such by penalties upon the counterfeiting of it, and once dignified as a legal tender in payment of debts and dues, it should be restored to its first state, or called in at its nominal value and melted. In the judgment of this Department it should be thus called in and melted."

Some six or seven millions of these coins are now held in various parts of this country, awaiting the action of Congress. They are owned chiefly by banks, bankers, trust companies, charitable societies, traders, and men of varied business, who took them in the regular way and at their face value, and they repose in confidence upon the rather tardy justice of the Government.

The crisis, of which Secretary McCulloch lately warned us, seems unpleasantly near.

The customs, which were collected in gold and set apart by law to pay the interest on the public debt, are now, under the Silver bill, chiefly paid in silver certificates, not even a legal tender, and worth but 85 cents on the dollar.

The Assistant Treasurer of New York reports for customs received during the last week of December, 1884, as follows:

Dec. 23, silver certificates..$254,000. Gold..$26,000.
" 24,   "   "   .. 211,000.   "   31,000.
" 26,   "   "   .. 161,000.   "   39,000.
" 27,   "   "   .. 93,000.   "   25,000.
" 29,   "   "   .. 167,000.   "   38,000.
" 30,   "   "   .. 202,000.   "   126,000.

Apparently we are near the time when the Treasury will be obliged to pay its Clearing-house balances in silver certificates. A quiet hoarding of gold has already commenced, and it attracts notice that the gold certificates, so freely paid out by the banks a month ago, are no more seen.

So soon as the $610,000,000 of gold, estimated to be in the country, rises to a premium and ceases to circulate as currency, we shall discover that our financial system is not very sound.

It seems to be well ascertained that fifty millions of silver dollars will meet the extremest demand which is likely to be made for that coin.

What, then, is proposed?

The Plan.

Keeping in mind that by the act of February 12, 1873, a fixed weight *of gold* was made "*the unit of value,*" and that the gold dollar of $25\frac{8}{10}$ grains is the sole standard; this is the plan.

Repeal the Silver bill.

It is not easy to estimate the mischief of that law, which, in its execution, forced the Secretary of the Treasury to buy and coin foreign silver, and thus, to our harm, aid the German Empire. We have been coining largely of German silver since the Coinage act of 1878.

Let the Treasury buy no more silver.

Let coinage *be free* for American silver, and coin no other, and receive no other on deposit.

Make the silver dollar of 480 grains, and coin fifty million of them.

Prepare silver certificates, payable in dollars of 480 grains, or in stamped bullion, as the holder of the certificate may prefer. Make them exchangable for the silver certificates already out, and for the silver dollars already in circulation, and also for American silver bullion of standard fineness, at the rate of 480 grains to the dollar. Make the certificates a legal-tender, Bank of England notes —mere certificates—are a legal tender.

The silver already coined is of standard fineness and can be held as bullion, to be put into bars or coin as convenience requires; and since the silver certificates and the silver coin outstanding (within some given time) may be exchanged for the new silver certificates calling for a dollar of 480 grains, no disturbance in the currency could possibly arise while the new certificates were being prepared, or while the 50,000,000 of the new dollars were being coined.

Pay off the gold certificates in gold, and issue no more. Let gold coinage be entirely free.

During the year 1883, the mines of the United States yielded of gold $30,000,000, and of silver $46,200,000; in all, $76,200,000, and it is estimated that the yield in 1884 will be about the same.

With $872,000,000 of coin and bullion available for coinage on the 1st of October last, $346,681,016 of legal-tender, and with an annual product of $76,200,000 from the mines, we are in no danger of a lack of currency, without resorting to the expedient of borrowing money which we do not want, and paying interest upon bonds issued for nothing but to make a basis for National Bank circulation.

The National Banks.

The National Banks were of inestimable value to the country in its days of need, and the late Secretary Chase deserves enduring renown for the priceless services which he rendered in establishing his system of finance against collossal difficulties.

But now, as the bonds, which secure the bank notes are paid off, the notes will, of course, be gradually retired, but the yield of the mines will more than supply the vacancy, with silver certificates; and instead of bank notes secured by paper promises, on which the people pay interest, we shall have a currency in their stead secured by the actual deposit of the precious metal without interest.

As the gold and silver increases in the country, the "greenbacks" can be paid off in gold whenever the paper currency becomes redundant, and the silver certificates may take their place; thus the Government will, in due time, become divorced from every function as a banker, and give the people the best and safest currency in the world; made up of gold coin and paper certificates backed by silver deposits.

The banks would go on with their business as now, obtaining their currency in gold and silver or silver certificates in whatever way they found it most for their interest, and no one need fear lest banking facilities would cease.

The Government vaults would hold the *metal* securities for the paper circulation, just as they now hold the *paper* securities for the bank paper circulation.

If the silver men cannot see their own and the country's gain in this plan they must be blind indeed.

It will be asked whether the new dollar may not also fluctuate in value?

It may fluctuate as often as the tide, but like the tide, it will maintain its general level for a long time, as we think; and since we can but darkly see into the distant future, we act as best we may, upon probabilities gathered from past experience, and leave the coming generation to deal with new conditions as they arise.

The silver, for economic reasons, would seldom be shipped to settle balances, but gold would more naturally perform that function, and at home the silver certificate would pass current in parity with gold and, until the returning tide would level up any temporary depression caused by the export. Free coinage would increase the demand for silver and stop its downward tendency, and the refusal to allow the coinage of foreign silver would prevent a flood of it from abroad.

To escape the danger which is apprehended, it is now proposed to stop the coinage of silver entirely. The inevitable effect must be to lower the price of silver, bring gold to a premium, and withdraw it from circulation. Those of us who lived in the war-time well remember how all the coin vanished in a night, even to the copper cent, and that for a considerable time we paid stage fare with postage stamps and transacted other business with "shin-plasters;" and that the premium on gold ran up until on the 11th of January, 1864, it reached from 152¾ to 152½, and on the 11th of July, of the same year, it sold at from 276 to 285.

The complaint that silver is not "treated well" by the Secretary is a childish cry. This is not a sentimental question. The treatment, both of gold and silver is determind by the demand for, and the supply of the two metals. Defects in this plan, which present discussion or future experience may reveal, can be remedied by Congress.

When this central fact, that all the trade balances of Christendom are settled by the gold standard, *and by no other*, shall have been comprehended, and also that every scheme through statutory law, to force silver much above its intrinsic value must come to naught, then the way to prosperous legislation upon the finances will be plain.

It may be said that the execution of this plan will be attended with expense to the Treasury. When the false idea is exploded, that the Treasury is a money-making corporation, and the true idea prevails, that the Treasury was made for the people, and not the people for the Treasury, we shall have advanced considerably. The Treasury now shows that it has already made more than twenty-two millions of profit on the purchase and coinage of silver. This profit all came from the people ; let some of it be returned to the people in a dollar worth what it claims to be.

It is the duty of the Government to furnish the people with a safe and convenient currency, and to make a question about the small expense to provide a safe.deposit for the securities of that currency is preposterous.

If the silver advocates would destroy themselves let them stop all silver coinage under the delusion that they will thus force England and the other nations of Europe to come to our assistance.

The price of silver depends upon the demand for it. There will be no very large demand if it cannot circulate as coin. If coinage is free and confined to American silver, and the coin is of the weight above indicated, and the certificates issued upon it are of the same denominations, large and small as the " Greenbacks," silver will in that form circulate without driving out gold, and when gold is needed for shipment, no panic would be caused or harm done or hoarding take place, and the Secretary of the Treasury might be empowered to use any but reserved assets in the Treasury to provide for the gold obligations of the Government.

It is conceded that the Congress of the United States in the plenitude of its power, overriding the veto of the President, did by the act of Feb. 28, 1878, make it possible for the Goverment, LAWFULLY, to discharge all its gold obligations by payment in silver dollars worth but 85 cents of their face value. Perhaps it will do so ; but in so doing, it will violate the plighted faith, injure the prosperity, and degrade the honor of the country.

EDWARDS PIERREPONT.

NEW YORK, January 5, 1885.

The Speech of Edwards Pierrepont

IN

The Alumni Hall of Yale University,

UPON

The Presentation of a Portrait of one of its Founders

ON THE 50TH ANNIVERSARY OF

THE GRADUATING CLASS OF 1837;

And the Reply of President Dwight.

The Speech of Edwards Pierrepont,

IN

The Alumni Hall of Yale University,

UPON

The Presentation of a Portrait of one of its Founders,

ON THE 50TH ANNIVERSARY OF

THE GRADUATING CLASS OF 1837;

And the Reply of President Dwight.

On the 28th of June, 1887, at a meeting of the Alumni of Yale University in Alumni Hall, there was a crowded assembly over which Senator Evarts presided and made the opening address : He was followed by the Hon. Edwards Pierrepont and others. In closing his address, Mr. Pierrepont turned around, and addressing President Dwight, who arose—presented a portrait of the Rev. James Pierrepont, one of the original founders of the University.

President Dwight, in reply, said : "In behalf of the Uni-
" versity, allow me, sir, to accept this valuable and interesting
" gift at your hands, It is most of all interesting that it comes
" from you, sir—you, an honored representative of the University
" and one whose affection for the College has lasted through
" these fifty years.

"We number you, sir, as one of the illustrious men whom
" Yale has given to the world. It is a privilege, sir, to you and
" to me, that we are descended from this Honorable Man.

"I had not intended to have addressed the Alumni to-day ;
" but we have heard from Mr. Pierrepont the criticism that we
" do not graduate the students early enough. The truth is,
" that the years of our boyhood are wasted ; from two to four
" years wasted ;—were it not for this, we could enter the Uni-
" versity as early as those distinguished men whom Mr. Pierre-
" pont has named."

NOTE.—*The foregoing and the following is from the New Haven Morning News.*

ADDRESS OF EDWARDS PIERREPONT.

SUGGESTIONS FOR YALE UNIVERSITY—THE ENTRANCE EXAMINATIONS—AN ANECDOTE OF THE LATE SAMUEL J. TILDEN—WHAT HE SAID ABOUT THE PRESIDENCY AND HIS CLASS AT YALE.

At the Yale alumni meeting to-day Hon. Edwards Pierrepont followed Senator Evarts, the presiding officer, and spoke as follows ;

Mr. Chairman—The warning horologue of time strikes the half-century for the class of 1837 :

We now stand where old Yale and all its cherished memories are fast receding into night,—and we soon shall see the widening dawn of the eternal day, and with increasing joy as the morning comes, if our life has been a good one.

This great university has so long been accustomed to hear only praise from its graduates that a few words of friendly suggestion may usefully break the monotony of admiration.

I open the catalogue of this year and read from page 27, eighteen closely printed sections, with a statement, that, "all candidates for admission to the freshman class are examined in all those books and subjects." The boy of 13 who commences his preparation must have a stout heart, or be appalled at the task before him ; but there is an encouraging note at the bottom stating that next year *more* will be required.

I venture to say that not a member of the class of 1837 could pass an examination for the freshman class to-day ; and that there never was a time when he could have passed such examination. If there is any member of the class present who thinks that I underrate his accomplishments, he will, of course, correct me.

The requirements for graduating are in harmonious severity with the requirements of admission. Would it not be well to have many of these exactions for a degree postponed over to the resident graduate?

This is a university :—Encourage resident graduates, and all who wish to become teachers, professors or eminent scholars, to remain here ; but nine-tenths of Yale graduates propose a widely different career in life, and for them I fear that you are going to make the entrance and the honorable exit quite too difficult, and thus prevent them from commencing the real work of life until too late.

Education at a large university is of priceless value. If the noble men who so generously endow various colleges about the country would bestow the same amount to increase facilities in universities already established they would largely enhance the value of their gifts. You cannot make a great university *to order*, by the expenditure of any amount of money or the employment of any number of professors :—you may cite any quantity of logic against this proposition, but the fact will remain.

A university requires age ; it must grow up. If the rich merchants of London should contribute ever so liberally to make another Westminster Abbey, and should copy every turret and tower and statue they could not make a Westminster Abbey.

In a large university one professor can teach 200 students as easily as twenty, and thus the expenses in this way, as in many other ways, are greatly diminished.

Besides, that subtle influence, that magnetic force equally necessary for the development of a healthy body and a healthy mind, can only come of the congregation of numbers. Not only contact of mind with mind, but contact with many minds, is absolutely essential to a perfect growth. But academical plodding should cease for those who are to be men of affairs, at the age of 20, and those studies and observations of the world, should begin which are suited to the career proposed.

Eton college is one of the oldest foundations in Christendom. It is 447 years old. No college has sent out so many who have become eminent. No one can enter there who is not under 14. The science of physiology has demonstrated that knowledge acquired and impressions made upon the brain in early life are deeper, far more lasting and at readier command than those of later life, and that the young man who proposes to himself a career on the great stage of the world as a leader of men, must quite early enter the crowded arena where aspiring youth contest for the supremacy.

The strong man who has not made his mark before he is 45, will never make it; and the young man who has not set his ambitious foot upon the "ladder leaning on a cloud," before he is 25, will never ascend it. It should not be difficult for the student of fair ability to obtain his degree, without injury to his elasticity of mind or bodily health, by the time he is 20; but if you impose burdens too heavy for this, the years draw nigh in which the numbers of illustrious names on your roll of graduates will be few.

Look back three hundred years and more, and see what history teaches upon this subject, and you shall not find a single instance of a man, illustrious in great affairs, who did not very early begin his great career.

Gustave Adolphus ascended the throne of Sweden at 16 ; before he was 34 he was one of the great rulers of Europe.

Condé conducted a memorable campaign at 17, and at 22 he and Turenne also were of the most illustrious men of their time.

Maurice of Saxony died at 32, conceded to have been one of the profoundest statesmen, and one of the ablest generals which Christendom had seen.

The great Leo X was pope at 38; having finished his academic training he took the office of cardinal at 18—only 12 months younger than was Charles James Fox when he entered parliament.

Martin Luther had become largely distinguished at 24, and at 36 had reached the topmost round of his world-wide fame.

Of Napoleon it is superfluous to say, that at 25 he commanded the army of Italy. At 30 he was not only one of the most illustrious generals of all time, but one of the great lawgivers of the world. At 46 he saw Waterloo.

Wellington, be it remembered, was born the same year.

From the earliest years of Queen Elizabeth, to the latest of Queen Victoria, England has had scarce an able statesman who did not leave the university by the time he was 20, and many of them left at an earlier age.

Lord Bacon graduated at Cambridge when 16, and was called to the bar at 21.

The great Cromwell, by all measure the ablest ruler that England ever had, left the University of Cambridge at 18, was a student at law in London at 20, and in parliament at 29.

John Hampton, after graduating at Oxford, was a student at law in The Inner Temple at 19.

William Pitt entered the university at 14, was chancellor of the exchequer at 22, prime minister at 24, and so continued for twenty years, and when 25 he was the most powerful uncrowned head in Europe ; and like his great father, Lord Chatham, he was charged with "the atrocious crime of being a young man."

Charles James Fox was in parliament at 19.

Peel was in parliament at 21, and Palmerston was lord of the admiralty at 23.

Gladstone was in parliament at 22, and at 24 was lord of the treasury.

John Bright, the best orator and one of the ablest statesmen of England, wrote me on the 28th of July, 1879, that he never was at any school a day after he was 15 years old; that he commenced thus early the affairs of life; and his letter explained how he had acquired his unparalleled style of oratory.

The late Lord Beaconsfield left the cloister and entered the great world early—as did John Bright—and commenced his political career by writing a book at 19, in which he predicted that he would be prime minister.

He was the original of Tennyson's

   * * * Divinely gifted man.
Whose life in low estate began,
   Who breaks his birth's invidious bar,
      And grasps the skirts of happy chance,
      And breasts the blows of circumstance,
   And grapples with his evil star.
Who makes by force his merit known,
   And lives to clutch the golden keys,
   To mould a mighty state's decrees,
And shape the whisper of the throne.

The only statesman now thought of in England, who, if alive, could solve the Irish question.

But let us learn from our own country:

Washington was a distinguished colonel in the army at 22, early in public affairs, commander of the forces at 43, and president at 57.

Hamilton was in Kings college at 16, when 17 he made a notable address on public affairs to the citizens of New York; at 20 he was intrusted with a most important negotiation with General Gates: was in Congress at 25, and Secretary of the Treasury at 32.

Webster was in college at 15, gave earnest of his great future before he was 25, and at 30 was the peer of the ablest man in Congress.

Henry Clay was in the Senate of the United States at 29, contrary to the Constitution.

Chief Justice Marshall was a member of the house of delegates at 27. At 42 he was special ambassador to France; at 45 Secretary of State, and at 46 Chief Justice of the United States.

Judge Story was in Harvard at 15, in Congress at 29, and Judge of the Supreme Court of the United States at 32.

William H. Seward commenced the practice of law at 21; at 27 was president of a State convention, and at 37 Governor of the great State of New York.

John Quincy Adams, at the age of 14, was secretary to Mr. Dana, then minister at the Russian court; at 30 he was himself minister to Prussia; at 35 he was minister to Russia; at 48 he was minister to England; at 50 he was Secretary of State, and President at 57.

There have been twenty-two Presidents of the United States. Five of them were elected at 57, and six attained that great office before the age of 50. Three military men, past 60, have been elected: two died very soon, and the other was General Jackson, and he was but 61 when elected.

Only one civilian out of the whole number gained his first election after he was 60, and that one was James Buchanan. The chance for the Presidency after 60 is small, and growing less.

General Grant was elected President at 46. But when a very young man, in the Mexican war, he so distinguished himself at the battle of Molino del Rey that General Scott named him for promotion on the field, and at the storming of Chapultepec his courage and ability caused him to be specially commended by General Worth, and for these young acts of skill and valor he was made captain in the regular army. He was but 39 when he gained his victory at Fort Donelson, and only 41 when he took Vicksburg—a victory, which in its grandeur and its consequences, was not surpassed by Ulm or Austerlitz.

Jonathan Edwards acquired early renown as the greatest metaphysician in America, and as unsurpassed by any one in Europe. He commenced the reading of Latin when 6 years old. At ten he wrote a remarkable paper upon the immortality of the soul. At the age of thirteen he entered Yale College, where he graduated four years later.

Before he was seventeen he had completely reasoned out his great doctrine concerning the freedom of the will. Before he was nineteen he commenced preaching at one of the first churches in the city of New York. At twenty-four he was installed over the church in Northampton.

From Leo the Tenth down to Gen. Grant and Prince Bismark, I find not one name of large renown in war, church or state, whose career of greatness did not conspicuously begin in very early manhood.

The late Governor Tilden, of New York, was for a short time a member of our class, and was always proud of it ; but he left us very soon to study law and engage in public affairs. After he failed to be declared President he called upon me in London, and conversing familiarly, he said : " The class of '37 is a great class. It has furnished a Chief Justice of the United States, two Attorney Generals, the Minister to England, the Secretary of State, and a President ; out of the President the class has been cheated, and ought to resent it." I replied : " But you deserted us. If you had remained and graduated, perhaps you would have held the White House." " No, " he rejoined, " I should not have amounted to much. My health was not very firm, and I found that I was considerably older than the better part of the class and I left. That was the turning point of my life. Those four years gave me a start which would have been lost in college." Mr. Tilden was a sagacious man.

Inventors, discoverers, poets, are proverbially young ; though Longfellow says that Goethe finished Faust when past 80—yet in the next breath he says :

> " Whatever poet, orator or sage
> " May say of it, old age is still old age,
> " It is the waning, not the crescent moon,
> " The dusk of evening, not the blaze of noon ;
> " It is not strength, but weakness ; not desire,
> " But its surcease ; not the fierce heat of fire,
> " The burning and consuming element,
> " But that of ashes and of embers spent."

But Goethe was a marvel of precocity ; when but 6 years and 2 months old, the terrible earthquake which destroyed Lisbon occurred, and he amazed the people of his native town by his discourse upon the event as against the goodness of Providence. Before he was nine years old, he could write in several languages, including French, Latin and Greek. He was in the university at sixteen and was made a Doctor of Laws before he was twenty-two. At twenty-five, he projected the writing of Faust and published the first part of it twenty-seven years before he finished the play.

A thousand pities that he ever did finish it.

To ruin an innocent young girl, in humble life—lured by the jewels and flattery, and wicked love of Faust—with the Devil to help him—was not a grand achievement ; and the compact with Satin, followed by crimes, and sorrows and woes unnumbered, without a single ray of hope, but in death, to light her repentant soul from its dark entanglement, is not a healthy presentation of human life, or of the abounding mercy of God.

Mr. President, I have now to present to the University, through you, the portrait of one of its original founders. He lies buried in the crypt of Center church, over which he ministered with so much fidelity and success from early life until he died ; of whom in Hollister's History of Connecticut it is said : " Descended from an illustrious family, and gifted to a high degree with intellectual endowments, eloquent speech, a graceful person, handsome features and manners, the most courtly and winning, he appears to have been from early youth too intently occupied with the mission of saving the souls of his fellow-men ever to think of himself. I suppose of all the clergymen whose names belong to the early history of New England, Pierrepont was the most lofty, and pure in his aspirations and of the most spiritual temper. With none of the sterness of Davenport, without the despondency of Wareham, and free from the impetuous moods that proved such thorns in the pillow of Hooker, his words like the live coals from the altar in the hand of the angel, touched and purified the lips of those who listened to his teachings."

And of whom Dr. Leonard Bacon, in his " Historical Discourses"—speaking of the call to the Center church—says: " He had graduated less than three years before at Harvard College ; but it is evident that, notwithstanding his youth, he was regarded as competent to do the work of the ministry in *any* of the churches of New England."

It seems fit that I should present this portrait through you.

From him whom it represents, you are directly descended in the female line, and I in the male line ; you direct from his beautiful daughter Sarah, and I from his son Joseph, her brother ; this daughter became the distinguished wife of that eminent divine, President Jonathan Edwards. If from the viewless heights of unimagined bliss his spirit can look down to earth, we may believe that it adds something to his happiness to know that two eminently gifted presidents of this college— Woolsey and Dwight—are of the blood of its founder.

I present the portrait that it may hang in this hall or wherever else in the University you may wish to place it.

Printed in Dunstable, United Kingdom